SEDUCTION OF SUICIDE

Understanding and Recovering From Addiction to Suicide

By

Kevin Taylor, M.D.

ISBN: 1-4033-1000-9 (e-book)
ISBN: 1-4033-1001-7 (Paperback)
ISBN: 1-4033-6960-7 (Dustjacket)
ISBN: 1-4033-1002-5 (Rocketbook)

Library of Congress Control Number: 2002105694

This book is printed on acid free paper.

Printed in the United States of America
Bloomington, IN

1stBooks - rev. 10/10/02

To my best friend, Morgan Winfred Taylor

Table of Contents

Preface: A Personal Reflection

"God, grant me the serenity to accept the things I cannot change, the
courage to change the things I can,
and the wisdom to know the difference."
—Reinhold Niebuhr

Suicide is a dark and difficult subject. It can strike anywhere, any time. It kills some 30,000 Americans each year and is a leading cause of death among young people. Its incidence is on the rise among children and young people aged 15-24, especially young black males[1] It is a major social problem, and it leaves in its wake terrible wounds and confusion to the survivors.

Much has been written about suicide, and yet most people are still too frightened to talk about it or study it directly. Those who write about it want to explain it—to make sense of it. They may decide that they do understand suicide, but any such

---

[1] United States Public Health Service, *The Surgeon General's Call to Action to Prevent Suicide* (Washington: GPO, 1999), 3.

belief inevitably crashes into confusion. In the end, they are forced to conclude that they don't understand suicide at all. In spite of the vast amount of attention given to the subject, professionals have a hard time finding a common denominator for suicides.

About all we really know about attempted vs. completed suicide is that women are more likely to attempt suicide and men are four times more likely than women to complete it.[2]

Most of those who write about suicide fall into two categories: those who try to fix it (the experts) and those who are touched by it (the attempters and survivors). The goal of the expert is to understand suicide in order to prevent it or make it go away. If these experts are at all honest with themselves, they have to admit that suicide is terrifying. They're afraid that their patients or clients may "do it", leaving them liable for huge lawsuits. Survivors, on the other hand, want to understand suicide for different reasons: they want

---

[2] *Ibid.*

closure. They cannot ask their own dead loved ones what went wrong: what did we do? What could we have done? As for those who have attempted suicide, they also want to understand, and their goal is hope. They want never to go down that road again.

Of the three groups (experts, survivors and attempters), experts probably know the least and write the most, while attempters probably know the most and write the least. They are silenced by the deep, pervasive shame that faces them at every turn. Ironically, experts are actually reluctant to study attempters because of the medical-legal liability issue.

For example, drug studies on depression routinely exclude suicidal patients. Past studies on suicide have also excluded attempters on the grounds that they were not the "real thing" — that is, only completed suicides count! (And of course, that group cannot be interviewed.) As a result, most studies of suicide have been limited to theoretical discussions or reports of brain autopsies of completed suicides. While these studies are, of course, useful, they are obviously limited.

Suicide is such a dark topic that throughout history, it has been passed around like a hot potato. The church "owned" suicide for most of the last two millennia, and its solution was to make suicide a matter of sin. Suicides were, for example, forbidden burial in consecrated ground—a matter of deep shame to their survivors. This attitude still pervades our culture. Starting in the Middle Ages, the law followed suit, making suicide or attempted suicide a crime—indeed, the crime of suicide is still on the minds of many people. Our forcible commitment of suicidal people reflects this legal ownership. The hot potato has now passed to the mental health profession, which is largely ill-equipped to handle it. So: what *is* suicide? Mortal sin? Crime? Mental illness? All three? Few people ever stop to ask this question. Most only want to know how to prevent suicide from happening at all.

One more useful and promising question is "what other conditions are associated with suicide?" This excellent question has led to studies on risk factors for suicide and generated much-needed research on depression and alcoholism, the two big killers associated with suicide. This in turn has led to the nascent, all-important suicide prevention movement, which is literally a life-saver.

But the basic question still goes unanswered: what is suicide? *Why* is suicide?

If suicide does belong to the field of mental health, then surely it is a mental illness. But the Diagnostic and Statistical Manual of Mental Disorders IV, the Bible of mental illnesses published by the American Psychiatric Association, barely mentions suicide, and then only in a few passing footnotes. It fumbles the hot potato. And this reflects the trouble that the mental health professions have with suicide.

Historically, psychiatry has taken two different approaches to explaining suicidal behavior: Freud's psychodynamic view and Durkheim's sociological explanation.[3] Freud believed that suicide is triggered by an intrapsychic conflict that emerges when a person undergoes great psychological stress. This stress emerges either as a regression to a primitive ego state or as an inhibition of hostility toward others. In the latter case, the person turns aggression inward on the self. Durkheim, on the other hand, thought that societal pressures are major determinants of suicide. He divided suicide into three types: egoistic, anomic, and altruistic. Egoistic suicide results from an individual's failure to be integrated or to identify with a group. Anomic suicide arises from a perceived or real breakdown in societal norms. Altruistic suicide results from real or perceived social solidarity (think, for example, of traditional Japanese *hari-kiri*).

---

[3] H. Kaplan, B. Sadock, and J. Grebb. *Synopis of Psychiatry* (Baltimore: Williams and Wilkins, 1994), 807.

But put aside the theoretical discussions and the philosophical questions (what *are* you killing if you kill yourself?) and another possibility emerges. When pushed for an explanation, many people who have attempted suicide say that suicide is an attempt to escape the pain—a longing for death because life looks impossibly difficult and hurtful. This poignant longing is hardly a new thing.

Never weather-beaten sail

More willing bent to shore;

Never tired pilgrim's limbs

Affected slumber more

Than my weary sprite now longs

To fly out of my troubled breast.

O come quickly, sweetest Lord,

And take my soul to rest.

Put this way, suicide doesn't sound like a mental illness at all. It sounds like a desperate soul's desire for rest.

Years ago, we had to face a similar problem: another large-scale killer that defied precise definition or neat categorization or simple explanation, but had devastating and far-reaching effects, not only on its victims but on all who loved them. That disease was alcoholism. Between 1935 (when Alcoholics Anonymous was founded) and the mid-1950s, when the American Medical Association finally defined alcoholism as a disease, we faced very much the same sort of confusion. Although alcoholism had been a huge killer for centuries, it was seen only as a manifestation of something else—usually stress or depression. We only began to make progress with alcoholism when we began to deal with it in its own right, as a disease.

Suicide, I believe, deserves the same focus, and the same approach. We must stop seeing suicide as the result of something else. Even though depression and alcoholism are two of the biggest risk factors for suicide, suicide does not equal depression alone nor alcoholism alone. The time has come for us to study suicide directly, to learn about it, not to run from it or to miss the mark by studying only its risk factors. When we finally start looking at suicide itself, we will almost certainly find that it is more than one thing. We will likely find that, like alcoholism and depression, suicide comes in many forms and stages—that it is not merely a disease, but a whole cluster of diseases.

This book discusses one type of suicide: suicide addiction. This is a radical concept and one with which many people will have very real problems. Suicide addiction goes against all common sense. Suicide is among the last things that one would expect to be addictive. But in fact, in a small number of cases, it seems to be the only answer to the question "why?"

Suicide addiction is probably only one very small slice of the pie. It does *not* explain all cases of suicide—only a few. In fact, it may not "explain" very much at all, since we know so little about the real causes of addiction. But some suicides do seem to fall into an addictive pattern. Those who do show a common pattern of childhood trauma, other addictions, and mood disorders:

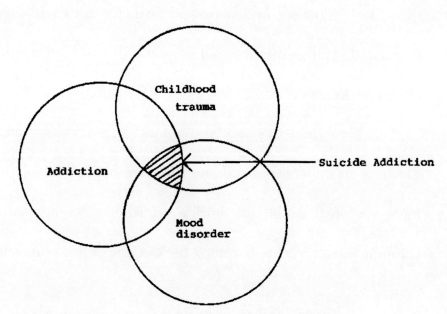

Figure 1: Possible matrix of predisposition to suicide addiction.

This highly unusual disorder lies at the center of these three overlapping disorders. Once it starts to develop, it acts like an addiction modulated by a mood disorder, with deep early trauma roots. And because it behaves like an addiction, our best hope for helping people with this strange, singular disorder lies in what we have learned about treating addictions.

What evidence do we have for such an explanation? The evidence lies in the minds of suicide attempters. This book gathers and presents the stories behind the theory. This is not a scientific study; it is purely descriptive. If you're looking for hard facts and figures, or if you have problems with radical new ideas, put this book down now. If, on the other hand, you believe, as I do, that suicide is an unknown frontier, to be explained with an open mind, and if you want to see inside the hearts and minds of those who have tried to kill themselves, read on.

A word about myself.

I am a practicing physician, and as such I want hope and healing for my suicidal patients and their families. In my 25 years of practice, I have encountered certain suicidal patients who made me very uncomfortable, primarily because I couldn't "pigeon-hole" them into standard psychiatric categories. Existing psychological theories simply did not work for these patients. I sensed that something else was going on, something different, requiring a new view.

But my interest is far more than professional. I am myself the survivor of seven suicide attempts. I need hope and healing for myself and my family. At the most personal level, traditional views of suicide never offered hope or healing, even though I can now see how some aspects of those theories apply to me. But they did not explain my own experience with suicide.

When I hit bottom in 1982, I began to understand some of what happened to me and those of my patients who didn't fit the theories. This book offers my understanding. It is a composite of my own struggle with suicide and the experience of 50 of my patients who experienced the same struggle between 1982 and 1997. These people are by far the most interesting, most challenging, and most rewarding of my patients. They willingly shared their stories for this book. I have, of course, changed their names, places, and ages and any dates they mention, in order to protect their privacy. Respecting the traditions of Alcoholics Anonymous, I have also disguised my own identity.

My addiction to suicide started in Grade 9, when I was 14. From that day until September 30, 1982, when I was 38, suicide was the most powerful thing in my life. Medical school and psychiatric residency, including two tours as Chief Resident, did not fix me. A wonderful wife, three beautiful children, a lovely home, and two nice cars did not fix me. After three overdoses and four attempted hangings, I hit a very painful rock-bottom in January 1982. Nine difficult but rewarding months in Woodlawn Psychiatric Hospital in Houston, Texas, learning to live instead of die, did me much good — but they too did not fix me.

What fixed me was a gift of grace. My near-fatal love affair with suicide ended with God's help, brought to me through the Twelve Steps of Alcoholics Anonymous. When I reached out to my sponsor Steve and my therapist Tom in mid-September 1982, I could admit to them what I had tried so long to hide from God and my fellows. In an agony of fear and shame, I told them of my drive to kill myself.

Two weeks after that, after daily AA meetings and several therapy sessions, I awoke free of suicidal thoughts on

September 30, 1982. By God's grace, I have stayed mostly free of suicidal thoughts for 20 years. To this day, I cannot explain this change, and I no longer try to understand it. I am simply grateful to God and live one day at a time, enjoying His grace and thanking Him for it. I have lived on borrowed time for 20 years. I often ask myself, "Why am I still here?" The answers come to me slowly, when I am spiritually ready for them.

Practicing medicine as a psychiatrist and addiction specialist has been a spiritual adventure, these last 20 years. I found my path crossing the paths of other people like me, and I found common elements in our experience. My wife Morgan and I appeared on "The Oprah Show" in the mid-nineties, on the subject of suicide. That event prompted us to tell our stories in this book.

Finding these 50 others like me has helped me understand that I am not alone. I believe that meeting these people has been another sign of God's grace and generosity toward me.

Each has touched my life in a special way, healed me a little more, and reminded me why I am still here.

Here are our stories.

Chapter 1:

Kevin's Story: To Hell and Back

"The frightening thing about suicide is its reminder
that we are none of us so far from it."
—P. Lopate[4]

My life was over. I knew that much.

January 1982, the neurotrauma unit. I came up from the depths,
surfacing into a cold gray day. The IV hurt. The short backless
hospital gown left my ass flapping in the breeze. My arms and legs
were like overboiled pasta, flopping helplessly. Nurses came and
went. I never looked up, never spoke. What was the point? Why
should I do what everyone had always expected of me? I was dead.

And then the thoughts and feelings hit, slamming into me like
breakers after a storm. I was *not* dead. I was full of fury at being alive,
back from death not once, but twice. I hated that bastard God and
knew with all my soul he hated me back, every bit as venomously.
But that had nothing on my hatred for myself. Hopelessness choked

---

[4] P. Lopate, *On Suicide* (San Francisco: Chronicle Books, 1992), 21.

1

me like coal smoke—probably the first fumes of the damnation that awaited me, if the God-people had it right.

Pain burned deep inside me, searing the inside of my head. It was too intense for tears, for words; it would not be released, and it could not be ignored. Everything *hurt*.—life in particular. If this was living, I wanted out, desperately.

Time passed. I could, with difficulty, focus my eyes. I could read the blue hospital band circling my wrist: the attending physician's name was Dr. Joe Calvin. Shit! My tennis buddy is now my doctor and chief guard. Abruptly I hated him too. He knew the truth. Everybody knew the truth. Shit.

I spent the next few days as a prisoner in Madison Heights, my own hospital. The attendants, there around the clock, might wear white uniforms, but I knew better than that: they were guards. I hated them too: dumb bastards. Some wanted to preach and pray over me; others pretended nothing had happened. Which was worse? I didn't know; I simply hated them all.

Late one night, I got the preaching-guard out of my room by conning her into fixing me a milkshake. That left me free to call home and give my wife Morgan hell. "I know you're behind this crap!" I screamed at her. "I feel like a goddamn five-year-old. Don't you know who I am? I don't need this!" I hated Morgan too.

This was death row, and I was both the condemned and the executioner. Every meal seemed my last one, fattening me for the kill. No more appeals, no prospect of a pardon. I had been judge and jury; I had passed judgment upon myself with no scrap of mercy. I thought of Hester Prynne wearing her scarlet A for adultery. I wore a black S for suicide. "At least adultery is an act of living," I thought.

Unit secretary is a one-of-a-kind job on a psychiatric unit, about halfway between mother confessor and traffic controller, with a dash of cruise director. Robin was a good one. She cared about her work, but more importantly, she cared about her patients and their doctors— even me. As a doctor, I counted on her to route all the goddamn paperwork—charts, bloodwork, orders, consults. Robin would make it all happen, as though by magic.

I knew enough to believe in her, even if I could not believe in me. I trusted her, and I respected her opinion. She, of all people, could assess the psychiatrists like a Kennel Club judge at a dog show. If she thought well of me, that would carry some weight. And so, when the nurse's voice squawked through the white-box intercom strapped to my metal bed, "A Robin to see you," something inside me yearned for her presence, as a prisoner on Death Row might want to see the chaplain.

She came slowly, softly, to the side of my bed. Her eyes were full of tears and pain drew lines across her forehead. She took my hand, very gently, and looked into my eyes. I could not resist that quiet look. I felt full of shame and yet oddly safe. I had no words, no explanations, and she asked for none. No bullshit; no small talk, no social "I'm fine", because I wasn't fine and Robin and everyone else in the hospital knew it.

"Kevin Taylor, I care about you," she said. Her voice was firm and compassionate, and I believed her—who knows why? "*We* care about you." I believed her again, without needing to know who "we" were. I'd been a practicing psychiatrist for seven years; I can judge tears, laughter, frowns, smiles, blankness, pain-lines, you name it. Facial expressions and body language are my stock in trade. I knew she was for real. "Why don't you let us help you?" she whispered, her eyes brimming.

At that moment, something inside me unknotted, and warmth flowed back from my chest to my cold, hurting head. I felt my eyes grow moist and a tear rolled down the side of my face—a tear of peace. *My way almost got me killed, twice. My way got me back in this hospital two times, almost dead. What have I got to lose? Why not let them help?*

I rolled my wheelchair through the 8 Calvin psych unit door, the same door I had locked and unlocked for seven years, on my rounds to see my patients. The door clicked and locked behind me. I had no key. It didn't matter. I was home.

The Dilantin and phenobarbital I'd taken in my overdose left me horribly uncoordinated. I overshot whenever I reached for anything. I couldn't walk; I couldn't use a knife and fork. I couldn't take a person's hand and shake it. For someone who'd been the Rollins College Ping-Pong champion for two years running, this was extremely scary: neuromuscular meltdown, oh no…"No way I'm going to live like this," I promised myself, as I deftly aimed a spoonful of food two inches to the right of my mouth. If this was life, I'd sooner not, thank you.

Suicide was alive and well within me. Next time, I wouldn't fail.

I have never been a gun person. I preferred drug overdoses and hangings But now, guns looked promising. End of barrel in the mouth, reach for the trigger, blam! It's over. I had run this scenario through my head over and over in the past, always stopping short. I hadn't the guts to use the gun. Now I was finding the guts. No fear; just rage, raw and powerful. "Blow your head off" said the executioner, exultant and terrified. I hated who I had become.

God catches you in the strangest places…Three feet from the nurses' station, for example. I must have crossed that same spot thousands of times in the last seven years. Now I call it my God Spot. It wasn't a voice, merely something between a feeling and a thought. Sometimes the solution to a problem pops into your mind, effortlessly, after what seems like an endless struggle. It feels like the tumblers of a lock clicking into alignment and the lock opening.

Something becomes possible that had not been possible before, however hard you'd worked at it. It was like that.

Two overdoses. Two best shots at suicide. I should be dead, but I'm not.

Abruptly I saw God, patiently and painfully watching me, staying with me, protecting me from each overdose. God just being present, not hating me, but suffering with me. God *wanting* my wellness and fullness of life, holding back, waiting for me to choose.

I didn't create myself. And I'm not in charge of when I die.

I kept it to myself at first, this knowledge, not sharing it with anyone. But in that single moment, something in me changed. I set foot on a great journey that day, one I had never thought about before. I had always asked to be understood, not to understand. I had always fled from consciousness, not embraced it. I had wanted to escape the painfulness of living. Now I could think about turning straight into it, like a boat setting out to sea—the start of the greatest of adventures, truly living.

I left Monroe, heading for Houston and the Woodlawn Psychiatric Hospital, on January 24th. At the airport, I met the eyes of my three beautiful children, who were there to see me off. I had chosen, 18 days before, to leave them by killing myself. Now, seeing them clearly, I felt a sudden pang of connection, a deep sadness for what I had put them through. I didn't want to leave them ever, but now I had to go, for their sakes and my own.

As I felt for them, I started for the first time to feel for myself. The child in them touched the child in me, and the child in me was a child in great pain. *How could you try to kill me?* But for the first time, I could see the pain as a gift, a healthy something to be accepted, not an evil to be evaded.

Morgan wasn't at the airport. She had done her bit to save me; now she was back in her childhood home, Savannah. How could I blame her?

My father was with me on the flight to Houston. I had my last drink on the plane, a double gin martini. It felt like the last drink given a condemned man on his way to execution—and in fact it was. For a new man to have life, the old man had to die.

The White House of Woodlawn Psychiatric Hospital was built in 1919. It sits out front, while behind it sprawl one-story red brick buildings on grounds spotted with old trees. South Unit, the newest, is furthest back on the campus. Walking from White House to South Unit with a guard at my side took forever. All I could feel was fear: *Will I ever leave this place? Who's behind those locked doors? I don't know anyone here!*

South Unit had no loving children, no concerned parents, no friendly co-workers—nothing to numb the pain, even for a second. Here I had to come up against it full force and utterly alone. *I'm drowning! I'm all alone. I can't do this. I want to die.*

I was on suicide watch. This time, I couldn't flee into the safe darkness. They'd left me no way to kill myself. I had to surrender all vestiges of my dignity—belt, keys, anything sharp. I ate with plastic utensils handed out, one meal at a time, by a tech stationed five feet from the dining table. And then there was Nurse Rhoda, my very own daytime nightmare. She was one tough lady, and I hated her. I thought bitter and scandalous things about her, as I struggled down the hall holding my pants up with my hands.

At night, I couldn't sleep. I felt as though reality was closing in around me like a cloud of biting insects; I slapped them away, but they would not leave me in peace. I slipped into a sort of oblivion now and then, but I spent what felt like eternity, night after night, staring into my own soul with a depth of self-loathing I cannot describe, until darkness closed over me.

And then it was morning, and morning was *hell*. Floods of awareness, and awareness meant reality—and reality sucked. I scanned my tiny room, looking for some exit, any way out of this—some rope of hope to hang myself with. Nothing. Suicide would have to wait.

Suicide watch ended, weeks later, with the ceremonial return of my belt. What a relief! Now at least I wouldn't have to hang onto my pants. I was actually grateful for something—a feeling I hadn't known for such a long time…And then I got real silverware, a metal knife and fork that didn't bend uselessly against every piece of mystery meat. "This is heaven!" I thought, cutting up my first meal as a free man. Heaven as a metal knife and fork…well, I was starting to learn.

Therapy hurt a lot. It stirred up those reality-bugs, the ones I wanted to swat away. But somehow, I managed to cling to my God-spot and my two God-things, back in Monroe. Little by little, my self-judgement and self-condemnation loosened their grip; they were no longer strangling me. I could feel them loosen their grip on my neck—the same neck I had slipped into a secret noose, four times, in my office on the floor below 8 Calvin psych unit.

As life started to stir in me, I felt a wriggle of curiosity. Two questions terrified and yet intrigued me: I was afraid to ask them, and even more afraid to answer them, but they kept stirring irrepressibly. What went so terribly wrong in me? And how did a smart guy like me end up in a place like this?

* * *

I was born in Costa Rica in spring, 1944. I have a photo of myself as a toddler, taken at our house: a happy blue-eyed blond baby with eager, trusting eyes and a huge happy grin, standing on a wooden patio chair, wearing nothing but my father's Army hat and a diaper with two big pins.

Something must have gone terribly wrong between that picture and the next, taken when I was two, after our move to Monroe. In that next photograph, there are no more smiles. The little boy has his head down; he looks fearful. He is dressed head to foot. The Santa Claus in the Monroe court square spoke Spanish. My mother said I finally smiled when I heard that language.

My first memories are all fearful: hiding under the coffee table in terror and tears during a thunderstorm; Mom was away, and there was only the maid there with me. I think I knew then that the world is not a safe place. Going to Snowden school: now, *that* was *terror*. Such a small word for such huge fear! First day of second grade: I dug in my heels and refused to leave the house. My father, wearing his big hat, walked me into my classroom to meet my new teacher. He left me there and walked out, as I screamed—but silently, inside my own head— "Don't leave me!" Something deep inside me froze that day in 1950, and I've spent the rest of my life trying to find some way to thaw that frozen part out.

By Grade 4, I had started to find both my brain and my feet. I learned that my intelligence could set me free. Getting As in my classes felt so good; they made my parents smile and earned my teacher's pleasure. Good grades could fill up the cold hole in the middle of me. They made the world safer. "As long as I can make As, I'll be okay," I whispered to myself. But even so, there was a tiny niggle of doubt—a corner of insufficiency. Mom had told me when I was four that my father had been the smartest student ever in his medical school. Had he made even more As? I wish she hadn't said that...

That year, Rosie came to us—more likely, was sent to us. She was my angel; I called her "my black mama" without understanding either the depth of my own needs or the implications of the title I gave her. She was always there. She made me feel safe.

By ninth grade, my shaky sense of confidence was just beginning to think about stabilizing. I could think about the future. I had my course all charted: straight As through school, med school just over the horizon. My sails were set and the waters ahead looked smooth and easy.

And then, just as the Titanic encountered its iceberg, so I encountered Mary Sims Dawson.

Grade 9 Latin. Latin scared me. Pop quizzes scared me. Bs scared me. Even the possibility of an F sent cold terror down into my frozen gut. When I saw that big red F on the pop quiz in Latin, it meant not just Failure, but Fatal and Frozen as well. There went my ship, torpedoed. So much for med school. So much for winning my parents' approval. So much for trust and confidence and hope.

I have to kill myself. The thought came from nowhere—or rather, it came from my own brain, the brain that had been going to set me free. Now that my brain had let me down, this thought came to rescue me. It consoled me. My sense of terror faded away; the trap opened, letting me go. I was free again. I had an option, a hope, a new course to set sail for, one that *I* controlled. It was a secret power, one I could hug to myself, and it killed the pain.

Senior year. I was the lead man in the senior play, and again terror gripped me. "Why, for God's sake, didn't I turn this down?" I demanded of myself, over and over, as opening night grew closer. I couldn't do this! Allen Macdonald, my favorite English teacher, thought I'd be good in the part, and I'd trusted him. But he couldn't possibly understand the risk. He didn't know what was at stake. The thought of suicide popped out of my mind again, stronger than before. Again, it comforted me; it gave me a way out, a solution. It gave me hope. I clung to the thought of suicide as a secret daily "fix" right up to opening night, when the play proved successful.

Rollins College was my coming out, and Morgan was my teacher. If I lacked confidence, she had it in abundance. An outgoing girl with a huge smile and a wonderful Savannah southern drawl, Morgan never met a stranger, only friends. For me, it was both love and jealousy at first sight. I hadn't a clue what to make of her. Could she thaw that frozen chunk deep inside me? Or would she rip all the sails of the ship I was sailing toward medical school? I didn't know which to fear more.

My first drink! I was 17; it was my cousin's debutante ball in Greenville, Mississippi. Bourbon and coke filled the cold emptiness in my gut—a hole I didn't know I owned until that night. No more staring at my shoes. No more playing the wallflower, looking out longingly at the dancers twirling in each other's arms. No more pain.

Now I had *two* drugs to fix me, booze and suicide, two secrets to hug to myself, two safe places.

Senior year at Rollins, carrying a full head of sail: if not all As, at least a very respectable 3.4 grade-point average. After graduation, Morgan and I married in 1965. We settled as newlyweds into our first apartment. Morgan started teaching, and I started med school.

"Bullfrog" Johnson taught biochemistry. Bullfrog Johnson had taught my father. Second day in school: Bullfrog Johnson raised his head from looking at his roll book. "Taylor?" he said, "where are you? Are you Fred Taylor's boy?" I put up my hand, slowly. "Yes, sir," I said, and heard my own voice shaking. "Son," Bullfrog Johnson said, looking straight at me over the top of his reading glasses, "you will never beat your dad's record at this school."

There it was, seeming to explode in my head: that big F. I'd failed even before I'd written my first paper or exam, and my failure had been broadcast to all my 200 classmates on the second day of med school. I froze in shame. *End of med school. I have to kill myself.* I hated Bullfrog Johnson for that. God rest his soul, he was only being tactless. He couldn't understand.

16

For the next weeks and months, suicidal thoughts roared through my mind like fire through dry grass. I could focus on nothing else. I couldn't study, couldn't think straight. All my dreams had collapsed; the ship had sunk. I was lost in terror, helpless. There was no safety anywhere. I dreamed only of ways to kill myself. I held out for four months before I finally had to give in. I sank on my maiden voyage.

Leaving med school was the ultimate disgrace. Not only was I humiliated, but I had disgraced Morgan, my parents, and my family name. As the oldest of three children, I had been the Hero Child, destined for greatness. Now I was finished. The day I quit school, I planned my death by overdose, carefully calculating dosages from my now-unneeded pharmacy textbook. As I worked through the dosages, my sense of dishonor and failure melted away. Humiliation loosened its grip on me, and I could breathe again. A great calmness came over me. I had found an option again. I had some hope.

Teaching Algebra I in high school was fun and kept me out of Vietnam. In school, algebra had been a straight-A sort of safety for me. Teaching it to 8th and 9th grade girls felt safe too, even though I'd never taught anything but Sunday School before. For a while,

17

thoughts of suicide died down to a small flicker at the back of my mind. But the flicker, lit in Latin I, never quite went out.

That summer, I drank Budweisers with my friend Ben—a real "in yer face!" gesture for two second-generation fundamentalist-church boys. Ben died horribly 25 years later, an alcoholic, all alone. I still miss him.

Back on course, second try: a new medical school let me break free of home, with Morgan at my side. I *could* reach that shore. This time, I'd beat the terror. I ate my way through biochemistry, downing masses of Empirin with codeine #3. "Take that, Bullfrog," I muttered with each pill. I came in first in gross anatomy! I could make the As I craved. I didn't *need* suicide; I'd be okay. It was false pride, of course, but I didn't figure that out until later.

Our first child, Kevin Jr., was born, and I lost my best friend. Morgan taught during the day and mothered at night. Now she wasn't *my* mom, but the baby's. So I looked elsewhere for comfort. Julie was cute, Julie was young, and making love to Julie made me feel good. I had three drugs to fix me now: sex, booze, and suicide. All three were powerful; all three were huge secrets. That summer, Dr. Newton taught me cardiology and dry gin martinis. I've forgotten the cardiology, but I can still taste those martinis on a hot night.

Finishing med school almost finished me. When Dean Caldwell called out "Kevin Taylor, M.D.!" a wave of terror hit me in the gut. I hated every possible medical speciality, eliminating each and every sort of internship and residency. I was adrift again, with no place to call home. For the first time, I realized that I didn't *want* to be a doctor. I'd got my M.D. only because my father had one.

Straight internal medicine internship was pure hell, while the first month on emergency was awful. Pathology was better, in that it meant no patients and less of my having to be a doctor. But it didn't fix me either. My first autopsy was of a blue-eyed blond boy, the same age as my own child—a child like me. Weeks before, I'd watched him struggle for life on the ward. He'd lost the fight. "No way I can cut that kid up," I thought in desperation.

I took my first overdose later that night, in the summer of 1971—only 12 pills, but for me, a huge step forward. Neil Armstrong had nothing on me! This was a new option, a new fix. I was half scared to death and half exhilarated. Above all, I was *hooked.*

As for my profession, there was one specialty that I thought I could manage: psychiatry. "More teacher than doctor," I thought, remembering how fun and safe it felt to teach algebra. "Besides, it might help fix me." This is a hell of a bad reason to become a shrink, but it's also surprisingly common.

Going back to residency in Monroe felt like returning to the scene of a crime. And suicide swept through my mind constantly: a continual fire.

First-year psychiatry resident, 5 North, Monroe Mental Health Institute. Damn. I'd never been on an inpatient psych unit. I'd never even seen a schizophrenic, much less had to manage one. I shivered in secret fear as the door clicked and locked. Pat, the 3-11 tech who was showing me around, looked interesting. Morgan was expecting twins in a few months, and I was about to lose my best friend again. I'd sworn off extramarital sex after Julie and was almost shocked to find myself in an affair with Pat after a few months. But again, sex was a powerful drug, powerful enough to still the pain in my gut. The two matched up perfectly. And at least, sex helped dampen my urge towards suicide.

I was Chief Resident—my second tour of duty. Maybe it wasn't internal medicine, but at least it was something I could do. I began to dream of a chair in psychiatry at Harvard. I'd be the hero yet.

Allergies. Snotty, sneezy, stupid, draggy allergies. They don't ever kill you; you just wish they would. I always prayed for something more fatal, or at least more interesting, but God wasn't listening. The headaches were awful—headaches of every sort: little ones, big ones, short ones, long ones, dull ones, pounding ones. "Migraines", I self-diagnosed with fear and excitement. "I'm getting migraines, like my father. Forget Harvard with these babies."

But Darvon fixed the headaches, so I took Darvon—before meals, during meals, after meals, between meals, before Darvons and after Darvons. Darvons kept the headaches at bay and Harvard on the horizon.

Assistant Director of Residency Training, Department of Psychiatry, 1975. Not Harvard, but on the way. Private practice at Madison Heights in the afternoons. A foot in both worlds, Darvon in my pocket and plenty of prescription pads, Harvard still in sight...I had the world by the tail, it seemed.

21

Goodbye Pat-the-tech, hello Natalie-the-shrink—well, I had always thought psychiatry might fix me…For eight years, we were together daily. Not once could I tell her a word about the Darvon in my pocket and the suicidal thoughts burning through my mind. So much for closeness…

Oh, '76 was a banner year: my mother almost died of a massive heart attack, my dad ended up at Woodlawn, on my referral. Darvon, more Darvon, plus Ativan, more Ativan. There weren't enough pills in the world to quiet the growing terror in me. I was running straight onto the rocks, facing the certain prospect of disaster: failure, dishonor, humiliation, despair. I could see only one way out: "Brilliant young psychiatrist kills himself. Whole world mourns!" It was better than Darvon, better than drink, better than Natalie.

Friday, August 13, 1976: I left the note of apology on the passenger seat of my red TR7, where Morgan and Natalie took turns sitting. I had 5000 mg of my own Elavil samples, washed down with my mother's favorite, a cold bottle of Coke. It almost worked.

Waking up in the intensive care unit of Madison Heights. They'd had to bring me back several times during the ambulance ride. As I started to surface, so did the despair—and then the rage. A nurse was trying to fix the IV in my right arm. I took a swing at her. I swore and screamed in the safety of my own head "I'm not supposed to BE here!" My god had failed me. Death had let me down.

And here I was, branded by my own actions: I'd wear this SUICIDE label till the end of my days. For the first time, I realized just where I was and what I had done. Another thing to be ashamed of, another failure. It burned deep in my mind; my own soul stank with it. I would have to live with this until I died—but I couldn't die.

I spent ten days on 8-Main at Lee Memorial, the crosstown rival nut ward. My time there worked wonders, or so they thought. I said nothing about my 50 pills a day, nor of Natalie, nor of the steady flickering flame at the back of my mind. Of all people, of course *I* knew the buzz words, and just how I could feed them back to a shrink: "stress", "depression", "compulsivity" and (his favorite!) "Oedipus complex." Dr. Harris was pleased with me. Freud would have been pleased with me too. And since they were pleased with me,

I was pleased with me too. Besides, I thought, as I counted my pulse looking for signs of withdrawal, this whole pill and OD business— just a mistake. No big deal. End of discussion.

Three days later, back in my white coat, with the flowing color-coordinated label over the left breast pocket: Kevin Taylor, M.D., I marched confidently through the halls of Madison Heights, making my rounds. I was now dedicated to sniffing out suicide and eradicating it from every floor of the hospital. With fifty pills inside me, homemade filters stuffed into my nostrils to keep the allergens at bay, no underwear (to ward off the heat rash caused by all those pills), suicide burning brightly at the back of my head, and Natalie at my side, I was the Hero Child. I would, by God, exterminate every symptom of emotional pain that crossed my path.

Rope! Lots of rope! I browsed through the aisles of Simpson Brothers Hardware. There it was: the perfect rope. *Keep cool. Nobody will suspect a thing.* What a rush! What a fix! A new frontier…Knots usually weren't my thing, but with practice between patients and after hours, I got noose-tying down to a fine art. In my biofeedback lab, right beneath the 8 Calvin psych ward, there was a handy piece of black drainpipe exposed. That, with a small brown stool, made a perfect gallows. *Obviously I'm all hung up on psychiatry—enjoy that one, Freud*, I thought, surveying my handiwork.

Again and again in the years from '76 to '82, I would go into suicidal trances. Still in my white coat, I would go to Calvin 7, leave the elevator, turn first right and then left, slip through the back door into Room 703, enter the biofeedback lab, slip the noose over my head, and try to kick the stool out from under my own feet. The hangman in me wrestled with the condemned prisoner in me, while the addict in me stood to one side and copped a magnificent high. Four times I came very close. Once, the hangman won, and I came out of my trance on the floor, the stool three feet away, and rope burns on my neck. For a moment, I was healthily terrified. But then the flame steadied and leapt high again.

From then on, I was in a losing battle with my god and lover, Death. Suicide stayed with me every waking moment, at home, at work, on break, whenever. It was only a matter of time.

Wednesday, January 6, 1982. In my own office, Calvin 703. I reached into the top left-hand drawer of my desk. Days before, during rounds I had found and confiscated a bottle of Dilantin and phenobarbital from one of my patients, an impulsive young man on Calvin 8. I had a bottle of booze in my desk as well. I took the two together, read my Bible for a while, and waited to walk straight into my lover's arms.

* * *

So there I was in the winter of '82, off suicide watch at Woodlawn, in Houston, Texas, feeling absurdly grateful for metal cutlery and my belt. Off suicide watch meant off South Unit, and off South Unit meant starting my classes. Off to school again. Some things never change. This time, I had no mom, no dad, no Morgan; only a guard—but a friendly guard. I felt childishly happy to have a friend to walk with me to school. I felt—safe.

No grades! This school has no grades! I can't make an F! I shouted to myself. All I had to do was suit up and show up and I'd be okay. It was a wonderful gift, a blessing. *A uniform—I need a uniform.* I chose my blue tennis warmups—*with* underwear, now that

I didn't have to worry about heat rash from those fifty pills. Art therapy had taught me that blue was my safe color. And the pants' drawstring waist let me keep my precious belt safe in my own room.

I was still mostly brain-dead from years of pills, sex, and suicide. I was also a very slow learner— "emotionally challenged" they'd call it today. I had to struggle with the most basic insights, learning them the hard way, by direct experience. My wonderful mind was no help at all.

Woodlawn was a "do it, don't think it; enjoy it, don't analyze it" sort of place. The kid in me loved it. The adult side of me hated it and wanted out *now*. In this internal war I was, for the first time, siding with the kid.

In the past, my kid-side had survived on sports—church baseball, Ping-Pong with my dad, basketball with my high-school gang, volleyball at Rollins, even racquetball and tennis, played late at night after rounds on Calvin 8. *Volleyball, here I come!* I laced my tennis shoes on with a burst of energy and enthusiasm, a strangely familiar feeling I hadn't know for years.

The ball floated toward me, absolutely perfect; I leapt to spike it, straining high—and took the ball right square on my skull. I hadn't reckoned with the effects of years of Ativan and weeks of Dilantin toxicity on the 37-year-old male body. Devastated, knowing myself a failure, I felt everyone's eyes on me.

I was back at age 9, playing baseball for the first time. The pitcher walked me. I was on first base, safe but scared. The first baseman whispered "Play off the bag." So I did, and he tagged me out with the ball he had hidden in his glove. Everyone laughed. I was crushed. *That was the first day I felt like crying like this.* I'd walked off that baseball diamond determined never to come back, but I did, at 11, and went on to play nine wonderful years of ball. *I did it then; I can do it now.* And I did, and had nine wonderful months of volleyball. I was learning. Something was starting to happen.

Something was also starting to draw me to chapel on Sunday mornings—I didn't know what. I couldn't understand what the attraction was. Few other patients came, but still, I kept on going. Was it some old church tape, something bouncing around in my unconscious from childhood? I'd grown up in a church where Sunday morning means Sunday school: that fact had been etched into my mind. Now that the drugs were out of my system, the etching was still there. So I sat in the chapel, obedient as a trained dog, long after the bell had rung.

That Sunday was nothing special—very plain, very ordinary. I'd sat through chapel, my mind as much on the week ahead as it was on the service. I still don't know what happened. I just know that it hit me again: another God-thing, like the brief God-things I'd had on 8 Calvin—but this one was right off the scale.

All these years, I blamed God for deserting me. I was so angry with him—so furious at him. But he was there all along with me. He didn't desert me. I deserted him.

And then the gentle certainty, rising from the depths—a voice of great quietness and love, that I knew was not myself but God speaking: *My good child, my dear one. Thank you for seeing that.*

I'd always seen God as sitting above me in judgment, looking over his glasses in scorn, waiting to take pot-shots and find fault with everything I did and was. I imagined God raining Fs down on me, whatever I did, however hard I tried. I saw God as setting up a standard that I could not possibly meet, and judging me against that standard, without kindness or mercy. Now I found a new God, a friend, companionably beside me. And I knew he had been there all along, waiting for me: patient, silent, constant—with faith in me, as I had never had faith in him. He had endured my unfair judgment of *him*, waiting for me to release my blame, my rage. He had sent people to love and minister to me: Rosie, Morgan, Robin, even Nurse Rhoda, the guard who walked with me. He had given me such gifts: my beautiful children, my joy in sports, a world full of wonder. For a moment, I knew a gratitude so intense it floored me, and I wept.

Maybe some of us turn our lives around 100% in a single moment, but I'm not one of them. For me, it had to be two steps forward, one back. I'd left a real mess behind me, and I still had a whole lot to learn.

May, 1982. Morgan was pissed, *really* pissed. I didn't think that was fair. After all, I wrote her at least once a week, even when I didn't want to. Of course, I also wrote to Natalie, who really *understood* me. I still fantasized about shedding wife and kids and setting up a bachelor pad with megawatts of stereo equipment. I

poured my heart out to Natalie, detailing the horrors of my existence.
I made the hospital sound like something out of *One Flew Over the
Cuckoo's Nest*, with a dollop of Dante's Inferno thrown in for good
measure. Natalie poured on sympathy. Morgan didn't.

Kevin Johnson—Dr. Bushy-Brows—scared me even more than
Mary Sims Dawson and Latin I. He meant *business*—no B.S.
allowed!. Worse still, he'd treated my father. *I've got my dad's
shrink!* I screamed into my pillow, the night before my therapy began.

Kevin didn't appreciate my plan for the bachelor pad. That pissed .
me off. He wanted to "explore it". Explore it! I wanted to *do* it. *Don't
throw this therapy shit at me, doc!* But I locked my anger away,
keeping it safe from being seen—or healed. It took me five months to
get up enough nerve to admit to him that I was angry at him.

He could use those bushy eyebrows like a marksman uses a rifle.
"You know," he said, raising one of them, "I'm not sure you're
capable of commitment." Rage roared through me. What about Julie?
What about Pat? What about Natalie? *Don't you know who I am*? But
I feared that maybe he did know.

Eyebrow #2: ready, aim, fire: "You never really made a commitment to your marriage or to Morgan." Direct hit. He was right, dead right, and the knowledge stunned me.

That goodbye letter to Natalie was the first honest and healthy pain I felt at Woodlawn. Oh, I'd done lots of pain before, but there's the pain of sickness and the pain of healing, and this was the first I'd done of the latter persuasion. Still, it hurt like hell, from my toes to my teeth. I was like a kid losing his favorite toy. My whole world fell apart.

Morgan came to visit—our first therapeutic visit. We had four hours together, with a guard close by. Within five minutes, we were raging at each other on the tennis court. She almost left me there. *Don't you know who I am?* But I feared that maybe she did know. That same struggle, between wanting to be understood and not wanting to be seen with any clarity at all...We came so close that day to breaking our marriage. My life fell apart a little bit more.

On the other hand, life in the puzzle factory was definitely improving. I was starting to gain confidence, starting to feel better. My teachers seemed happy with me. Freud would have been pretty pleased, I imagined. So I was happy with me too. In therapy with Bushy-Brows one day, I was spouting off cheap insights with great enthusiasm, showing off my Woodlawn Patient of the Year persona, when he trained his eyebrows on me, sighting for bear again.

"And tell me, Kevin: do you plan to do something about your drug addiction before you go back to Monroe?"

Nice technique, I thought approvingly. *At least a 9.5. Drug addiction? Me?* I cast my mind back over my time at Woodlawn. Not once had I craved a drug, not even once. *Wrong man. Not me!*

Leaning forward in his chair, eyebrows up, Bush-Brows moved in closer. "I want you to contact the Impaired Physicians Program here in Houston," he said, looking me straight in the eyes. At once my heart went out to those poor impaired physicians, who I was clearly called upon to help. They *needed* me. How could I possibly refuse?

In Lynn's car, on my way to my first meeting of the International Doctors in Alcoholics Anonymous (IDAA), I was on pins and needles, waiting to meet the poor doc whom I'd help that night. As we drove, Lynn told me his story—the depressions, the drugs, the divorce, the shock treatments, the agony." Then he leaned toward me,

33

asking in that "I know something you don't know" voice: "Do you know what was wrong with me?"

"No, what?" I said.

"I'm an addict!" he proclaimed.

"No shit!" I thought, amazed. "I'm one too!" At that moment, years of denial melted away like snow under strong sun. *I* was the poor doc who got helped that night. I'd come home.

Paul strolled up to me after that first meeting, a big smile on his face, and thrust out his hand. "Woodlawn," he said with a sort of questioning authority. "Two years ago."

"Yep," I answered, much as I'd announce my alma mater.

"What unit?" he asked.

"South."

"Me too. What doc?"

"Johnson."

"Me too. What room?"

"Last one on the left."

"Me too."

This was giving me goose bumps. It felt as though God had sent me my very own angel that evening in the form of a sponsor.

Fourth step: personal inventory. I didn't want to do it. Paul said, do it. I did it, and the fifth step too. Dr. Bushy-Brows was starting to make more sense. Affirming the changes in me, he encouraged me to stick with Paul and the A.A. meetings. I was starting to *like* my therapist. The first time, I cried with him, it felt so safe—a warm-fuzzy feeling I'd never experienced before.

Morgan and I, meanwhile, took the best step we'd taken in years: we put our marriage on a one-day-at-a-time standing. What freedom! We gave each other the freedom to stay or go each morning. We chose, that first morning, to stay, both of us, and we have made the same choice every morning since.

As denial melted away, each stretch of truth became clearer. I realized that I'd been addicted not just to drugs, but to women too: for me, mood-altering sex was exactly like mood-altering pills. If I fell back into those two traps, I'd end up killing myself. And then there was work…I realized, sadly, that working at Madison Heights would threaten my sobriety. It was too big a risk. Morgan, our son Kevin, and my dad—bless them!—struggled to dismantle my old office. But with 703 Calvin gone, would I ever be able to work again?

August 10, 1982. It was a long, long struggle, but I faced the reality: it was time to go back out into the world. All I could do was to trust in God to carry me through. "If you think I need another year here on South, I'll do it," I told Dr. Munford on rounds that day, meaning every word of it. He paused, looking at me thoughtfully, and said, "We've set your discharge date. September 10." My heart almost stopped.

Saying goodbye to Woodlawn was almost as painful and terrifying as stepping through those doors and onto suicide watch nine months before. "I don't want to go!" part of me screamed inside my head, as I'd screamed to stay home from second grade, years ago. But another part of me knew that I had to go, just as I'd had to leave my kids at the airport back in January. To grow, I had to let go and move on.

My final goodbye was to Dr. Munford, who had been my doctor and attending psychiatrist. A G.P. turned psychiatrist, he brought common sense, firmness, and great wisdom to his work. I had come to trust and love him deeply, hoping some day to become more the man he was. "Kevin," he said in our last moments together, "You will always have us with you." I cried, thinking of E.T. touching Eliot's forehead and saying, "I'll be right here." I had seen that movie five times that summer and wept each time. E.T. had helped me understand so much. Now *my* E.T. was saying goodbye. It hurt like hell.

"I do have one concern for you that I want to share," he went on. I nodded, too close to tears to speak. "I don't think you're finished with your struggle with suicide."

Terror hit me."NO!" I screamed inside my head. The flame had been out for months; now it was awake again. Or had it ever really gone out? Driving away from Woodlawn with Morgan, I realized that it had been there all along, but burning so low I hadn't noticed it. I'd been distracted, too preoccupied with the Twelve Steps of A.A. and other new and healthy things to pay it any attention. But every mile we drove left the flame a little stronger. By the time we got to Monroe, it as burning bright and strong.

Steve introduced me to the I.D.A.A. group in Monroe and took me under his wing. I started therapy with Tom. But they weren't Paul and Kevin, and Monroe wasn't Houston. I wanted to go home to Woodlawn so badly...

Like Rip van Winkel, I was a stranger in my own home and city. What could I say to my children? "So sorry—I missed your childhoods." Who were these young people I barely knew? Looking back over the wreckage of my life, all I could see was how much I'd lost, or missed, or screwed up. The pain was intense.

Monroe Mental Health Institute, 3 North; back in the white coat, Medical Director. The same hospital where I'd started psychiatry was now the hospital where I had to start all over again. But this time, without mood-altering women or pills or booze. Locking the door behind me, glancing down at the keys in my hand, I found myself longing desperately for the guard with the keys who had walked me to class at Woodlawn.

Waking up at 5:00 that morning in September 1982, in the same bed I had lain in waiting for death, back in 1976, with the shutters closed, I knew They were back: the thoughts. Suicide roared through my head. I wanted so desperately to hang myself in our attic, or to shoot myself in the mouth, as I'd planned back in January on 8 Calvin. But this time, I refused to take a pill or find a mood-altering woman. If I had to die, I wanted to die sober. I'd worked too hard on those Twelve Steps of Alcoholics Anonymous.

Lying there paralyzed, I faced the worst moment since Woodlawn. *What do I do now, God? I don't want to die. I don't want to live.* What would all those people at Woodlawn tell me? I thought of those groups, the therapy sessions, the doctors' meetings, Paul, Dr. Munford, Bush-Brows—even E.T. I knew then: *I've got to call Steve.* I think that was the toughest phone call of my entire life.

Later that morning, Steve showed up for breakfast in his blue tennis warmup— "in case you tried to run" he told me later. We talked and ate and ate and talked. We've been talking and eating for the last 20 years, now. I have no plans to stop.

In therapy with Tom the next day, I finally opened up. I told him about my suicidal thoughts. Part of me was terrified that he'd lock me up; but at the same time, I secretly hoped he'd send me home to Woodlawn—my place of safety. Instead, he simply listened and loved me. He's been listening and loving me ever since—again, it's been 20 years, and I have no plans to stop. Just the other day, I told him I was ready to commit to long-term therapy, remembering the time Bushy-Brows confronted me about my inability to commit myself. I miss Bush Brows. I can't imagine life without Tom.

For weeks after that morning, things were tough, but I hung on one day at a time, feeling the gentle brush of wings as my angels circled around me. I went on working my A.A program and steps. It isn't a one-time process; you keep discovering them over and over again. I kept giving it what I hoped was my best shot. One day, at an A.A. meeting, the Third Step jumped out at me, almost off that page: "Made a decision to turn our will and lives over to the care of God as we understood him." *It's not there! There's nothing in there, not a word in that step, about alcohol, drugs, or mood-altering women.* It hit me right between the eyes. *That steps says to turn "our will and lives over to God". But I haven't done that.*

Now I could *see*—see all the way back to that day in Latin 1 when I, at age 14, had had my first thought of suicide. I suddenly understood. *Suicide had been my out*. I had felt unable to face life on life's own terms; well, I could always kill myself. Even at Woodlawn, I had thought, *well, if these Twelve Steps fail me, I can always kill myself.* Suicide had been my escape route, the thing I'd hugged to myself, my secret "out" from life's difficulties.

But the Twelve Steps don't work that way. They don't accommodate hold-outs. You can't hold out from God; you can only surrender completely, or not surrender at all. There are no negotiated truces, where you get to hang on to part of your will and give over the parts you don't care so much about. I had to trust completely, as I'd never trusted before. No outs; no cheap and quick solutions. I did not create myself, and I am not in charge of my life and death. That's God's business. Finally it all made sense.

September 30, 1982. I sat down with my coffee to start my meditation. This time, the difference in my mind-set was astonishing. *No suicidal thoughts.* I couldn't believe it. *Oh, thank You. NO suicidal thoughts!* I had lived for 24 years with that flame flickering at the back of my skull, and now it was gone.

I will never fully understand what it was happened that day—and I don't feel any need to. I accept it as the gift it was, thanking my God day by day. I will live this day as I hope God wants me to, and only *this* day, until God decides that my time on this earth is over.

(But were the thoughts gone forever?)

Chapter 2:

Can Suicide Be Addictive?

"There are also others…for whom the mere idea of suicide is enough; they…function efficiently provided they have their own…means of escape always ready: a hidden cache of sleeping pills, a gun at the back of the drawer…".
A. Alvarez[5]

Can suicide by addictive? What a bizarre question! Drugs have their attractions; so does alcohol, so does sex. It's easy to see how someone could become addicted to something that makes them feel good. But suicide *hurts*; it's messy and painful. How could anyone become addicted to it?

We think of it as the last act of hopelessly depressed or deranged people, and indeed, sometimes that's what suicide is. Think of a severely depressed 60-year-old alcoholic, whose wife just died of cancer. His kids won't speak to him. He has nothing left to live for, and the prospect of life without his wife is terrifying. So he gives

---

[5] A. Alvarez, *The Savage God* (New York: Norton, 1971), 154.

away all his possessions, puts the barrel of his shotgun in his mouth, and blows the back of his head off. Suicide? Definitely. Addictive behavior? Definitely not.

Or think of a 25-year-old schizophrenic, who's gone off his meds and has tumbled into a world of brilliant, terrifying psychosis, full of confusion and chaos. He is deteriorating rapidly. He hears voices telling him to mutilate himself. "If your eye offend you, pluck it out," they whisper to him, and he pulls out his own left eye. "Throw yourself down," they scream to him, "and God will send his angels to bear you up." He jumps from the 10th floor of an office building. Suicide? Definitely. Addictive behavior? Definitely not.

Most suicide attempts are the result of depression or psychosis. This book is not for them, or for people who have to deal with them. But for some people, suicide is not what it seems to be. It is a totally different experience. For some, suicide becomes a mood-altering experience, an escape from pain, a fix as powerful as crack is to cocaine addicts. How it works is complex and not well understood, as we'll find later on.

But for some people, myself included, with a history of multiple suicide gestures or attempts, diagnoses of depression, personality disorders, or other "conventional" mental illnesses don't fully explain what is going on. People like us continue to have secret patterns of suicidal fantasies, obsessions, rituals, and attempts, despite all sorts of treatment by well-meaning mental health professionals. Antidepressants, anti-anxiety medications, shock therapy, individual or group psychotherapy—none of these can stop our relentless preoccupation with death.

Kevin: *For ten years I knew that I would die at my own hands before age 40. I could see absolutely no other way out. Many times a day, I secretly pictured the newspaper headlines: "Brilliant Young Psychiatrist Kills Self. Whole World Mourns." Crazy as it was, the fantasy somehow got me through each day.*

How does such a state of mind develop? Why do some people seem to be trapped in suicidal thoughts and behaviors? No one knows.

But the stories of about 50 of us who have lived with suicide addiction suggest a possible progression, in definite stages: onset, early, middle, and late stages, each with definite common characteristics.

For us, suicide was our drug. For many of us, the drug of suicide was more powerful than other drugs, than alcohol or sex. We put it at the top of our mood-altering experiences. For us, it was there always, a powerful lover, the way out when we needed it.

Kevin: *When all else failed, I knew that suicide was there, that I could count on it, more than the drugs or the affairs. It was all mine. I didn't have to share it with anyone. I carried it with me at all times, tucked away in a secret place in my head. No one could take it away from me. No one could have it.*

Childhood Onset

The onset of suicidal thoughts can be difficult to pinpoint. But for virtually everyone in our group, the problem started sometime in childhood or the early teen years, rarely later. Most of us could remember some precipitating instance early in life, sometimes a very painful experience, but often something quite minor. Whatever it was, we thought to ourselves, "Well, then. If it gets bad enough, I can always kill myself." It was, for us, a comforting thought. But it was also the start of a struggle that would go on for years.

Kevin: *For me, it was when I was 14. It was a normal day at school, nothing special. Grade 9 Latin I class scared me. The teacher terrified us all by pulling pop quizzes just before the bell. One minute left to go, and I had no idea how to decline this particular word. When I saw the red F on my quiz the next day, I died. Med school means all As, no Fs! No more med school, no more life. I'd never be able to face my parents. I'd have to kill myself. I felt instantaneous relief and peace. Suicide was planted somewhere in the back of my mind, that day.*

Raquel: *When I was 12, I went to a sleepover at my friend's house, and her father and brother molested me. I thought I was bad and that someone would surely find out that it was my fault. I was afraid to live or to tell anyone. My next thought was suicide. It became my most powerful drug.*

Jacqueline: *When I was 13, they were trying to hospitalize me. I recall being analyzed and having psychological testing. It's very vague to me, but I remember wanting to jump out the hospital window.*

Chastity: *My bird died. I was 7. I just kept thinking about going to sleep and not waking up, or sinking into a swimming pool and never coming up to the surface. My teacher called my mother to talk about what was wrong with me.*

Suicidal thoughts seem to be harmless enough, in many children, and they may be common among children who are experiencing painful moments. Children talk of hurting themselves, sometimes as a joke, sometimes to get attention, or sometimes to express their pain to adults around them. The moment passes, and the thoughts pass too, with little impact.

But for others, these thoughts are not harmless and do not pass with the moment. Instead, the thoughts of suicide produce an alteration in mood—a brief "fix" which is dramatic and catches our attention. Experiences like these are highly personal. From such a moment onward, the child tucks his or her thoughts of suicide away at the back of the mind.

What makes the thought a fix? We didn't know at the time. In fact, we assumed that most children had the same experience. We couldn't, however, compare notes with other children, because we felt impelled to keep these thoughts to ourselves—often in shame, because in our culture suicide is a failure and a disgrace. But some of us played with the thoughts for a little, running them through our minds several times a day, then tucking them away for another time, hugging them to ourselves.

Looking back, almost all of us knew that something in us had changed in some fundamental way. We were not the same people we had been. We were not finished with the thoughts. Somehow, the thoughts had become part of us.

Early Stage: The Fantasy

Next time we encountered a painful situation or felt trapped or scared, we could pull out our thoughts of suicide and feel their comfort. This time, however, we started to run the thoughts around in our minds, tasting them. We started to fantasize about suicide. That felt even better.

Authors have described fantasy from a wide variety of perspectives. Fantasy is a complex business. Normal children spend hours in their own worlds of fantasy and play, using it to explore the world's possibilities, to develop their own sense of identity, and to try on new roles. In this way, fantasy can be an adaptive, healthy way of growing. Children can also use fantasy to process pain and to communicate that pain to the adults who care for them. Play therapy makes use of this process to give children in treatment a chance to release their pain and heal.

But for some children, fantasy becomes pathological—a way to escape the process of growth, exploration, and challenge. Spending longer and longer periods in these fantasies, these children become lost or trapped—arrested in fantasy without integrating their experiences into their lives. They use fantasy not to help them grow, but to evade pain—not to cope with reality, but to escape it.

Chastity: *I lived in a fantasy world. Dracula was one of my favorite characters. Everything dark and sinister called to me. It wasn't bad; it felt good. At 17, I went into renal failure in the hospital. My pressure was 60/20. They called in my parents and sisters. I felt very good, very warm and peaceful, as though God was holding me in His arms. I seemed to look down on myself and my family from a great distance, through a kind of glow—no worries, no pain.*

In 1983, Patrick Carnes described sexual addiction as a "fantasy addiction".[6] For sexual addicts, sexual fantasy both avoids reality and produces a mood alteration. Obsessive sexual fantasies powerfully alter their mood and turn their vision away from an external reality that they cannot cope with or control, toward an inner reality of excitement, power, control, and omnipotence. In the fantasy state, sexual addicts are in *control*. They can write their own scripts and replay the scenes as often as they want, in as many ways as they want. They control everyone in the scene, and in the most powerful way— sexually. They can change the scenes to suit themselves. They alone have the power. In their fantasies, they are God. These fantasies are tremendously exciting and mood-altering—a real fix, to which they become addicted.

For us, suicidal fantasies became the equivalent. Whenever we felt trapped by reality, we used suicidal thoughts to escape. Over time, we expanded and developed our fantasies. Just as sexual addicts fantasized about bodies in sexual postures and actions, so we

---

[6] P. Carnes, *Out of the Shadows* (Minneapolis: Comp Care, 1983), 4.

fantasized about ways of killing ourselves—overdoses, hangings, shootings, car accidents. We replayed the scenes over and over in our heads, varying the details, trying new ways. We controlled everyone in the scene, in the most powerful way—living and dying. We could change the scenes to suit ourselves. In our fantasies, we were God. Over time, the power and control became more and more powerful and exciting.

Jacqueline: *I developed at least seven fantasies about suicide, some more powerful than others. The most consistent one was overdosing on sleeping pills and other drugs. But I also thought a lot about hanging from a specific tree in a cemetery, or of disappearing into a forest and hanging myself. Drowning in a large pond also came up a lot.*

Paula: *I had six or seven fantasies of suicide and ended up trying most of them. Overdosing, drifting painlessly from this existence to the next and then being found in a*

> *peaceful pose—that was my favorite. However, I also*
> *thought a lot about cutting my wrists, drowning, carbon*
> *monoxide, and hanging myself. I ended up trying all of*
> *these.*

Raquel: *I fantasized about overdoses, lethal injections,*
gunshots to my head, and car accidents. I visualized
washing the sheets on the bed, making up the bed
perfectly, giving myself the lethal injection, getting into
bed, then pulling the covers neatly up to my chin.

The relationship of fantasy to our suicidal preoccupations was complex. But one crucial part of the relationship was secrecy. Secrecy fueled the fantasies by keeping external reality at bay. The more secretive the thoughts and fantasies, the more power they possessed and the stronger the fix. Most, if not all, of us never told another human soul of our suicidal thoughts and fantasies—not until we hit bottom and started to recover. We kept it all to ourselves, hugging the secret close, ducking into a wholly private, personal, internal, unchallenged world where no one and nothing could get to us.

Chastity: *My family knows nothing about my suicide attempts.*

Jacqueline: *My family lives in a different country. All these years, I kept my thoughts of suicide and my hospitalizations away from them. It would just hurt them.*

Sharing the secret thoughts and fantasies would strip them of their power—would force us out of our inner reality back into the painful, reality-based external world. Exposing our obsessions would bring us face to face with our buried feelings. That was what we wanted least of all. And so we consciously kept our suicidal thoughts secret, minimizing or denying them when others caught us. We rationalized our thoughts to ourselves. After all, everyone thinks of suicide now and again. And besides, we weren't planning to *do* anything...

Many of us weren't aware of how often we thought about suicide. Like alcoholics, who fail to notice how much they drink, we assumed that others thought about suicide as much as we did. We weren't aware of how different our thoughts were from theirs.

Later, when we started to put thought into action, we tried to re-establish secrecy as quickly as possible, glossing over our actions, to replenish the fantasy's power. Unknowingly, people who were trying to care for us "enabled" this process. They helped us to discuss depression, interpersonal conflicts, or other issues. They missed—and we carefully concealed—our fantasies, our denial, and the full extent of our suicidal involvement.

Kevin: *On August 16, 1976, I woke up in ICU after three days in a coma from a massive Elavil overdose. Half awake, half asleep, I suddenly realized that the people taking care of me knew what I'd done. I was trapped. I knew they weren't going to let me put on my white coat and go to my office. I would have to play their game—the depression game—and hope that would satisfy them.*

But they were not going to find out about the drugs, the

women, or the suicide stuff!

Fantasy, secrecy—and power. For us, living in fantasy meant being omnipotent; the key statement was "I can *always* kill myself." The more all-powerful the thoughts and fantasies were, the stronger the high. Paradoxically, the way we took charge of our lives was to take charge of our deaths—at least in our fantasies.

Children manifest this sense of omnipotence as they move out of a view of the world as centered on themselves and into a view in which they are not the center of the universe. Ideally, God should hold that place. Over time, children's inward-focused reality gives way to outward-focused reality, little by little, year by year.

But in deeply traumatized children, the process goes awry. This journey from inner reality to outer reality becomes difficult and may stall along the way. These children desperately need a sense of safety, protection, and power over some area of their own lives. And what could be more powerful than control over your *whole* life—your very existence?

Like these traumatized children, we harbored childlike omnipotent thought patterns. Playing God was heady stuff. Living in fantasy, we were King for the Day; it both exalted our mood and numbed reality. In fact, nothing was a stronger and more exhilarating drug than playing with life and death. "Taking it to the edge," "daring God to take me," "seeing how far I can go"—these were themes we played with. We harbored an alarming confusion over "who is creation" and "who is Creator", keeping an omnipotent, almost delusional belief in our control and mastery over our own lives and (ultimately) our deaths.

Kevin: *For years, I thought I was not afraid of death. When I developed high blood pressure, I took secret delight in it, knowing I was moving closer to death. At lunchtime, I would take my TR7 out across the levee and "open her up" to 125 miles an hour, daring God to take me. It was crazy, but it sure was a rush!*

We were people with very confusing double lives. Outwardly, we could be highly successful, high-functioning individuals—doctors, nurses, health-care providers, or other professionals, showing all the signs of being happy and contented in our lives. But inside, we were struggling, out of control, desperate at times. We were looking for ways to master life while slowly succumbing to ever-increasing fantasies of suicide.

Adults on the outside, trapped children on the inside, we could not speak out and tell our secrets.

Jacqueline: *No one in my residency knew my secret life. They thought I was quiet, didn't share much. I even booked out holidays to cover it all. It was worst at night—the thoughts and fantasies, the driving around, the cemeteries, the rope, the pills. I was two different people.*

Paula: *Until the end, I was a very responsible tech in an OR. I was good at my job. Being an alcoholic and addict, I* *was great at keeping secrets. No one knew what was going on. I lived in two different worlds.*

Kevin: *On the day of my last suicide attempt, I made rounds on all my patients, went to my office, took off my white coat, and swallowed an overdose. I thought about the noose hidden above the ceiling tiles—the rope I used to try to hang myself four different times. I could never tell anyone, not even my mistress, about the pills and that rope.*

Along with omnipotence, fantasy includes a component of control. Control, and the illusion of power, are well described components of sexual addiction. Sexual addicts show the illusion of power and control over others in "paper sex", using pornography, sexual fantasy, and sexual visual memories to make sex objects do whatever they want, within their minds. Inside the fantasy, the addict completely controls the scenes, the behaviors, the thoughts, the feelings of his or her objects.

Likewise, we experienced illusions of power and control within our private worlds. We set up the scenes, visualized the behaviors, played out the scenarios, and completed the stories to our own satisfaction. Nobody else could do a blessed thing to stop us. *We* were in control. Nobody knew what we were doing. Nobody could interfere or stop us. The sense of control was intoxicating.

Kevin: *The day I walked into Simpson Brothers Hardware Store to buy rope—that really got me. I was wearing my white coat. On the outside I was cool and casual, completely in control—and hoping no one would ask me what the rope was for. On the inside, I was turned on, getting by with something big, something very secretive. When I got out of the store with the rope, I was really pumped!*

In later stages, many of us acted out fantasies of control with our therapists and family members, who had discovered our suicidal behaviors. We refused to disclose the truth of our fantasies, always keeping the other off guard, daring them to guess the secrets, to piece together the puzzle, and to uncover our obsessions. We played a deadly game of control with those who loved and were trying to help us, challenging them to discover our secret suicide places or rituals. The game enhanced our feelings of control and fueled the mood alteration.

> **Jacqueline:** *On the day of my suicide attempts, I would call my therapist's office and leave a message on his machine—sort of like saying goodbye, hinting at it, but never telling him where I was. It was months before I told him the name of the cemetery where I'd planned to hang myself.*

Closely related to the issues of control and power was the anger—actually, the frozen rage—that so many of us kept inward. We had trouble feeling and expressing our anger and distinguishing it from rage. Others have called it "frozen rage," "numbing out," or "trance-like dissociation." Whatever the term, we harbored obsessive fantasies and acted out mood-altering rituals with an ice coolness, totally out of contact with our own anger and rage. The emotional high of suicidal thoughts helped to numb the reality of feelings we couldn't afford to face up to.

On the rare occasions when something happened to expose our secret world—usually after a suicide attempt—we responded with incredible rage. It's as though the roots of our rage were exposed, however briefly. We lashed out fiercely at those who saw us. But then, almost immediately, we sealed over the vent and returned as fast as we could to our addictive world—our world of secrecy, power, control, and hidden rage.

Transition: The Problem of Tolerance

The problem with most addictive behavior is that the addict begins to need more and more of the fix—that the dose needs to get bigger to have the same effect. At first, thinking "I can always kill myself" was enough. We could think of it in secret, without any apparent consequence. "Nobody got hurt," "no one knew what happened," "it doesn't make any difference" —it wasn't a *real* problem, just an idiosyncrasy, a little something to make life's problems easy to bear. And with that little something, we could go on (and often did go on) to become successful, accomplished, well-educated people with good jobs and marriages and families—or at least a really handsome veneer.

But over time "I can always kill myself" lost its power, little by little. It wasn't enough, any longer, to ward off that sense of fear or insufficiency. It did less and less to numb the painful moments in life, to loosen that trapped feeling, to give that emotional high. So we had to increase the dose—to think about suicide more often, to extend the fantasies. The theme began to be "I'll bet I could—" as we came up with more elaborate scenarios, new possibilities. We began to look for suicides in the newspapers, in novels or biographies, in family histories. Increasingly curious, we tried to get into the heads of other people who had killed themselves, to study their methods. Slowly but surely, we began to identify with suicide itself, becoming fascinated with death itself.

Many of us grew up with the belief that suicide is the ultimate, unforgivable sin. We'd been taught this in church. Now we started to question this doctrine. We became more and more curious about what

lies on the other side of death—even death by suicide.

Chastity: *My cousin died of an overdose, and an uncle burned*

up in his car, drunk—he was too drunk to open the door

handle and get out. I've always wondered what they

were thinking and feeling.

Paula: *I read in the newspaper about fatalities, noting the*

method that worked best. I read anything I could get my

hands on about the afterlife, being drawn most often to

stories of near-death experiences. I was most comforted

by New Age philosophies and clung to them, rejecting

all concepts of hell or punishment for suicide.

Kevin: *In high school English class, I wrote an essay on death*

in which I slowly "came to" and figured out, paragraph

by paragraph, that I was indeed dead, inside a coffin in

the ground.

We could overcome the tolerance problem by "doses of danger" —increasing the mental risk-taking to get the adrenaline pumping, creating the high we needed. To do this, we started to explore new ways of self-killing—painless ways, fast ways, clean ways, hidden ways. These mental exercises were both scary and intoxicating. We were crossing new frontiers now, into a dangerous, exciting unknown.

Middle Stage: The Ritual

It was only a matter of time before the problem of tolerance drove us from fantasy to ritual, from thought to behavior. It was one thing to *think* about suicide; moving from that to actual action was, in effect, crossing an important and powerful boundary and moving into a new country altogether. We transferred all the old attributes of fantasy— secrecy, omnipotence, control, and danger—from our thoughts to our behavior. And from that step, there was no turning back.

Each of us developed a number of rituals, limited only by our own creativity, often elaborately detailed. They were detailed and mechanical, but also carefully designed to leave the impression of spontaneity and impulsiveness. We planned our deaths oh-so-carefully to leave the impression that our suicide "came out of nowhere".

Chastity: *The sequence went like this: count the pills, then the vials; go into the bathroom, lock the door, dry off the sink top; spread the pills out, grouping like with like; line up the vials, drawing up larger and larger doses; get the tape ready, pick the vein; inject the drug carefully.*

Our rituals centered around the means of suicide: hanging, cutting, shooting, overdosing, jumping, setting up an accident—we spread all the possibilities out on the table, considering them carefully, picking each one up, examining it closely, setting it down—for the moment. We translated our obsessive fantasies into obsessive planning, working through the details, weighing each option carefully and precisely, and working in total secrecy. We were like cat burglars planning the perfect heist. As we devoted more and more time to planning, we turned deeper into our own inner obsession, becoming more self-absorbed and less connected with the outer world.

This shift into ritual brought with it a tremendous high. The first trip to the hardware store to buy *"the* rope" —that was like the first venture of a compulsive shoplifter. The adrenaline rush from the danger was terrific. Completing a purchase in the illusion of total secrecy, with "no one ever knowing" what we'd done, gave us a sense of power, triumph, and deep satisfaction. We were hooked!

From that initial high, ritualization developed rapidly. We tried on new suicide tactics the way a person might try on new clothes, each new one more elaborate, more dangerous, more fantastic—and more intoxicating. Of course we didn't want to get *hurt*, so we started to obsess about the perfect, painless, permanent suicide. What a rush! Talk about playing God—having power over life and death itself…

Methods had to be painstakingly reviewed. Does hanging hurt? Where's the best place to put a bullet? Does carbon monoxide make a person cough and choke? What about pills? These questions grew to monumental proportions, overshadowing the rest of our lives.

Perfection demanded no interruptions—nothing to spoil the scenario, nothing to betray the secret. Which meant, in turn, that timing was everything. How long would it take to fill the car with a lethal amount of carbon monoxide, fed in from the exhaust? How quickly would the pills take effect? What if I threw up?

Not being found was essential and required elaborate planning. We looked for and practiced with windows of opportunity. Painstakingly, we tracked the patterns and times of the people who might foil the perfection of the plan. Hiding and watching, studying who came and went, checking times, establishing patterns—these all consumed our energies.

Jacqueline: *I had an impulse to drive to a certain cemetery, walk around, and visit a site where I wanted to hang myself. I had picked out a specific branch on one particular tree. My thoughts of hanging increased, and I got the idea to buy rope at a grocery store. I saw this rope and went past it a few times; then I left and thought more about hanging. I finally bought the rope* *and kept it at home, to have a noose ready. Later, I went to the cemetery many times with the rope and some pills, as late as ten o'clock at night, avoiding daytime when people could see the rope. I got caught up in all the types of rope—blinds, cable, wires, straps—even in the clothing I'd wear, like stretch pants.*

Each meticulous exploration of the perfect, painless, permanent suicide left us freer to take action, to ritualize each new obsession. Having crossed that boundary between thought and behavior, we started to experiment—a deadly form of trial-and-error. We might shop for a gun, buy it, hold, caress it, finger the trigger, feel the squeeze, visual the act itself—all powerfully intoxicating acts.

Remington: *I would stroke my hand up and down the barrel of my gun, like a lover stroking his partner. Then I'd touch it to my lips and nose, squeezing the trigger ever so carefully—taking it right to the edge. Nothing has ever felt the same.*

The rituals grew steadily over time, growing ever more elaborate, depending only upon the limits of our imaginations. We refined them slowly, fine-tuning them, making them more detailed, more personalized, more perfect. Each small step in the process had its emotional charge, which we lived for. And we sealed our rituals away from reality, keeping them out of the light of day and away from the healing power of love.

As we moved more deeply into sickness, our double lives also grew steadily more polarized. On one hand, we went on working in the "real world", often with increasing successes and accomplishments. On the other, we were consumed with plans for suicide.

Paula: *I always worked hard to be good in the OR, and I worked long hours. I was good at procedures and could do cut-downs in my sleep. I was very careful about my work. In contrast, I secretly gathered medication from any source that I could, counted the pills frequently and* *checked the PDR for lethal doses. I drove recklessly into dangerous places like the projects, with my car windows open, late at night. I wrote suicide notes, sometimes in calligraphy. I carefully chose "music to die by" and kept a ready reference list at all times.*

One of the major obsessions was the *where* of suicide. It had to be not only the perfect method and the perfect time, but also the perfect location—the perfectly safe place. As you might guess, we had been traumatized children, who had lacked that sense of safe places and safe people in childhood. Nowhere and no one felt truly safe now. Long before we first thought of death, we had come to see the world as a cold, hostile, problematic place that cared for us not at all.

The search for *where*, then, was a search for a refuge from this unsafe world, a place away from people, none of whom we could really trust. Strange places that most people would find lonely or frightening took on, for us, qualities of serenity and safety. Cemeteries, secluded rural spots, private offices after hours—these places could fill the bill. Finding and securing a safe place was an essential part of the process.

Jacqueline: *Cemeteries were always quiet and calm. I thought about my dad. I felt safe.*

For some of us, the *where* was closely linked to past trauma, especially if a family member had committed suicide during our childhood. Such a trauma was so painful, so inexplicable, so devastating, that we never really recovered. The death represented the ultimate abandonment, and itself pulled us toward suicide. Desperately wanting to explain the inexplicable, we began to explore the dimensions of the suicide, usually by going back to where it had happened. Maybe by going back, we could be close to the person who had left us?

Jacqueline: *My father drowned himself in a pond on our farm. He was 41. I will be 41 my next birthday. I couldn't stay away from that pond. It called to me. I wondered what* *it was like for him, what he felt, what he was thinking. At the hospital, I looked out the window and the lake called to me the same way.*

Late Stage: The Attempts

In the end, we had to test the limits. For many of us, the stage of actual suicide attempts or behaviors lasted for years. It ended either in death or recovery, but only after many institutional stops along the way.

Why try to kill ourselves? Partly to evade a reality we felt we couldn't cope with; partly for that sense of power and control; and partly because of the high.

Paula: *The decision to commit suicide always gave me a jolt of adrenaline unsurpassed by any of my other addictions. I felt powerful and defiant. It was, and is, the greatest feeling I have ever experienced.*

We hid our first attempts from others, only disclosing them much later, when we were ready to recover. The actual attempt momentarily broke through the trance of fantasy, bringing us back to reality. Having survived and covered up the attempt, we swore off suicide. It wouldn't happen again.

But still we had no notion of the nature of our addiction. "This was a big mistake" or "I'm working too hard" or "Maybe I'm depressed?" or "I'd better stop playing with fire" —we thought things like these. We didn't seek professional help. In fact, we avoided it. Instead, we got busier with work or church, exercised more, made new social contacts.

Kevin: *After my first overdose during my internship, I decided that internal medicine was my problem. I didn't get any professional help, but decided to go into psychiatry, convinced that would fix the problem.*

But in fact, we'd crossed another boundary. We'd become suicide attempters in our own minds, and the shame of it was tremendous.

And that shame rapidly refueled the problem. At first, we were in shock; we swore off and were temporarily "on the wagon". But the knowledge that we'd tried suicide ate away at us, marking us in inescapable ways.

Most people never try to kill themselves. Those who do join a painfully exclusive club, one linked by bonds of deep pain. Society is terrified by suicidal behavior, because suicide is so confusing, so final. For mental health professionals, suicide represents failure; it is something to be controlled or avoided, not understood. The church calls suicide the one unforgivable sin. *Nowhere* is it safe for suicidal people to talk about their feelings, much less about their actual attempts. And we carried this knowledge deep inside us.

Paula: *If I were conscious when I started to realize that a suicide attempt was not going to work, I would be seized by a frantic desire to cover up my intent by destroying notes or other evidence of my overdose. I would be filled with feelings of self-loathing because I could not even do this correctly. If I regained* *consciousness in an ER or ICU, my acute humiliation came out as anger toward the staff trying to help me. I intensely desired to take back the attempt, or to become invisible.*

Driven ever inward by the shock, the shame, and the label that separated us from the rest of the world, we sensed that something must be horribly wrong with us. Something deep inside us must be deeply broken, evil, repellant. We came to that moral split where we confirmed through bad behavior that we were indeed bad people. The worse the behavior, the deeper the shame, and the deeper the moral split. After all, what behavior could be worse than murder—murder of the self? In our overwhelming sense of our own badness, we lost any sense whatsoever of our own sickness.

Chastity: *When I got sick in the fifth grade, I believed that God was punishing me for being a bad sinner and that if I wasn't good enough I would burn in hell. The suicidal fantasies sealed the deal.*

Kevin: *Growing up, I always saw God sitting up there with a six-shooter, frowning down and taking a bead on me, waiting to take pot shots at me whenever I screwed up. I screwed up all the time with the suicidal thoughts. Once I attempted suicide, I really was a goner.*

But nothing had really changed in us. As soon as life presented us with another crisis—anything threatening or difficult—we went right back to the old patterns. We needed that drug too badly. We were still deep in denial. Before the attempt, we'd thought that the suicidal thoughts and plans were just a game. After the first attempt, we could pretend that it had been a big mistake, a fluke. Now we knew better, but we still failed to grasp the gravity of our situation, our sickness, or what was to come.

Kevin: *After my near-fatal Elavil overdose, I spent ten days in a psychiatric unit talking about my depression and my mother. Thinking the overdose was just a big mistake, I* *was discharged and resumed my busy practice. Within three days, I was back to using 40 pills a day and the suicidal thoughts rushed back with full force. I knew it was just a matter of time. I was shocked, and I felt utterly hopeless.*

Those of us who survived our second suicide attempts often sought professional help. We often had no choice. We'd been caught; the professionals knew about our attempts. We were under pressure to come up with explanations for our suicide attempts, just as drunks show up at psychiatrists' doors for both to figure out why the drunks drink too much.

The professionals assumed, reasonably, that what ailed us was probably depression. We agreed quickly—and in fact, many of us were *also* depressed. Of course, the problem was both different and deeper than depression, but that was something we didn't want anyone to look at too closely. Thus we began a phase of psychiatric treatment that usually turned into pure hell for patient and practitioner alike.

Mostly our psychiatrists prescribed antidepressants—which did help clear up treatable depression, for those of us who suffered from that too. For a while, we seemed to be doing better. But sooner or later, we slipped back into the cycle of fantasy, ritual, and suicide attempts. As we repeated the cycle over and over, we slipped more deeply into hopelessness and desperation. Nothing seemed to help.

Kevin: *I put myself on high doses of desipramine [an antidepressant], hoping it would cure my depression and stop the suicidal thoughts. I thought I felt a little better for a few weeks. Then the fantasies of suicide came back. Nothing had changed.*

Jacqueline: *I just assumed that the antidepressants weren't working. I kept on thinking of suicide, more and more; and I got mad because the drugs wouldn't stop the thoughts.*

It didn't matter whether we were honest with our psychiatrists about the return of suicidal thoughts. We could tell our psychiatrists only that we were depressed again; the antidepressants weren't working. They tried other antidepressants. Or we could be honest about having suicidal impulses; our psychiatrists then assumed we were depressed and tried other antidepressants. But each new trial ended in failure. For us, the success or failure of the drug lay in its ability to stop our suicidal fantasies, not its effect on any depressive symptoms—and in that sense, the drugs made no difference. Our psychiatrists, who were totally in the dark, were baffled. They felt defeated.

Since antidepressants didn't work, our psychiatrists came up with new theories, focusing on anxiety. (Hardly surprising, since by this time both we and our psychiatrists were quite anxious!) So we tried other drugs, often benzodiazepines (tranquillizers like Valium). Again, some of us seemed to do better for a while. But sooner or later, the cycle started up again.

We felt more desperate than ever; we seemed to be running out of options. Benzodiazepines helped a little, but we needed larger and larger doses and developed tolerance problems or an addiction to these drugs—another push in the steady downward cycle.

> **Kevin:** *I started with Tranxene but quickly found Ativan. Over the years, I built up the dose to 18 or 20 mg a day. For a while it helped the thoughts, and I was sure I'd found a cure. But the drug addiction became a nightmare of its own and made my suicidal fantasies even worse. Ativan really accelerated my spin towards the bottom.*

The repeated cycle of fantasy, rituals, and attempts landed many of us in psychiatric wards. While this seemed to help, in fact it often complicated our problems. Most of us were distrustful of psychiatry, which had failed to help us. In the hospital, we had to give over more control to larger numbers of caregivers—nurses, therapists, psychiatric technicians, even other patients. Moreover, in the hospital our suicide attempts really were completely out in the open, no longer known only by ourselves and our psychiatrists.

Our treatment teams, on the other hand, were terrified. Nothing frightens hospital staff more than suicide. Not only does it remind them of their own mortality; it tells them they have failed. It also means "potential lawsuit" and "threat to job and career."

In light of all this, we rapidly went underground and again became secretive about our problem. We focused on looking good and getting out. And in fact, many of us improved temporarily, finding relief in the hospital's structured institutional life. Knowing that talking about suicide left everybody feeling nervous, some of us managed to repress our suicidal thoughts and fantasies—and found a flicker of hope that maybe we really *were* free of "this suicide thing" after all. Others knew perfectly well that nothing had changed, and we focused on outfoxing the staff to get released.

Looking good, saying the right things, following directions, taking our pills—these were acting jobs. But we'd been actors for years and years. It worked for a while. The voices in our heads seemed to be muffled. Facing discharge, we felt new hope (or codependent enthusiasm!)

Bottoming Out

Back in real life—and the plummet was nightmarish. Suicidal thoughts and fantasies flooded us with more power than ever. We started a cycle of suicide attempts and hospitalizations, and each hospitalization signaled another failure for our psychiatrists, our treatment teams, and ourselves. We were increasingly desperate and hopeless; they were increasingly hostile.

Paula: *Many of my caregivers felt duty-bound to "preach the gospel" to me—not from compassion, but almost as if to ward off the demons. Some of them took care of my physical needs with no mention of my emotional agony. Many were cold and withdrawn. Some expressed passive-aggressive anger by telling me how to do it better next time. Some were compassionate but totally at a loss to understand how someone who had so much going for her could do this to herself. I experienced open hostility from other patients, especially when they learned my profession or how many attempts I had* *made. I had a great deal of shame in "coming out of the*

closet" in this atmosphere.

We regressed to fantasizing that we could somehow be magically fixed, while at the same time harboring deep fears that nothing could make us better—that we were doomed. Our psychiatrists and treatment teams grew more and more frustrated and angry, and just as frightened as we were. They tried new labels— "borderline personality disorder", for example. This is a deeply ingrained pattern of destructive behavior patterns and very, very difficult to treat. By then, in our desperation, we probably fit that pattern. But the label only made things worse. Our treatment teams, with that diagnosis, effectively distanced themselves from us. The therapeutic alliance— vital to any real progress—was first stressed, then broken. Other teams tried to take over, and we brought to them not only the underlying problem, but fresh and very deep wounds from the previous therapeutic disaster.

Paula: *When I wrote it all down, I couldn't believe it. Here's*

what I wrote:

Suicide attempts:

1967: age 15, attempted drowning

1976: age 24, overdose

1986: age 34, overdose

1989: age 37, overdose

1992-1995: 14 or more attempts, including one hanging, one

carbon monoxide, two wrist-slashings, the rest overdoses.

Psychiatric hospitalizations:

1976: 6 weeks, depression

1986: alcohol rehab, plus 6 weeks for depression

1989: short admission for bipolar stabilization

1992- present: at least 20 admissions.

Jacqueline: *I'm still ashamed of it all and I really don't want*

to admit it to myself or anyone else, but here goes:

Suicide attempts:

April 1992: alcohol plus Ativan

April 1992: tried hanging myself with my shoelaces in the hospital shower

April 1993: drank liquid detergent

July 1994: overdose on Trazodone

March 1995: tried hanging myself from a door in my apartment

June 1995: overdose on sleeping pills

July 1995: overdose on sleeping pills

Psychiatric hospitalizations:

April 1992: 3 weeks for depression

October 1992: 5 days for depression

October 1992-April 1993: 6 months for depression

April 1993-1996: at least 14 or 15 hospitalizations of 3 to 10 days each for suicidal thoughts and plans

And so the cycle continued: new psychiatrists, new drugs, more suicide attempts, more therapeutic failures, more hopelessness. Many of us drifted into new addictions to prescription drugs or alcohol, or to sexual acting-out or addiction, or any combination of these—anything to numb the pain. But these also only added to the sense of shame and the out-of-control spiral, as we headed steadily down toward destruction.

In the final months, we exhausted more emergency psychiatric resources than any other group of psychiatric patients. A dozen or more suicide attempts, with numerous (and humiliating) emergency-room visits and psychiatric hospitalizations—all to little or no avail. We faced the anger of a helpless, frustrated medical and psychiatric community, which could not cope with us.

We were in hell. In the end, either we died, or we hit bottom and started on the long, hard road back from the grave.

Raquel's Story

I was born in the 1960s to alcoholic parents, the youngest of three children. Two of us are now alcoholics and addicts, and my next-oldest sister also has a problem with suicide. On my mother's side of the family, there is a long history of suicidal preoccupations and failed suicide attempts.

One of my earliest memories is of incest; it started when I was 4 and stopped when I was in Grade 1. When I was in Grade 2, my mother had what the doctors called a "nervous breakdown." They treated her with drugs, and she turned into a zombie. My older sister became my caregiver. My father, an alcoholic, only created chaos during his short visits.

I was so scared that I obsessed every day at school: would my mother be alive or dead when I got home? Even though my sister had developed perfect mothering skills by the time she was 9, I could not understand what had happened to my mother. I loved her, and I missed her terribly. "Mental illness" was not one of the vocabulary words I learned in school.

We went to a private Roman Catholic school. The nuns knew what was going on in our home. They gave us shoes, coats, and uniforms, and let us attend school for free.

At 11, I was a whopping 120 pounds. It was very hard for me to make friends, and I was severely teased. I did have one girlfriend, and even got invited for a sleepover for her 12th birthday party. Her father and brother molested me that night. That was the first time I tried to kill myself—the start of my lifelong obsession with suicide, and also the onset of my addictions to drugs and alcohol.

Whenever I felt out of control, my fears became overwhelming. I felt trapped, and I rapidly spun into feelings of helplessness and hopelessness. These feelings triggered my suicide cycles—fantasizing, obsessing, planning, and actual attempts.

Fantasizing about suicide gave me a euphoria like that from a shot of morphine. It lifted my mood; I forgot my problems. I could do whatever I wanted, say what I pleased, because I knew I wouldn't be around to face the consequences. When my mood began to slip, I started to obsess about suicide. I felt impelled to prepare for my death. It had to be clean, neat, and pain-free. I'd wash all the bed linens and make up my bed in military or hospital style, all tight and precisely folded. Or I'd tidy and scrub the whole house, so that when they found me dead, it would be in a perfectly clean place.

Planning never took much time: I kept a plan in my head at all times, in case of emergency. I started that at 16, on a date. The boy offered me drugs, and I accepted. I woke up the next morning out in the woods, my groin hurting badly. Even now, I am afraid of being alone or lost in woods.

After that, I started to carry a bottle of aspirin or Tylenol to take immediately, if I needed it. As a nurse, I could find out the lethal dose of a drug, and I made sure to have an overdose available at all times— in my purse or pocket, in my car, and at home. Having these drugs around me gave me a sense of safety that I found intoxicating. Whenever I felt out of control at work, I could reach into my pocket and touch the two vials of heart medication that I thought would kill me instantly. I felt better at once. The sense of control I felt from being able to kill myself gave me the strength I needed to keep going.

The actual attempts were powerfully mood-altering. After I tried to kill myself, I would feel a sense of peace, contentment, and serenity filling my thoughts. I felt great power, as though I were laughing in the face of God, the world, and all those unbelievers who said "she only does this for attention."

Having to wake up and face nurses, doctors, and my family—that was never part of my fantasy. It was hell on earth. Most people seem to think that if you try to kill yourself, your family members will cry over you and beg your forgiveness and try to keep you happy for the rest of your life. After I'd made several attempts, my family would simply call the hospital and ask which room I was in this time. They'd tell the nurse they might visit later, if they had time. I was left to the wolves.

The only thing my caregivers understood about my suicidal behavior was that I had to be crazy to try to take my own life. They had no sympathy. In most cases, in fact, they were pissed off because I'd given them more work. They were already overworked and underpaid, running around frantically trying to save the lives of people who wanted to live. And there I was, wanting to die. They resented it. I took a lot of abuse from health-care professionals, and I felt I deserved it. I was an ICU nurse; I should know better. The shame I felt started the suicide cycle all over again.

One time, I woke up to find that I wasn't dead but very much alive and in the same ICU that I'd woken up in for the previous six suicide attempts. And my anger exploded. God help the ICU nurses who were around at that moment! I was physically violent toward myself and others. I screamed like a madwoman for hours or days. They had to put me in every type of restraining device known to man, some with keys, some without. I said and did things that I only vaguely remember.

Failure and shame came crashing down on me like a ton of bricks. When the nurse came with my family members, I swore solemnly never to try suicide again. Whenever I said those words, I lied. My family was furious with me and wished I would die and get it over with—and that was exactly what I wanted. There they were, my mother, my husband and children, staring at me with such pain and anger that, for a moment, I saw clearly how self-centered I really was. I felt deeply ashamed.

After each bout in the hospital, people were afraid of me. My family didn't trust me—why should they? I was watched and babysat at all times. My friends, co-workers, and family ridiculed me: "Why would a smart girl like you do a stupid thing like that?" Or "You know better than that now, don't you?" Back to shame and worthlessness, and the suicide cycle started up again.

Here is how it all ended:

I was sitting on the couch in late June, going over in my mind the events of the last few months. I had been released from a treatment center after a series of shock treatments for my depression and suicide problems. I had come home, to a small town in Alabama. My husband and children expected much more of me than I felt I had to give them. I knew in my heart that my marriage was over, and that devastated me. It was only a matter of time before I screwed up again. Along with my suicide addiction, I had problems with alcoholism, drug addiction, and addictions to sex, love, food, and gambling. I had to repeat any action that altered my mood, whatever the consequence.

I walked off and left my family for a sexual relationship in another state. Nobody knew me there, and I thought I could start fresh. I didn't find out until too late how physically and mentally abusive he was. I started working in a hospital, as a critical care nurse. My home life was hell, and I missed my husband and children terribly. I drank and took a lot of Xanax, which I got from a local physician. I started to steal narcotics from work. I fantasized about suicide all the time. I even tried to see my children one last time, but my husband called the police and got them to take me away.

At work, the authorities intervened because I was stealing drugs. The man I lived with couldn't work—he had to know where I was at all times—so we were broke. The only thing I had left of any value was my wedding ring. It meant more to me than my life, but I sold it to pay for a divorce, so that I could see my children again.

That day, sitting on the couch, all I could think of was my losses. I had lost my husband, my children, my job, my home, my car; now my nursing license was in question. I was broke and stuck in an abusive relationship with a man I did not love. I had left the husband and children I loved so dearly. I was devastated.

As I upended a liter of 100-proof vodka and swallowed the last drops, I thought *what the hell have I done with my life?* I felt trapped, helpless and hopeless. My stash of narcotics had run out long since, but I found five 1-mg Xanax tablets. I crushed them, being very careful to leave them in large pieces, and mixed them with tap water. I had a large-gauge needle and syringe, and I filled it with the Xanax mixture and injected it into an artery in my arm. The pain was intense.

I opened my eyes in an ambulance. I could hear a woman screaming and realized it was me. An EMT was looking down at me and saying, "Stay with us, girlfriend." I went under again. The next time I surfaced, there were doctors and nurses standing over me. I knew at once that I was in the same hospital where I'd been stealing drugs. They wanted to know what had happened, and why. I asked them to leave me alone, because I had absolutely nothing left to live for. No more questions.

They worked passionately for 24 hours to save my right arm. In the end, they had to take it off below the elbow.

After a few days, I *really* woke up. My doctor explained that because of my built-up tolerance for narcotics, they could not give me enough narcotics to ease the pain of my amputation. The doses needed to control pain would kill me. Instead, he did a nerve block. I couldn't feel anything. I began to realize not only that I was going to have to go on living, but I would have to live with the loss of my arm—my own doing.

That night, the volcano erupted. I ripped out the catheter, tube, and IV line they had attached to me. I cursed and fought everyone who came near me. The nerve block wore off, and I was in excruciating pain. The staff gave me drugs and tied me down, and the doctor was called back to redo the nerve block. Everyone was pissed off, me included. They concluded that I was suffering DTs and put me on a continuous infusion of IV narcotics. Of course I didn't argue with that!

For days, I went on ripping things up and cursing people. All the nurses hated being assigned to me. I hated them right back.

One night, a nurse from another floor won the big prize—me. She was all in white, and she was quiet, understanding, and kind. I let her bathe me, but when she tried to talk to me about God, I asked her to leave. That night, I felt overwhelmed with sorrow and loneliness. I had not slept in days; I was angry, tired, and confused. I knew I could not leave the hospital and care for myself, but I had no one left to ask—no friends, and my family was sick of me. I was licked. My life was totally unmanageable. I surrendered.

The nurse in white heard me crying and came in. She took me in her arms, cradling me and talking to me about God for a long time. She read me passages from the Bible about others who had overcome horrible circumstances with God's help. I felt hope—something I hadn't known for such a long time. I prayed a simple prayer, asking God to take control over my life. I told God that I should have been dead already, and whatever He wanted me to do I would do without question. I asked forgiveness for my sins and told God that I had no idea what to do or where to turn. Then I closed my eyes, and I slept for a long time.

That was the turning point for me, the beginning of my recovery from all my addictions, including suicide. To get from that point to where I am today has been very difficult, but I've had help. Today, my worst day is much, much better than my best day in addiction. I go to Twelve Step meetings—Alcoholics Anonymous, Sex and Love Addicts Anonymous, and Suicide Anonymous - and do the things suggested. I read recovery literature. I have a great sponsor who I talk to daily. I pray to my God morning, night, and as needed. If I have problems I can't do anything about, I give them to God, and He takes care of them.

I am trying hard to rebuild trust with my family. I tell my mother where I go and when I will return. I call my children every day that I don't see them. I see the pain in my ex-husband's eyes. I am kind and understanding with him and always do what I say I'm going to do. He knows that I love him, but his anger and distrust are bigger than he realizes.

I *like* myself today, and I am so grateful to be alive! Life is worth living, and my happiness is surely a gift. I do not regret the past, because it brought me to where I am today. And where I am today is a good place. I believe that it is only by God's grace that I have been given another chance to live happily, joyously, freely—one day at a time.

Chapter 3:

A Theory of Suicide Addiction

> "For others, though, the first suicide attempt becomes a haunting memory...They have attempted the ultimate solution once and, having tried it once, they sometimes feel compelled to try it again."
> —Quinnett[7]

Nature and Nurture

If suicide addiction exists, it most likely results from a combination of genetic predisposition and psychosocial predisposition. That is, we have an inherited tendency towards suicidal and addictive behaviors; this, combined with stressors in our lives, predisposes us toward suicide.

We don't (yet) know what the genetic component is like. Studies of suicide do show familial links, but this area needs further research. A brief historical overview:

---

[7] P. Quinnett, *Suicide: The Forever Decision* (New York: Continuum, 1992), 112.

- From 1949 to 1977, Kallman's work dominated the field of suicide research. He found "no cases of twins who both suicided" and convinced the scientific community that suicide probably had no genetic basis.[8]

- In 1977, a Danish twin study by Juel-Nielsen's group found no cases of fraternal twins who both suicided. But 20% of identical twins *had* suicided.[9] The researchers concluded that depression best explained their findings, but the study did open the door to the possibility of genetic factors in suicide.

- Danish and Amish adoption studies between 1979 and 1985 opened the door still further. Kety's group found that Danish adopted children whose birth families had a history of suicide had a higher suicide rate than the general population, and that

---

[8] F. Kallman and M. Anastasio, "Twin Studies on the Psychopathology of Suicide," *Journal of Nervous and Mental Disorders* 105 (1947): 40-50; F. Callman, J. Deporte, *et al.*, "Suicide in Twins and Only Children," *American Journal of Human Genetics* 1 (1949): 113-26.

[9] N. Juel-Nielsen and T. Videbech, "A Twin Study of Suicide," *Acta Geneticae Medicae et Gemellologiae* 19 (1970): 307-10; A. Bertelsen, B. Harvald, *et al.*, "A Danish Twin Study of Manic-Depressive Disorders,: *British Journal of Psychiatry* 130 (1977): 330.

suicides tended to cluster in certain families.[10] Egeland's group examined Amish families over 100 years. While suicide was strongly linked to mood disorders, the suicides also clustered in four family trees.[11] Both studies suggested that there might be genetic factors in suicide. More anecdotally, in our suicide group, five individuals had family members who had attempted or completed suicide.

Cross-Addiction

In 1981, Cloninger described Type II alcoholism, characterized by early onset (before age 25), criminal or antisocial behavior, and multiple treatment efforts.[12] This type of alcoholism shows strong

---

[10] F. Schulsinger, S. Kety, *et al.*, "A Family History of Suicide," in M. Schou and E. Stromgren, eds., *Origin, Prevention, and Treatment of Affective Disorders* (New York: Academic Press, 1979).

[11] J. Egeland and J. Sussex, "Suicide and Family Loading for Affective Disorders," *Journal of the American Medical Association* 254 (1985): 915-18; B. Mitterauer, "A Contribution to the Discussion of the Role of the Genetic Factor in Suicide Based on Five Studies of an Epidemiologically Defined Area (Province of Salzburg, Austria)," *Comprehensive Psychiatry* 31 (1990); 557-65; S. Kety, "Factors in Suicide: Family, Twins, and Adoption Studies." in S. Blumenthal and D. Kupfer, eds., *Suicide Over the Life Cycle* (Washington: American Psychiatric Press, 1990), 127-33.

[12] R. Cloninger, "Neurogenic Adaptive Mechanisms in Alcoholism," *Science* 236 (1987), 410-16.

genetic links, with a father-to-son transmission. Research by Cloninger and others has confirmed a significantly higher rate of suicidal behavior and impulsivity in Type II alcoholics, together with a possible serotonin deficiency. These interrelationships suggest underlying genetic factors that predispose individuals toward suicide, impulsivity, depression, and alcoholism.[13] We need more research to clarify what genetic factors might be at work, especially given the high rate of "cross-addiction" between alcohol and suicide among members of our group.

Serotonin Disorders

In 1976, Ashberg's group discovered low levels of the serotonin metabolite 5HIAA in the cerebrospinal fluid (CSF) of people who had attempted or completed suicide. This led to a series of studies hoping to find a biological marker for suicide.[14] These studies confirmed

---

[13] L. Buydens-Branchey *et al.*, "Age of Alcoholism Onset," *Archives of General Psychiatry* 46 (1989): 225-36.

[14] M. Asberg *et al.*, "5 HIAA in the Cerebrospinal Fluid: A Biochemical Suicide Predictor?" *Archives of General Psychiatry* 33 (1976): 1193-97; M. Asberg *et al.*, "Cerebrospinal Fluid Studies in Suicide: An Overview," *Annals of the New York Academy of Sciences* 487 (1986): 243-55; G. Brown, F. Goodwin *et al.*, "Aggression in Humans: Correlates with

Ashberg's original findings and showed that 5HIAA deficiency tended to be more prevalent among impulsive violent young males. This strengthens the possible link between poor impulse control, violence, and suicide.

Bipolar Links

In 1990, Goodwin's group reported that suicide is rare in mania but more frequent in mixed states (mania and depression) and in rapid cycling (quick shifts from mania to depression).[15] Dunner's group (1976) and Rihmer's group (1990) found that suicide is more frequent

---

Cerebrospinal Fluid Amine Metabolites," *Psychiatry Resident* 1 (1979): 131-39; G. Brown and F. Goodwin, "Cerebrospinal Fluid Correlates of Suicide Attempts and Aggression," *Annals of the New York Academy of Sciences* 487 (1986): 175-88; J. Mann *et al.*, "Evidence for the 5-HT Hypothesis of Suicide: A Review of Post-Mortem Studies," *British Journal of Psychiatry* 155, Suppl. 8 (1989): 7-14; L. Ricci *et al.*, "Monoamines: Biochemical Markers of Suicide?" *Journal of Clinical Psychology* 146 (1990): 106-16; M. Stanley and B. Stanley, "Postmortem Evidence for Serotonin's Role in Suicide," *Journal of Clinical Psychiatry* 51, Suppl. 4 (1990): 22-28.

[15] F. Goodwin and K. Jamison, *Manic-Depressive Illness* (New York: Oxford University Press, 1990).

in bipolar II disorder than in bipolar I disorder. There may be genetic

links between unstable mood disorders and suicide.[16]

Psychosocial Factors

The strongest predictive factor for suicidal preoccupation, suicide

attempts, and self-mutilating behavior is childhood or adolescent

trauma. This topic is discussed more fully in Chapters 4 and 5. A

number of authors, including van der Kolk, Putnam, and Teicher have

found links between (on one hand) sexual abuse, witnessing domestic

violence, disrupted attachments, and total neglect and (on the other)

suicide attempts, cutting, self-destructive behaviors, and depression.[17]

Generally, the earlier the trauma, the stronger the link with self-

destructive and suicidal behaviors.

---

[16] D. Dunner *et al.*, "Heritable Factors in the Severity of Affective Illness," *Biological Psychiatry* 11 (1976): 31-42; Z. Rihmer *et al.*, "Suicide in Subtypes of Primary Major Depression," *Journal of Affective Disorders* 18 (1990): 221-25; D. Jacobs, *Suicide and Clinical Practice* (Washington: American Psychiatric Press, 1992), 18.

[17] B. van der Kolk, J. Perry, and J. Herman, "Childhood Origins of Self-Destructive Behavior," *American Journal of Psychiatry* 148 (1991): 1665-69; F. Putnam, "Conference on the Psychobiology of Post Traumatic Stress Disorder, New York Academy of Sciences," *Clinical Psychiatry News,* Nov. 1996, 22; M. Teicher, "Conference on the Psychobiology of Post Traumatic Stress Disorder, New York Academy of Sciences," *Clinical Psychiatry News,* Nov. 1996, 20.

The Biochemical Pathways

The biochemical pathways mediating suicide addiction are as yet unknown, but three research areas are promising:

- A number of authors have found elevated levels of endogenous narcotics in subjects with stressful/traumatic behaviors. Coid's group (1983) reported that habitual self-mutilation correlates with heightened levels of met-enkephalins, a group of endogenous opioids.[18]. Wiles's group (1981) showed that surgical stress (possibly cutting) elevates plasma beta-endorphins—another class of endogenous opioids.[19] Christie's group (1982) showed that prolonged stress in animals activates brain opiate receptors that are analogous to those binding narcotic drugs, leading to 3-H-leu-

---

[18] J. Coid, B. Allolio, and L. Rees, "Raised Plasma Metenkephalin in Patients Who Habitually Mutilate Themselves," *Lancet* 2 (1983): 545-46.
[19] J. Willes, J. Petren, and J. Cambier, "Stress-Induced Analgesia in Humans: Endogenous Opioids and Naloxone Reversible Depression of Pain Reflexes," *Science* 212 (1981): 689-90.

enkephalin dependence.[20] Mutilation and other self-destructive behaviors—possibly including suicidal thoughts, fantasies, and actions—may also cause the release of endogenous opioids. Over time, this would likely give rise to tolerance and addiction.

- In 1983, Carnes described the relationship between adrenaline levels and sexual addiction. In arousal, sexual addicts undergo an obsessive trance and preoccupation phase, which is associated with risk, danger, and violence and is accompanied by the release of adrenaline.[21] It may be that the risk, danger, and violence associated with suicidal or self-mutilating behavior also causes adrenaline flooding. Over time, subjects would experience withdrawal, tolerance, and addiction to the adrenaline "rush".

- Finally (and least likely), there may be a role for the peptide hormone oxytocin. In 1992 Insel reported evidence that

---

[20] M. Christie and G. Chesher, "Physical Dependence on Physiologically Released Endogenous Opiates," *Life Science* 30 (1982): 1173-77.
[21] P. Carnes, *Out of the Shadows* (Minneapolis: Comp Care, 1983), 10.

oxytocin is involved in mother-infant bonding.[22] In 1991, Caldwell discovered that sexual fantasies and behaviors may release oxytocin as a chemical reminder of the maternal bond.[23] Possibly, very early trauma that alters or disrupts the maternal bonding process may alter oxytocin levels. It could be that suicidal fantasies (which are akin to sexual fantasies) might release oxytocin or affect its metabolism, leading to withdrawal, tolerance, and addiction.

Most likely, the biochemical mediators of suicide addiction have yet to be found. It seems highly probable that early childhood trauma produces complex alterations in a number of chemical reactions in the brain, including norepinephrine, dopamine, serotonin, cortisol, or combinations of these biologically active substances. These changes could occur in a number of centers or hormone systems—in the brain's amygdala, hippocampus, or hypothalamus, or in the pituitary

---

[22] T. Insel, "Oxytocin: A Neuropeptide for Affiliation: Evidence from a Behavioral Receptor, Audioradiographic, and Comparative Studies," *Psychoneuroendocrinology* 17 (1992): 3-30.

[23] J. Caldwell, "Central Oxytocin and Female Sexual Behavior," *Annals of the New York Academy of Science* 652 (1991): 166-179.

or adrenal glands. Changes in neurotransmitters or hormones could lead to chemical deficiencies or excesses, accompanied by suicidal thoughts, fantasies, rituals, and behaviors and to the classic addictive cycle.

The Suicide Addiction Cycle

Each suicidal cycle starts with a suicidal thought. But not all suicidal thoughts lead to suicidal cycles. Many people have the odd suicidal thought with no addictive impact, just as many people have the occasional drink without turning into alcoholics. What makes the difference?

The answer lies in trauma. Trauma induces shame and trapped feelings that lie dormant until something happens to trigger them. When this happens, the pain is intense—and the suicidal thought acts as a pain reliever. But as tolerance develops, we need a stronger fix of the painkiller, and so simple thoughts give way to complex thoughts, which in turn lead into the sequence of fantasies, rituals, and attempts.

In 1983, Patrick Carnes described a four-step cycle of sexual addiction. In his book *Out of the Shadows*, Carnes wrote: "Addicts progressively go through stages in which they retreat further from the reality of friends, family, and work. Their secret lives become more real than their public lives. What people know is a false identity…And essential part of sanity is being grounded in reality, so in the sense that addicts distort reality, the sexual addiction becomes a form of insanity."[24]

Suicide addicts describe our experience in similar terms. The addictive experience seems to progress through four steps, each becoming more intense with repetition:

1   **Preoccupation/trance induction:** We start by entering a trance—an altered mood state, a state of deep preoccupation. In this state, we dream of suicide, becoming more and more engrossed in our thoughts and fantasies. Over time, the fantasies need to become more elaborate and intense to give us the same level of stimulation. The state is akin to sexual fantasizing.

---

[24] P. Carnes, *Out of the Shadows,* 4-5.

2 **Ritualization/automatization:** We develop secret, highly ritualized special routines that over time take on qualities of automatic behavior. These reinforce the trance state.

3 **Compulsive/addictive suicidal behavior:** From ritual, we take the step into actual suicidal attempts or behavior—the goal of our preoccupation and ritualization. We cannot control or stop these actions.

4 **Despair/withdrawal:** The suicidal behavior leaves us feeling hopeless and powerless over our own behavior. These feelings are coupled with a break of the trance state—a "coming off" that leaves us facing an unendurably bleak reality.

Preoccupation/Trance Induction

While we harbored a constant awareness of the possibility of suicide, kept at the back of our minds, we still mostly managed to keep this awareness to ourselves and get on with our daily lives. But we knew that the thoughts were always there, waiting to be triggered. Many of us still felt a strange combination of fear that the thoughts would return and relief that we could still summon them up if we need them. Suicide is both enemy and friend. Drug and sex addicts feel much the same way about their "fixes."

What are the triggers? They depend entirely on our experience—whatever the underlying abuse was. It might be something quite neutral, like the sound of an airplane overhead or the smell of a leaf fire. It might be something that reminded us of feeling abandoned and helpless or having to cope with a parent's rage. Triggers are personal and particular, and often we had no overt knowledge of why they affected us as they did.

Often the triggers involve feeling trapped. We had sudden overwhelming thoughts of being trapped, with no way out. The trap was purely mental. Objectively, there was no trap: it was all in our heads. But to us, it was an extraordinarily vivid, painful, and terrifying sense of panic: *I have to get out NOW!* To which the mind responds: *There's no way out. There are no options. There is no one to turn to for help.*

Kevin: *Out of nowhere, it hit me deep inside, like a panic attack, but without the outward symptoms. I felt very*

ashamed, afraid I was about to make a fool of myself,
and everyone would see it. I couldn't run, I couldn't
cry, I couldn't speak out and ask for help. I just felt
totally trapped, with no way out. That's when the
thoughts of suicide started. They were the way I got by.

As the trance started, we moved into a tunnel-world, one in which we lost all peripheral vision of the outside reality. We shifted our attention from the world around us to our own internal world, refocusing on what was going on inside our heads: spiraling thoughts and fantasies of suicide. Outside reality gave way to inner reality; the logic of normalcy succumbed to the logic of the trance. As this happened, the pain and panic set off by the trigger gave way to a sense of numbness and relief—a strange combination of excitement and deep calm. Time stood still; or we seemed to be moving in slow motion.[25] From inside the trance, suicide held out the promise of peace and freedom. At the same time, all other options seemed to

---

[25] P. Quinnett, *Suicide: The Forever Decision*, 22.

shrink away to nothing. Suicide looked like the *only* solution to the problem at hand.

Raquel: *My awareness would narrow—sort of like wearing blinders—and I really stopped noticing the world around me. My feelings took over—feelings of anger, loss of control, revenge, and relief. My thoughts turned to ending the pain. Nothing else. Then the overwhelming desire to kill myself kicked in. It always seemed completely logical, the perfect solution, the **only** way out.*

Jacqueline: *I would cry intensely and then calm down into a trance-like state. An inner voice would tell me to go ahead and do it. I wouldn't care what was going on around me: I just blacked everything and everyone out of my consciousness as I floated toward a suicide attempt. My vision blurred. My hearing decreased.*

Ritualization/Automatization

As the trance deepened, we started to carry out suicidal rituals—behaviors that were like rehearsals for suicide attempts. Many of us recounted a sense of "loss of will": we felt pulled along by a powerful force that overtook us,[26] like a wave breaking, and rolled us along. We were helpless to stop. Our actions were robotic, automatic, as though we were under the control of unknown forces. Our own sense of will slipped away.

Automatic thoughts are "cognitions that intervene between external events and the person's emotional reaction to the event."[27] These (usually negative) beliefs, also called cognitive distortions, play a major role in most psychiatric disorders. In effect, the person superimposes an inaccurate and usually negative interpretation on events. A.T. Beck has reported specific patterns of cognitive errors, including (among others): excessive responsibility; assumptions about temporary causality; catastrophizing; and dichotomous thinking.[28]

---

[26] R. Heckler, *Waking Up Alive* (New York: Balantine, 1994), 71.

[27] H. Kaplan, B. Sadock, and J. Grebb, *Synopsis of Psychiatry* (Baltimore: Williams and Wilkins, 1994), 861.

[28] A. Beck *et al.*, *Cognitive Therapy of Depression* (New York: Guilford, 1979), 48.

Individuals with suicide addiction are subject to cognitive errors of hopelessness and deficits in problem solving. That is, when faced with a difficult situation, they automatically assume that they can't solve the problem and leap directly into hopelessness.

Daniel Goldman has characterized this "fast and sloppy" thought pattern as emotional hijacking.[29] Instead of taking time to assess the situation and reach a well-supported conclusion, we leap instantaneously to a conclusion that may have little to do with reality. It's a hair-trigger response. Faced with difficulties, instead of working through the problems and possibility, we think "I can't handle this!" and leap immediately into a hopelessness so total that suicide seems like the only solution.

> **Kevin:** *After I came out of one of the suicide attempts, it seemed really crazy to me. I knew I had overreacted, taken things way too far, but I couldn't see any other choices at the time. Looking back, I can see that the situation wasn't really that hopeless.*

---

[29] D. Goldman, 1994. *Emotional Intelligence* (New York: Bantam), 13ff.

Automatisms are "automatic performances of acts generally representative of unconscious symbolic activity".[30] Automatic writing is an example of this sort of behavior. It is, according to DSM IV (the manual of psychiatric disorders) a manifestation of possession or a trance state. In automatic writing, the hand and arm write without the writer's volition, often disclosing material of which the writer is not consciously aware.[31]

In a similar fashion, we turned robot-like and reported feeling "possessed" or "driven" in this stage of the cycle. We could not stop ourselves from acting in ritualized patterns—a dance over which we had no control, performed without volition. In it, we "wrote" what we cannot now remember.

Kevin: *I would find myself walking in the back door to my office, all alone, in my white coat, and going straight to my biofeedback room. I would stand on a stool, move*

---

[30] H. Kaplan, B. Sadock, and J. Grebb, *Synopsis of Psychiatry*, 304.
[31] *Ibid.,* 651.

the ceiling tile, get the rope noose down, and put it

around my neck—white coat and necktie still in place.

It all happened like a very long slow-motion replay of a

pitcher's wind-up.

Remington: *I would stroke the chamber of my gun, back and*

forth with one hand, while caressing the trigger with

the other. I'd be staring straight ahead in a trance.

Then I would eject the chamber over and over in a

perfectly timed military cadence.

Rituals are "automatic activities, compulsive in nature, anxiety-reducing in origin."[32] For all people, healthy or not, rituals help establish a sense of order and control. Habits do help us. We rely on them to organize our lives, to reduce ordinary anxiety, to help us be efficient and productive. Rituals can also help to anchor our spiritual values—to reduce our "spiritual static" and to help connect us to others in communion and to God.

---

[32] *Ibid.,* 304.

But for suicide addicts, anxiety is not ordinary, and life seems like a very dangerous place. Life feels chaotic and out-of-control, and anxiety is so severe that it strips the meaning from existence. In this phase, our emotions felt so overwhelming that we had to dissociate—to set the memories off to one side, apart from *us*, because otherwise we could not possibly cope. We distanced ourselves from the pain, splitting it off from consciousness. We became less aware of the outside world, one way of making it less complex and frightening, more manageable.

Ritual let us control the anxiety; it was like a mantra in meditation, allowing us to focus.[33] Through the ritual, we moved closer to the actual attempt, with its promised release from pain. As the ritual progressed, death looked more and more like a relief and an entryway into a better, safer world. The images intensified with alarming power.

Chastity: *Just before an attempt, I felt very calm; I thought I was doing the right thing. I had no awareness of*

---

[33] P. Carnes, *Out of the Shadows*, 11.

thoughts or feelings of anything, except for a kind of hyperawareness of exactly what I was doing. During a cycle I felt very peaceful and relieved. I thought I was going home to a better place. The angels beckoned me.

Buying pills, getting hold of knives, driving to cemeteries, loading guns—these actions took on special, bizarre qualities. We looked normal—calm and controlled. But at a deeper level, we were out of control. In a trance state, with narrowed attention and lapsed concentration, we had turned into the robots of our rituals. We saw ourselves not as human beings, but as objects. We had turned our backs on life and applied all that was good in ourselves—our talents and ingenuity, our creativity and intelligence—to death: the fix, the solution, the way out of the pain.

Suicidal Behavior: Compulsion and Addiction

During actual suicidal behaviors and attempts, we experienced strong ambivalence. We felt driven both by something deep within ourselves and, at the same time, strangely drawn to something outside ourselves. Was this compulsion, addiction, or something of both? To answer this question, we have to look at the nature of compulsion/obsession and addiction.

Compulsions are "uncontrollable impulses to perform an act repetitively."[34] A wide range of these behaviors have been documented over the years: compulsive drinking (dipsomania) or stealing (kleptomania), hand-washing, checking (e.g.) door locks, hoarding, and counting. All involve rituals. Compulsions share five characteristics:

1 An idea or impulse intrudes itself insistently and persistently into the person's conscious awareness.

2 The idea/impulse is accompanied by a feeling of anxious dread that often causes the person to take countermeasures against the initial idea or impulse.

3 The person experiences the obsession or compulsion as being ego-alien—that is, foreign to the person's sense of him- or herself as a psychological being.

---

[34] H. Kaplan, B. Sadock, and J. Grebb, *Synopsis of Psychiatry*, 304.

4   No matter how vivid and compelling the obsession or compulsion, the person still recognizes it as absurd and irrational.

5   The person feels a strong desire to resist the obsession or compulsion.[35]

Suicide addicts experience *some* of these characteristics. We tend to experience the first characteristic (intrusive ideas/impulses) and the fifth (resistance). Early in the addiction, we do feel that the impulse is alien to us (the third characteristic), but over time, we accept the impulses as part of ourselves.

But we do *not* experience the second and fourth characteristics. Intrusive thoughts of suicide don't make us feel anxious dread; they make us feel peaceful or high. And we don't see suicide as being irrational or absurd; we see it as perfectly logical—the inevitable way out. Suicide is, for us, partly compulsive, but only partly.

---

[35] *Ibid.*, 601-02.

Addictions are "maladaptive patterns of use, leading to clinically significant impairment or distress, manifested by three of the following in a twelve-month period"[36]:

1   tolerance (the need for increased amounts of a substance, for example);

2   withdrawal (distressing physical or psychological symptoms when the habit is discontinued);

3   use in larger amounts or over longer periods than intended;

4   persistent desire or unsuccessful efforts to control use;

5   spending a great deal of time in activities related to use;

6   abandoning or cutting back important social occupational, or recreational activities as a result of use; and

7   continuing the habit in spite of knowing that it creates problems.

---

[36] *Diagnostic and Statistical Manual of Mental Disorders*, 4th ed., ed. M. First (Washington: American Psychiatric Association, 1994): 181.

Suicide addicts acknowledge *all* of these characteristics. We develop tolerance rapidly, progressing to increased fantasies, then to rituals, then to attempts. (Withdrawal will be discussed below.) None of us expect to devote hours and hours to suicidal fantasies and attempts for years, and all of us try to control our addiction through secrecy, denial, psychiatric labeling, and treatment of other psychological problems. Suicidal fantasies and rituals steal us away from all the important things in our lives—work, family, friendships, activities—and this in spite of our full knowledge of the deadly consequences of our behavior. *That's* addiction.

The Hell of Withdrawal

Actually attempting suicide breaks the trance, and withdrawal starts. It takes the form of painful feelings and memories that the addiction had succeeded in blocking. Coupled with these is a sense of overwhelming shame and failure. The promise of permanent relief and peace has been broken and the fantasy slips away. We're left facing the cold, hard light of reality. And it is hell.

Some of us experienced this double whammy in a hospital; others faced it alone at home. Those of us who woke up in a hospital had the additional hell of being *seen* to be suicidal—something we had desperately attempted to keep private. But now everyone knows; the cat is out of the bag. Strangers invaded both our physical space and our secret world. Each encounter, each question or procedure, only compounded the shame. We had to face the issues, judgments, fears, and confusions of everyone around us—hospital staff, family, friends, other patients. Even those who tried to be kind fell short; they lacked full understanding and so could not connect with us. No one fully understood where we were, or how we came to be there.

We also had to deal with the biochemical backswing—the onset of irritability, rage, and suppressed affect. The result was utter despair.

Raquel: *After an attempt, it went like this: severe anger, rage, sense of failure, tears, anger at God. Next came the desire to kill the people around me, especially the nurses and* *doctors. I blamed everyone for not letting me die. And then came thoughts of trying it again, immediately.*

Those of us who avoided hospitalization had to face this hell alone. We kept the secret and hid our suicide attempts from others, simultaneously rejecting this reality ourselves. Reality looked overwhelming. Rather than deal with withdrawal and despair, we got back into the trance state as quickly as we could, and started the cycle again.

Treatment

The suicide addiction cycle is a complex mixture: it is both inherently traumatic *and* a response to previous trauma. We have become addicted to trauma, as it were. There seems to be a good chance that the addiction is mediated through a complex internal biochemical pattern established by childhood trauma.

That being said: what do we do to deal with the problem?

Suicide addiction, like other addictions, responds to a Twelve Step approach. At the core of any treatment for this or any other addiction, there has to be deep spiritual healing. We have to break our dependence on the "high" induced by suicidal behavior, and we have to give up the false peace that results from thoughts of suicide. The Twelve Step approach is ideal for establishing and maintaining day-to-day sobriety—controlling the addiction, so that we can get on with the underlying work.

For the other half of the picture is trauma therapy. We have to find out what went wrong—what got us into this mess in the first place. The underlying hurt has to be healed as well. This requires specific trauma treatment.

But before we discuss treatment, we have to look further into the problem: its sources and its other effects on us and those around us.

Remington's Story

I was born in a small town in Nebraska. My father was a fairly successful executive with a small company, and my mother was a housewife. Both of them were older; my father was almost 50 when I was born, and my mother was almost 40. I was her only child. My father had a son, my half-brother, who was 25 when I was born.

On the surface, we seemed like a good family. My father's picture was in the local paper a lot; he was involved in civic clubs and other activities. He always wore a nice suit. But he was also an active alcoholic. We had a whole different life at home. I've seen pictures of myself as a child, being held by different people, and you'd think I was a happy kid because there were always a lot of toys around. But if you look more closely at those pictures, you'll see that nobody is smiling. I remember how tense and quiet everything was. We never talked much about anything.

Fundamentally, my father used our home for drinking. There was a lot of tension, especially on weekends; lots of arguments, then long silences, then more arguments. I was frightened, angry, and very, very quiet.

My mother had no close friends, only acquaintances. Her sister and I were the people she was closest to. I turned into her surrogate spouse. She talked to me about my father, about her fears and anger. Gradually, the family became just the two of us, my mother and me, with my father on the outside.

My first exposure to suicide came when I couldn't have been much more than five. One Saturday night, my father was sitting and drinking, becoming more and more morose, talking about how everything would be better if he was dead. My mother took me aside and told me what we had to do. We searched the house, and we found my father's pistol. It was fully loaded. I remember the impact of seeing that revolver, and my mother taking it out of the house. We went to my aunt's house—we were there often.

About the same age, I remember going out on weekend nights with my mother to try to find my father. He led a double life: during the week, he was a well-dressed well-spoken successful executive, but on weekends, he would hit the lowest meanest bars he could find. We'd look for him there, my mother and I. I remember her saying, as we drove through the night, "Well, we need to find him so we can make sure he hasn't killed himself." That really frightened me. But I had to be good, I had to be quiet, because I was there to help my mother.

My salvation was my aunt—she was the person who really raised me. At her house, I could be a kid; I could play, and I had neighborhood friends. Friends could never come to my parents' house, because it had to be quiet so that my father could do what he did. I didn't want people coming there. I was ashamed of our house. It was full of junk, old ratty couches covered with sheets. No one ever visited there. Home was where my father lived and drank. I remember the fear; I remember the gun. We had to keep it hidden where he couldn't find it.

When I was six or seven, my mother developed breast cancer. I became her helper and withdrew from other kids. I played war games by myself—I had an arsenal of toy guns. That's what I was happiest doing. I was a mama's boy, unlike other boys. At first the other kids called me "sissy"; then they used worse words.

I was six when I first thought of suicide. It was after my mother's diagnosis; I was so scared and angry...Not having any friends and having to put up with other kids' tormenting made me feel deeply ashamed and angry. I didn't have a father; the only role my father could teach me was how to drink beer and be abusive. I turned inward, in my anger and shame.

I remember talking about suicide for the first time when I was seven. There had been a Cub Scouts meeting at my home, and the other boys were tormenting me. I ran up to my room and started to cry. They came to my door, yelling names and making fun of me. There was nothing I could do to stop them. After the meeting, I was in an absolute rage. I went to my mother in tears, yelling at her "I might as well kill myself!" At that moment, I crossed a line. Those words gave me a sense of control over what went on around me. I didn't speak those words again for a long time, but I held on to that knowledge. I never really put it away.

My mother's cancer was treated with surgery and chemotherapy. It was very frightening. I was the little man of the house, living with other kids' abuse and with the strains and silences of our family. My fear and anger grew all the time. I had no friends; I couldn't play sports—all I had was my solitude and my toy gun collection.

I decided that the only thing I could do was to be smart. I'd been told I was smart; I chose to be smarter. My school performance was the one thing that pleased even my father. So I threw myself into my schoolwork. I studied constantly. When I got into high school, I went all the time—I even went to summer school. That gave me a sense of being worth something.

My mother died when I was 14. It was terrifying, being left with only my father. I could retreat to my aunt's house, but not all the time. I shut myself up in my room, reading or playing with my toy soldiers. I also found that I could satisfy myself and find escape from my fears through masturbation—something I found entirely by accident. It relieved my sense of stress and tension. I masturbated often.

I also learned how not to feel—or at least, how not to show feelings. That's what I did the day my mother died. She'd been in the hospital for about a week, and it was clear she was dying. The cancer had spread throughout her body. She died early one Wednesday morning in 1965. My father and my aunt came home from the hospital and told me she was dead. I cried a little, but then I did what I had to do. I wasn't supposed to miss school. So I went to school the day my mother died. I finished out the week without letting the kids around me know what was wrong. I knew how to behave: I was supposed to carry on and do what my mother would have wanted me to do.

But I still had to put up with the taunts, the pushing and shoving, and the snickering…So I learned how to fight, and that helped some. But you can't fight everybody. I think the flip side of my suicidal impulses was the fantasies I had of killing my tormenters—shooting, stabbing, maiming the kids who made my life miserable. Those fantasies made me feel better.

I finished high school when I was 16. I don't know if I was really all that smart, but I'd certainly worked hard. My father decided that he would be proud of me if I went to one of the military academies. That would make a man of me. It would be a prize for him, to talk about the fine school his son went to, to boast that his son was an outstanding military officer. I hated the idea. I begged not to go, telling my father I didn't belong there. I wanted to go to medical school. He wouldn't listen.

In 1969, I was enrolled as a freshmen at one of those academies. It was horrible. I was hopeless at sports. I didn't know how to behave around other young men, and I was shut up with thousands of them. I remember being nose-to-nose with people who were screaming at me. I was frightened all the time.

During that first summer, a lot of students quit and several killed themselves. We had our own weapons; we maintained them and marched with them. One young man shot himself in the head with a blank cartridge; at very close range, the blank did exactly what he wanted it to. For months I obsessed about getting hold of a blank round, keeping it, and—if things got unbearable—using it on myself. That's how I kept going. I was doing well enough academically that I wasn't going to flunk out. If I had to, I could always use the blank round...Fortunately, I didn't act on that idea. Instead, I quit the Academy and went home.

The day I got back was the worst in my life. My father had remarried, and he invited me to a welcome-home dinner at the country club. Midway through his second Tom Collins, out of the clear blue, he told me that I was a goddamn worthless coward and he didn't want anything to do with me. I'd learned not to respond, and I took it very quietly and with some dignity, but I have never been more shamed in my life. I thought I deserved to die. I had let my father down, and I had taken my one chance to be Somebody and thrown it away. I was suicidal for quite some time after that evening.

I went off to the state college and threw myself into studying. I went to school twelve months a year. At college, I found something that helped for a while. I'd been active in church as a child, because that's what children were supposed to do. At college, I joined the church Student Union. I was a damn good churchgoer for a while, and that helped me. I started to think that just maybe, life was going to be okay.

I got accepted into medical school when I was 19. I thought that was really cool—to be in med school as a teenager. That was going to fix me. I became a summer missionary and went to Mexico. I was pretty good with the young people at camp, and that too made me feel better.

I went back to Nebraska, to med school, and met the girl I later married. In fact, I was already engaged to someone else, a country girl, but I figured I needed to move up a level. That says something about who I was. I found several new diversions that year: sex with a partner, alcohol, and marijuana.

Medical school wasn't what I thought it would be. For one thing, it was hard work. It was the first time I'd ever had to push myself academically. Because I wasn't perfect at it, I felt I wasn't any good at all. This was what I'd been aiming for, all my life, and I wasn't the very best at it. I was in a state medical school, too, so even if I did well, what did it mean?

I got my first gun. The medical school was in a bad neighborhood, so I needed the gun for self-protection. That was great, having my own gun. I kept it with me. If I went out at night, I took it along in my car. With it, I felt that nothing could get to me—that I was safe. I kept it close by me when I studied, playing with it—as I did later, when I was drinking.

Later, after I was married, I started to think that it could take care of me in another way. I remember one night I was sitting in the closet where I studied; my wife was downstairs. I picked up my revolver, turning it over in my hands and studying it, rubbing it; and I thought *This can take care of me. I don't have to feel this shit any more. I can take care of things.* From that moment on, I was never entirely free of suicidal thoughts. Suicide became both a way for me to pay for not being good enough *and* a way to protect myself. If the pain got too bad, I could find a way out.

During medical school, I obsessed about death all the time. I was so frightened. I found out that I had Medical Student Syndrome: everything I studied, I got. I got worked up for cancer, kidney disease, and other disorders, going through all sorts of invasive procedures, because I was convinced that I had some disease that was going to kill me. At the same time, I had this gun that I was going to use to kill myself. I gave up smoking marijuana because I had death fantasies that terrified me.

In medical school, I started drinking heavily. One of my classmates named me the Happy Drunk, because drinking made me happy. After tests, before tests, I was steadily using alcohol. My addiction to sex started about the same time. I had an affair with one of my classmates and broke it off the week before I got married. Later, I had affairs with nurses; they made me feel a little better.

My father died while I was in medical school. He died on New Year's Eve. I remember taking the call and saying, "Oh, well, happy New Year" as I hung up. That was that.

Medical school didn't fix me, so I went to North Carolina to do my ear-nose-and-throat residency. For a while, that went well. With more money, I started buying more guns. That was how I was going to kill myself. Guns gave me a sense of protection from whatever might threaten me.

As for addictions, I limited myself to guns, alcohol, and sex. As a young resident, I found it easy to find young women who wanted to be with young residents. None of these affairs ever lasted more than a month or so, but they came one after another. It was always unprotected sex, too—which, again, says something about my outlook on life.

I made it through residency and into practice. I went with a friend of mine to South Carolina. I thought perhaps making a lot of money would fix me. I didn't realize how frightened I was of going into practice. It was a multi-specialist practice, and I was the junior guy. I started drinking daily, drinking to go off to work, and having lots of sex. These affairs were more and more dangerous—sex in the woods, in a moving car. The ultimate was sex in a swimming pool during a thunderstorm, something I found immensely stimulating and dangerous as hell.

I had all the guns anyone could ever want. That's what I did with my money. I loved guns, lots of guns, and lots of ammunition. I was never a survivalist or a militiaman; guns were my way of protecting myself. The world was over *there* and I was over *here*, and I needed to keep a killing zone between us. I needed to keep that space. Besides, guns were powerful, and I needed that as well. So I bought guns, I traded guns, I hung around with gun owners, and we shot guns together.

My wife and I had real problems. She was the adult child of an alcoholic, and her way of dealing with everything was to use anger and shame. She always tapped all the right buttons. I came home late one night, drunk, and my wife confronted me. She shamed and scared me, and I was really pissed off. In front of her, I grabbed my .44 hand-cannon and put it to my head. I felt a sense of power: *back off, or I shoot.* What was she going to do? Be spattered all over with pieces of my head? That was power. It was vicious, but at the time it felt good.

Over time, I spent more and more time in my own inside place, because life was starting to fall apart. Medicine was drudgery for me.

People knew I was drinking, but they didn't want to confront me. When they did confront me, I denied the problem: "No, I haven't been drinking." I lost my job at the clinic and opened a solo practice, which my wife ran. It was pure hell, absolute misery. I couldn't get enough to drink, so I got more involved with the woman I'd been seeing. One night, I stayed with her and drank until two or three in the morning, and then admitted a patient to the hospital. I finally sobered up, went to the hospital to follow up, and found myself in a whole lot of trouble. Sent to counseling, I covered up by telling the counselor that it was just stress, a lot of things going on. I thought that the most honorable thing I could do was to kill myself.

One night, my wife and I had a fight about my drinking, money, and a number of other things. In the middle of the night, I started to sober up, and it felt awful. I pulled out my trusty .44. This time, I meant it. I waited for my wife to fall asleep. When I thought she'd nodded off, I cocked my gun and put my finger on the trigger. I rubbed the trigger lightly, with a sense of tingling anticipation. I can't describe it: it was a sense of *I'm going to get the hell out of here, and wherever I go it's going to be quiet and I will be at peace.* I don't know how long I sat there with my finger on the trigger—minutes or hours. I was trying to experience how it would feel, that last moment before I stepped out of life. I don't think I've had a feeling quite like that before or since. It was amazing. I *knew* that when I pulled that trigger, I'd be dead. I just wanted to savor the feeling before that moment. If that's not mood- and mind-altering, I don't know what is.

After dragging on for another year or so, I went to Colorado. I told myself that I wanted to go to the mountains and ski. What I really wanted was to go somewhere where *I* wouldn't be, and of course, when I got there, there *I* was. I went into practice with another surgeon. The same things started happening all over again: angry outbursts at patients and others; people picking up the smell of alcohol on my breath and not being sure what to do, not wanting to raise a stink about it. I did, however, get into skiing, which I loved.

I lived in the home town of John Browning, the inventor of the .45-caliber automatic pistol. Pure coincidence, I think. I even met Browning's 91-year-old son. I thought I was doing pretty well, but every time I had to come in from the slopes or from a ski trip, there *I* was, still drinking and playing with guns.

One afternoon, while my wife was still at the office, I got my trusty .44 out. I kept it loaded with the heaviest rounds I could fit in it. A .44 magnum loaded with hunting rounds is a formidable weapon. I sat in the bedroom, playing with it, really getting off on it. I suppose it was a form of masturbation. I was reasonably drunk at the time. I cocked the pistol. I don't remember the sound, but I do remember seeing an orange ball hanging in mid-air. It seemed to hang there for about 10 minutes. When it finally disappeared, there was a hole right through the bedroom wall about the size of a grapefruit, a hole in the far wall of the next room about the same size, and a crater on the other side of *that* wall. *Oh shit. I'm not going to be able to hide this from my wife...Where'd the bullet go? If that hit anyone, the next round goes into me.* Fortunately, I was on the second floor of the house. I searched and found a chunk of plaster-covered metal.

You'd think I'd have learned something from that incident, especially after my wife got home and found the damage. How she lived through it, I don't know. We seemed to get past it. But I couldn't let go of the gun or the vodka—I couldn't put them down. My practice was doing poorly. I made some money, but getting up in the morning to go to work was hell. I decided I had to do *something*, so I went to counselors and psychologists. We'd talk about my problems, and they'd always come to the same question: "Do you have a drinking problem?" I always answered, "No, not really. I drink some because I'm really depressed." And I always got away with it. Of course, I could never tell them that I knew that as long as I had my guns, I would be okay.

I managed to quit drinking for a while. I didn't get sober by any means, but I didn't drink for about five years. I was miserable. I kept holding on to the thought, *If it gets bad enough, I can always...<click>*

In 1988, one of my colleagues—a general surgeon, who was my hero, who had money, position, respect, cars, and women—took out his pistol, put the end of the barrel in his mouth, and blew off the back of his head. I grabbed hold of that suicide and couldn't let go of it. It was like the kid who'd shot himself with the blank at the military academy. I kept saying "Poor Gene!" but I kept thinking, *That's really cool, that's great, that he could just step out of all this shit.* I was obsessing about the suicide to anyone who'd listen to me. I couldn't leave it alone. People started worrying about me again. I got calls from the hospital chief of staff asking if I was okay, and I told him I was just upset about Gene's death. But it wasn't grief or sorrow: I was using his death as a mood-altering drug. *If he can do it, I can do it. I wonder what it was like. I wonder how he felt, that last minute.*

Soon after that, I started drinking again, and my wife and I separated. We'd both had enough. I was alone. I had a few friends, but I couldn't keep them. I took another geographical cure, saying *to hell with this private practice; I'm going to join an HMO.* But being an HMO doc was even worse. It paid better, and the work was easier, but I was even more miserable.

I finally managed to put Gene's suicide down, but the drinking was causing problems. I started taking the barbiturate Fioricet because my headaches were so bad. *But that's not because of the alcohol. Maybe I do have a problem with alcohol, but Fioricet will make it okay.* I was having lots of headaches and taking lots of Fioricet. I didn't kill myself because I just didn't have the energy—probably because of the barbiturate. I got incredibly depressed. I quit taking

Fioricet not because it made me want to kill myself, but because it made me so damned tired that I couldn't get around to it.

That brought me back to alcohol, and to angry outbursts at patients, other physicians, and the HMO hierarchy. I lost my job in January 1993. They paid me off handsomely, so I could sit on the couch putting back the vodka, always with a gun close at hand. I had nothing else to do, and I had plenty of vodka. I just hung there for a while.

It was then, I think, that God came back into the picture...Something started pulling me back. I decided that I couldn't just sit there and drink myself to death. So I started looking for a medical job again. I also met my present wife, and that was good. I couldn't find a job in Colorado—probably something to do with my drinking! But I found work in Kentucky, at a clinic. My wife and I were married, but she stayed in Colorado for her health. I said to myself, *I'm going to work again, and this time when I get there, I won't be there.*

I took off across the western United States, my car loaded with my clothes, a bottle of vodka under the back seat and my .44 under the front seat. God's grace must have been with me, because I made it all the way through the desert—through Colorado, across New Mexico, driving through the night drinking vodka. God must have been at work.

Finally I got to Kentucky and put the gun away for a little while—but I kept the vodka out. I started work in August 1994. My bottoming-out was in sight. First I carried the regular-sized bottle of vodka; then I graduated to the big jug. Then I was keeping two jugs in my car and drinking whenever I could get out of the office. I lost my job. It was real scary now, because before, I'd drunk when I needed to drink, but now there was no not-drinking.

My wife arrived from Colorado, and I don't know how I managed to hide my drinking from her. I kept the booze in my car and went out ten times a night for a drink. I started getting sick; I was vomiting, bloating, and bruising. I snuck out at night to throw up blood behind the apartment. One night, in the rain, I was down on my knees in the mud, vomiting. *God, you've got to help me. I can't stand this. I can't take it any more. I'm going to die, either from the bottle or from the barrel.*

146

But then I got myself a .45 pistol—I've always liked a .45 automatic, Mr. Browning's pistol from the West. I would sit at night just working the action and ejecting shells. My sex was with my weapon. Whenever my wife was out, I'd sit on the couch drinking vodka and playing with my gun.

God finally stepped in, through others like my self, who intervened with me. They didn't say "Remington, have you been drinking?" They said, "Remington, you're drunk. Here's what you've got to do." I remember a sense of relief; but there's a lot more that I don't remember. It was on a Thursday, I heard them say "Remington, you need to go to treatment and get some help." I went home instead.

I don't remember that weekend, except for little flashes of pain when I'd run into a wall. I remember sitting on the toilet, falling off, smashing into the wall, and urinating all over myself. My wife tells me I played a lot with that gun. I don't remember much of it. I do remember the taste of metal in my mouth.

I woke up Monday morning with a chipped front tooth and the gun beside me, cocked and with the safety off. It was very gently and gingerly lifted from my hand by a deputy sheriff. They put me on a stretcher and took me to the city ER. I stayed in-patient for a couple of days, and then I went to a treatment center for drug and alcohol addiction. It seemed like a lousy idea at the time. I remember saying, "Look, you've got to let me go home. My wife needs me." This, from a guy who'd been sitting on the couch, less than 72 hours before, with a cocked gun, dead drunk…I promised to go back as an out-patient—that was just part of the insanity. This time, thank God, they didn't listen to me.

Treatment lasted a long, hard 16 weeks. I played it every way but the right way. There was some real hard times. But I came through.

Today, I wouldn't trade what I've learned for anything. I'm learning more about what's wrong with me—about my alcohol and drug addictions, about my sex addiction. I was in love with suicide. I said that I was afraid of death, but in fact, I was in love with killing myself.

I am so thankful now to be alive, and to know and (for the first time) to believe that God does listen—that he was listening when I begged him for help. I still carry a .45-caliber pistol shell. By itself, it is absolutely harmless. In the proper vehicle, it could have kept me from having a wonderful life. That's amazing—that such a little chunk of metal might have kept me from having the life I have today.

Chapter 4

How Did We Get Here?

"...where a man's wound is, that is where his genius will be. Wherever the wound appears in our psyche,...that is precisely the place for which we will give our major gift to the community."
—Robert Bly[37]

What happened to us in childhood? We were not born this way. Something went terribly wrong, although not all of us could remember what it was.

It seems that all of us suffered some sort of childhood trauma, sometimes a traumatic life event, but more usually physical, sexual, emotional, or spiritual abuse or some combination of these. Unless these events are properly handled at the time, children can be left with unprocessed emotions that scab over without properly healing—rather like an abscess of the soul.

---

[37] R. Bly, *Iron John* (New York: Addison-Wesley, 1990), 42.

Life-Event Trauma

Children may be subjected to terrifying or damaging events—the death of a family member, for example, or war, or a car accident, or a frightening illness and hospitalization. Van der Kolk discusses these "uncontrollable, terrifying life events."[38] These events leave the victim with post-traumatic stress disorder, a specific disorder with definite symptoms such as flashbacks and dissociation. Some children seem to have particular problems with health.

Chastity: *I was bitten by a spider at age 5—had massive swelling and necrosis of my upper arm. Then I had my tonsils removed at age 9, exploratory laparotomy at 11, and multiple surgeries from 13 to 18, spending six months in the hospital. When I was 22, they resected my bowel. My hysterectomy and knee surgery both took place when I was 31.*

---

[38] B. van der Kolk, *Psychological Trauma* (Washington: American Psychiatric Press, 1987), 1.

Physical Abuse

Many of us grew up in alcoholic homes. We had memories of being beaten with a belt or strap by a father in an alcoholic rage, or of an enraged out-of-control mother slapping or shoving us or pushing us down the stairs, or of siblings tearing into us in a rage. At the same time, however, we were debarred from talking about the abuse at all. At home, we were up against familial denial ("oh, your dad didn't really mean it" or "well, if you bug your brother, of course he's going to hit you!"). But telling anyone outside the home was unthinkable ("we don't air our dirty laundry in public.") One of the most damaging things about abuse of any sort is its insistence on silence and secrecy. We're all supposed to pretend that nothing happened, to go on as though the incident, whatever it was, never occurred. Only years afterward is the victim free to see what's happened, and to speak about it.

Paula: *My father routinely beat my mother. When he was drunk, no one was safe. The police were at our house frequently.*

Thelma: *Even as a young child of two or three, I remember having thoughts of death and hopelessness. I had a great-grandmother, who I loved very much. One day I accidentally stepped on her foot and got whipped really hard. I felt ashamed, as though I had meant to hurt her foot. That day, I wanted to die.*

Sexual Abuse

Most of us had been sexually abused as children or teenagers. Many, especially the women among us, had been overtly abused through direct, forced sexual contact—intercourse, genital manipulation, or inappropriate touching. Some had been in forced incestuous relationships with their fathers, brothers, uncles, or grandfathers. Some were abused only once; others had to endure years of incest. Still others suffered rape by non-family members—and some incest victims were raped years after the incest stopped.

Kevin Taylor M.D.

None of us could talk about it. We all carried the shame, the horror, and the rage within us for years. We acted out our pain through multiple addictions and repeated suicidal behaviors.

Paula: *I was fondled by my grandfather, and later my father sexually molested me from age 12 to 17.*

Chastity: *A family member sexually abused me when I was 4— oral and anal. I felt a heavy weight on me. I couldn't breathe.*

Raquel: *One of my earliest memories is of incest; it started when I was 4 and stopped when I was in Grade 1...I did have one girlfriend, and even got invited for a sleepover for her 12th birthday party. Her father and brother molested me that night.*

Even more of us were victims of covert sexual abuse—emotional abuse of a sexual nature without direct sexual contact. Ken Adams describes this pattern in his book *Silently Seduced.* It includes any emotionally incestuous relationship between a parent and child. The parent unconsciously uses the child as a surrogate spouse, emotional lover, or inappropriate confidante.[39] These patterns are often subtle and easy to miss, even by well-trained professionals. The victims themselves have no idea what the problem was.

Once we knew what the pattern was, we could easily identify it in our own lives. Most of the men in our group had been abandoned by their fathers and emotionally seduced by their mothers. Becoming the "man of the house", we lost our childhood. At the same time, however, we were delighted and intoxicated by the power and responsibility granted us—think of a queen setting her prince-son on his father's vacant throne. We were programmed for life to be "mama's boy", mother's confidante and advisor.

---

[39] K. Adams, *Silently Seduced* (Deerfield Beach, Fla.: Health Communications, 1991), 8, 9.

Kevin Taylor M.D.

Kevin: *My mother always came to me for advice about my father's headaches. I felt special. Only years later did I realize that I was robbed of part of my childhood.*

Remington: *I was my mother's surrogate spouse from age 7 until age 14, when she died. We discussed my father's drinking and her plans to leave him. When I was 13, I frequently lay in bed with my mother, who wore flimsy, revealing gowns.*

Some of us were involved in relationships that were *both* covertly and overtly sexual. Some women, looking back, could see that they were both sexually abused by their fathers *and* played the role of surrogate spouse. This caused deep damage to their sense of self. In adulthood, these women—programmed to be "daddy's girl", "daddy's little princess" —lived on an emotional roller coaster, "riding to the top of romantic fantasies, then plunging into the despair of romantic disillusionment."[40]

Paula: *My father was covertly sexual with me for as long as I can remember. Then he sexually molested me from age 12 to 17. I've had numerous affairs and multiple suicide attempts.*

Emotional Abuse

"Sticks and stones may break my bones, but words can *really* hurt me." Emotional abuse, like sexual abuse, can be overt or covert—or both. We remembered being yelled at, told we were unwanted, told that we were stupid, told that we'd never amount to anything. We were brutally criticized for the slightest mistake or failure. More subtly, we could be given messages that compared us unfavorably to our sibs, or we could be teased in destructive, put-down ways. Or we were simply ignored—shut out and abandoned by parents who seemed not to care about us at all.

---

[40] *Ibid.*, 42.

Remington: *The worst day of my life was when I quit the Academy. My dad called me a goddamn worthless coward and said he didn't want anything more to do with me.*

Jacqueline: *My mother put me down—said I wasn't good enough, I wasn't intelligent enough. After my father's suicide when I was ten, my uncle began putting me down in front of others.*

We were left shamed to the very depths of our beings. These messages seemed to be embedded in our brains—tape-recorded into permanent memory. Any time we were under stress, we could hear the voices start up again, whispering our worthlessness, our wrongness, into our inner ear, draining our energy and self-confidence.

Spiritual Abuse

Spirituality is a critical component of any human being. It is the most precious and personal part of who we are as individuals. All cultures have spiritual values, creation stories, explanations of life. They describe humankind's awareness of some higher power, some sense of God. As the higher centers of our brains develop, this sense of spiritual curiosity— "a seeking" —emerges in children from every culture. At this time, children are highly vulnerable; they need nurturing and careful guidance, combined with the freedom to explore and grow in their awareness of God.

Probably few parents manage this side of child-rearing entirely successfully, but some parents do outright damage. Spiritual abuse, scarring our childish souls, left perhaps the deepest wounds of all. As children, we were made to feel ashamed for having spiritual questions, for showing curiosity, for trying to understand life, God, and the world. We were told how to think, not given the freedom to find answers for ourselves. Such patterns—rarely described in the literature—produced signs and symptoms of abuse that later had major implications for us as we struggled with suicide.

Kevin: *Growing up, I felt ashamed and stupid when I asked difficult questions about God. Other people seemed to have it all figured out. I felt completely left out—in the dark. I decided that I did not belong. The more others seemed to have the answers, the more left out I felt; and the more left out I felt, the more broken I felt. Not feeling safe to ask and seek, I finally just quit. God was there, but somehow I wasn't part of His group.*

Remington: *There was no spiritual guidance in my home, no family rituals or spiritual observances. They sent me to Sunday School for that. I can recall only two references to God by my parents—both directed at me—about God not being quick to forgive bad behavior. That message stuck.*

Jacqueline: *I was in church every Sunday—I had a strict religious upbringing. If I broke any of the church's* *rules, both my grandmothers and my mother condemned me.*

Shaming us for our spiritual curiosity wounds us at the deepest level, in the most personal part of our being. It risks cutting us off from what keeps us truly alive—a sense of connectedness, an ability to reach out to our Creator. Cut off from our one source of power, we die spiritually. We did not create ourselves, and we cannot sustain ourselves. Spiritual shaming unplugs us from our power source.

Intentionally or unintentionally shamed, we started our spiritual journey heading off in disastrous directions. We internalized core beliefs, all right, but they were the wrong ones: that we were damaged and broken, that there was something deeply wrong with us, that God was angry at us, that we didn't deserve to live, that we had no safe ground anywhere at all. These beliefs, running deep in our souls, shaped our feelings, thoughts, self-images, and psyches.

Chastity: *When I got sick in the fifth grade, I believed that God was punishing me for being a bad sinner, and that if I wasn't good enough, I would burn in hell.*

Kevin: *I always felt damaged—like I'd come from the manufacturer broken. No place felt safe. Not until treatment did I ever experience a sense of real safety. I discovered that my wife and others had been safe places for me all along!*

Mary: *When my brother died, I thought it should have been me. He was the good one. I was the bad one. I thought I did not deserve to live.*

Chastity: *I felt trapped in an alien body, hopeless to make up for my defectiveness and helpless to fit in or be anything but defective. I could never do enough to be normal.*

In *Breaking the Chains*, Fr. Leo Booth describes spiritual mind control—an experience that many of us remembered with a sense of deep anger and shame:

> Their message is: Don't think—accept; don't reason—obey. The argument is presented that "the leader" has been appointed or chosen by God to deliver "the message", and a faithful disciple is one who unquestioningly follows...As children, if they did anything that broke the rule, they were to confess it and receive the punishment. If they used slang or offensive words, the offending children must wash out their mouths with soap. Failure to go to church, falling asleep during the sermon, or forgetting a studied scriptural text resulted in a beating.[41]

That Sense of Safety

Children need a sense of safety—having a safe place and safe people. This sense of safety is essential for normal emotional and spiritual development. Healthy children develop "safe places" within

---

[41] L. Booth, *Breaking the Chains* (Long Beach, California: Emmaus Publications, 1989), 81-82.

themselves, in nature, or in the arms of loving family members. In times of conflict, crisis, or acute pain, they can turn to these places and feel safe, unconditionally loved, and solidly grounded. They also identify safe people who unconditionally love them and who they can turn to for nurturing and comfort. These may be parents, grandparents, favorite aunts or uncles. In troubled times, they can turn to these people and feel fully safe and grounded.

Abuse wounds trust, and the earlier the abuse happens, the greater the damage. Abuse in the first years of life is always a serious matter. Small children are vulnerable, open, trusting, and defenseless, which is why child abuse is so atrocious. It destroys its victims' ability to develop safe places or safe people during childhood. From that moment of trust-breaking on, the child cannot really trust authority and power; these have been twisted to do harm, not to protect and nurture the child. The child's ability to bond in trust, and his or her ability to reach out and to search are damaged. This loss leaves these children feeling exposed and vulnerable, always on edge, never fully safe. They have no "faith that there is order and continuity in life."[42] They are left with a sense of helplessness, a deep belief that they have no control over what happens to them—no sense of meaning or safety. Their only option, it seems to them, is to try to avoid life with all its dangers and pains—but in so doing, they also miss its rewards and joys. This is a truly tragic way to live.

Early childhood abuse is *always* spiritual abuse, regardless of the form the abuse takes—sexual, emotional, physical—because it disrupts the child's emerging spirituality. Abuse later in life, after the individual has formed basic spiritual values and established a sense of safety, also does damage to trust, but the damage goes less deep and is more easily reparable. Life may be terribly painful, but the individual has a God of love and power to be with, for strength and comfort. But when a child is abused, the child is given a god the child never asked for—a false god, an unsafe god, a god who punishes and does not protect, who is apparently indifferent to the child's suffering—who may very well be recruited to justify or increase the child's suffering.

---

[42] B. van der Kolk, *Psychological Trauma,* 31.

From that moment of abuse forward, then, the child internalizes an unsafe god, based on the child's perception of an unsafe world full of unsafe people. In this world, the child can only dimly imagine and long for a safe place, a safe God, in the next world.

The Longing for Home

In such a state of helplessness, locked in a world that felt bereft of meaning or safety, we wanted more than anything else to go home to safety in the life to come. This "fantasy of spiritual rebirth," as it's called, is akin to other fantasies in which the individual longs for a sense of completion or wholeness—that some change in state, or some lost object, can somehow put them to rights again. Wounded people often feel incomplete or less than total, or that something is wrong with them. For them, suicidal fantasies are paradoxically life-*seeking*. They are searching for a safe place where they can find wholeness. Things having gone so badly wrong, they want to start out right again.[43]

---

[43] B. Klopfer, "Suicide: The Jungian Point of View," in N. Farberow and E. Shneidman, *The Cry for Help* (New York: McGraw-Hill, 1961), 193-203.

Kevin: *Early on, I realized that suicide was about escaping damage, going to some safer place. E.T. was the movie of the year in 1982. I saw it five times in treatment. Each time E.T. pointed out there and said "E.T., phone home," I cried from deep inside my soul. I just wanted to go Home.*

Chastity: *Just before a suicide attempt, I'd feel very peaceful and relieved. I felt I was going home to a better place. The angels beckoned me.*

In 1938, Menninger identified three motives for suicide: to kill (aggression); to be killed (guilt); and to die (escape).[44] In studies of suicide, most completed suicides seem to fit into the third category.[45] We who struggled with suicide believed that what follows death is an after-life, not annihilation. And we believed firmly that we were

---

[44] K. Menninger, *Man Against Himself* (New York: Harcourt Brace, 1938)
[45] R. Maris, *Pathways to Suicide: A Survey of Self-Destructive Behaviors* (Baltimore: Johns Hopkins University Press, 1981)

going to Heaven, not Hell. We fit into the theories of escape and spiritual rebirth. That was what attracted us to suicide—the certain prospect of union with a safe and loving God.

But the church traditionally condemns suicide. Until recently, the Roman Catholic church considered suicide to be a mortal sin, condemning the soul to Hell. For many of us, this meant feeling caught in a trap, as though the church stood between us and God's love and safety. How did this come about?

The Bible says little about suicide. Neither of the Testaments, Old or New, specifically prohibits suicide. The Old Testament records four suicides—Samson, Saul, Abinelech, and Achitophel—without adverse comments.[46] Judas's suicide in the New Testament is the logical outcome of his betrayal of Christ.

But in the early days of Christianity, suicide became a major concern.[47] According to Alvarez:

The more powerfully the Church instilled in believers the idea that this world was a vale of tears and sin and temptation, where they

---

[46] A. Alvarez, *The Savage God* (New York: Norton, 1971), 69.
[47] *Ibid.*

waited uneasily until death released them into eternal glory, the more irresistible the temptation to suicide became...Why, then, live unredeemed when heavenly bliss is only a knife stroke away? Christian teaching was at first a powerful incitement to suicide.[48]

The suicide rate actually increased among members of the early church throughout the 6th century, bolstered by the belief that martyrdom afforded certain redemption.[49]

Augustine believed that if suicide were allowed in order to allow people to avoid sin, then suicide would become the logical choice for anyone fresh from baptism.[50] He feared that the church would suicide its way into extinction. Thus the church's ban on suicide grew, in part, from Augustine's concern for the survival of Christianity.

Augustine's authority carried conviction. In 533 AD, the Council of Orleans denied funeral rites to anyone who committed suicide while accused of a crime. Thirty years later, at the Council of Braga (562 AD), the church refused funeral rites to *all* suicides, regardless

---

[48] *Ibid.*
[49] *Ibid.*, **86**
[50] *Ibid.*

of social position, reason, or method. Finally in 693 AD, the Council of Toledo resolved that those who merely attempted suicide should be excommunicated.[51]

Many of us, therefore, grew up torn and traumatized. Augustine and other church fathers like Thomas Aquinas told us that "suicide is a mortal sin against God, who has given life."[52] But we still longed for reunion with a safe and loving God, who we felt we could find only in the life to come. We were spiritually racked and ripped apart, left with nowhere safe to go.

> **Kevin:** *I realized that suicide was a mortal sin against God, yet somehow I wanted to go to God in my suicide attempts. I just wanted to go Home. That dilemma left me paralyzed, with nowhere to turn. Part of my soul died.*

Possible Mechanisms: The Biochemical Connection

---

[51] *Ibid.*, 89.
[52] *Ibid.*

As van der Kolk says, "the earliest and possibly most damaging psychological trauma is the loss of a secure base."[53] More and more, research is showing that disrupting children's bonds of attachment may have lifelong effects, related to the maturation of the central nervous system.

From conception to age 5, children's brains undergo a delicate and complex process of differentiation and development. This process can be affected positively or negatively by the child's experiences. Separation from the child's primary caregiver causes the child deep distress—a phenomenon called the "separation call." This event seems to be mediated by endogenous opioids[54]—the same brain chemicals that come into play in addictions. The areas of the brain involved in social bonding are particularly rich in opiate receptors. It would seem that pain perception, separation distress, and affiliative behavior are mediated, at least partly, by the brain's own opiate system. Other research indicates that the hormone oxytocin is

---

[53] B. van der Kolk, *Psychological Trauma*, 32.
[54] *Ibid.*, 41.

involved in mother- infant bonding. Oxytocin is also stimulated by sexual behavior in adults.[55]

It seems possible, therefore, that chronic separation distress in infancy could predispose a person to look for comfort in actions that stimulate the opioid system or stimulate oxytocin release. These actions could include the whole range of behaviors discussed in Chapter 3—overeating, alcohol and drug consumption, sexual addiction, self-mutilation, suicide, anything that stimulates the production of endogenous opioids. Sex also increases oxytocin levels, a double bonus for the sexual addict.[56] Re-exposure to traumatic situations may "set off" internal opioid responses. It seems likely that these built-in narcotics play an important role in suicidal fantasies and sexual acting out. We who struggled with suicide consistently described "getting high" and "getting relief", both from suicidal fantasies and behaviors and from sexual acting out.

---

[55] T. Insel, "Oxytocin: A Neuropeptide for Affiliation: Evidence from Behavioral, Receptor, Audioradiographic, and Comparative Studies," *Psychoneuroendocrinology* 17 (1992): 3-35.

[56] B. van der Kolk, *Psychological Trauma, op. cit..*, 42, 72; J. Coid, B. Allolio, and L. Rees, "Raised Plasma Metenkephalin in Patients Who Habitually Mutilate Themselves," *Lancet* 2 (1983): 545-46; J. Caldwell, "Central Oxytocin and Female Sexual Behavior," *Annals of the New York Academy of Science* 652 (1991): 166-79.

Paula: *The decision to commit suicide always gave me a jolt of adrenalin unsurpassed by my other addictions. Alcohol, drugs, and sex all gave me a "high" like suicide, but suicide was the strongest. Once the decision was made, I felt energized, euphoric, powerful, and defiant.*

Sandy: *I don't need alcohol or drugs. Peace and euphoria come with the obsessive thoughts and gestures of suicide, which finally numb me. Thoughts of suicide make my life easier to endure.*

In 1991, van der Kolk reported linkage patterns between disruptions in parental care, trauma, cutting behaviors, and suicide attempts.[57] Subjects who reported self-cutting gave histories of major disruptions in parental care. Of the three types of childhood traumas associated with suicide—physical abuse, sexual abuse, and witnessing

---

[57] B. van der Kolk, J. Perry, and J. Herman, "Childhood Origins of Self-Destructive Behavior," *American Journal of Psychiatry* 148 (1991): 1665-69.

domestic violence—sexual abuse was most strongly related to all forms of self-destructive behavior. The earlier the abuse, the more likely the person was to indulge in self-cutting or suicide.[58] Experiences of domestic violence and total neglect also predisposed individuals towards suicide.

All in our group described abuse in childhood, often sexual abuse, and many of us had witnessed domestic violence:

Chastity: *I underwent oral and anal sexual abuse by a family member when I was four. I thought I was dying.*

Remington: *When my father drank, he became morose, argumentative, abusive, and hateful towards my mother. I remember the tension and silence in our home, alternating with violent arguments. I remember these when I was as young as 5. I stayed in my room with the door closed until my mother began to cry, and*

---

[58] B. van der Kolk *et al.*, "Dissociation, Somatization, and Affective Dysregulation: The Complexity of Adaptation to Trauma," *American Journal of Psychiatry* 153 (1996): 83-93.

then I would go to her bedroom and sit on her bed with her.

Trauma produces other problems in children, including difficulties with visual thought structure, impaired accommodation (or adaptation), "all-or-nothing" responses, and inflexibility.[59] Traumatized children are apt to re-enact scenes in their minds; they then have trouble with focusing attention. They are centered on their own internal world and cannot move away from seeing themselves as the center of the universe. Their responses to new situations tend to be automatic or rote in nature. They either fail to respond to situations, or respond overwhelmingly—the "all-or-nothing" response. But the strongest dysfunction seen in traumatized children is inflexibility.

Those of us who struggled with suicide had great trouble not seeing ourselves as the center of the universe. We had trouble adapting to new situations and were apt to respond to stressful situations in a catastrophic or overwhelming way, with little ability to be flexible or to think through the alternatives.

---

[59] B. van der Kolk, *Psychological Trauma*, 95-101.

Kevin: *Flexibility was not part of my life growing up. Grades were A or F. Woodworking was perfect or not at all. I thought it was a compliment when people called me a perfectionist.*

Dissociation, or the separation of experiences from consciousness, is a standard response to trauma.[60] The person forgets the memories and feelings associated with the trauma, often for years. These memories resurface in intrusive recollections and in states of feeling that often involve overwhelming anxiety and panic, delusions, and behavioral re-enactments. Dissociation is actually an adaptive response to immediate trauma; it's a way of "walling off" the self, protecting parts of the personality from further damage. But later, the trauma is "reawakened by some new precipitating cause…at a weak

---

[60] *Ibid.*, 185-86.

spot." It all comes back. Freud calls this the "return of the repressed."[61]

Many of us experienced a sort of trance-like state as we started into the suicide cycle. We developed tunnel vision, becoming less and less aware of the real world around us. We developed a robotic detachment from reality. The universe constricted, with our own lonely self at the center. We lost all flexibility, any capacity to think of alternatives, any sense of having any options but suicide—the "all-or-nothing" approach. Our responses turned automatic or robot-like. We found ourselves fixed at one moment in time.

Sandy: *Just before my worst suicidal thoughts, I feel like everyone but me is in slow motion. I'm in a trance, and people are oblivious to my existence. I'm invisible. It all feels like a dream. I can't control what I do. I'm on automatic pilot, but my remote control is broken. I'm*

---

[61] S. Freud, "Moses and Monotheism" (1939) in J. Strachey, tr. and ed., *The Standard Edition of the Complete Psychological Works of Sigmund Freud...* (London: Hogarth, 1954)

extremely detached from myself, as well as from the world I exist in.

Jacqueline: *I cry intensely, then calm down into a trance. I don't care what is going on around me. I block everything and everyone around me from consciousness as I start to float toward a suicide attempt. My vision blurs somewhat and my hearing seems to decrease in intensity.*

A National Institute of Mental Health study[62] found that early sexual abuse produced neurochemical, endocrine (hormone), and behavioral changes in girls aged 6 to 15. Depression and suicidal behaviors were common in the group. Usually suicidal thoughts and actions appeared first, and depression followed later. Sexual acting out, self-injury, immune system problems, and changes in blood cortisol levels were also common in the group. This falls in line with our experience.

---

[62] F. Putnam, "Conference on the Psychobiology of Post Traumatic Stress Disorder, New York Academy of Sciences," *Clinical Psychiatry News,* Nov. 1996, 22.

Thelma: *Sexually abused, I later became a sexual addict and an alcoholic. I also suffer from bipolar illness, with deep depressions and some manic episodes. Before my last hospitalization, everything seemed to shut down, both mentally and physically.*

Studies by Teicher at McLean Hospital report that individuals who had suffered physical abuse before the age of 18 show elevated scores on a checklist for symptoms of temporal lobe epilepsy.[63] Those who had suffered from sexual abuse scored even higher. High scores correlated strongly with suicidal ideation. Twice as many brainwave abnormalities appeared in the abused group.[64] These EEG abnormalities correlated strongly with self-destructive behavior.

The overall conclusion: **Those of us who are strongly drawn to suicide were at the mercy of powerful internal forces in our**

---

[63] M. Teicher, "Conference on the Psychobiology of Post Traumatic Stress Disorder, New York Academy of Sciences," *Clinical Psychiatry News*, Nov. 1996, 20.
[64] *Ibid.*

brains. These forces are beyond our control. They were set up as the result of abuse.

Possible Mechanisms: The Death Wish

Psychoanalytic theory offers no simple explanation of the traumatic mechanics of suicide. Two New York psychiatrists once observed that most of the 50 attempted suicides they had treated had involved people who had suffered early dramatic or tragic bereavements. These deaths usually involved close relatives—parents, siblings, or mates. In most cases, the bereavement had occurred before the patient finished adolescence. The psychiatrists called the pattern "the death trend", concluding that:

If one assumes that suicidal fantasies are possible forms of reacting to intense inner conflict and in some way represent problem-solving behavior, we may conclude from our study that the occurrence of the "death trend" in the patient's background would predispose him to act out self-destructive preoccupations.[65]

Freud thought that when children suffer losses at a vulnerable age, the task of mourning becomes more difficult and more hazardous.[66] A child who loses a parent or other loved one has to cope with a confused mass of emotions—guilt, anger, and a profound sense of abandonment. To relieve this hostility, the child splits it off from him- or herself and projects it on the lost figure. Thereafter, the child carries within him- or herself this murderous dead thing, which cries to be heard and waits to emerge at any crisis. The child's movements are controlled from some dark and unrecognized center. It is as though the child's one real purpose is to find a proper excuse to take his or her own life. Suicide attempts are, in this model, fundamentally an attempt at exorcism.

In fact, most of us had experiences significant losses at highly vulnerable ages.

---

[65] L. Moss and D. Hamilton, "Psychotherapy of the Suicidal Patient,: in E. Sheidman and N. Farberow, eds., *Clues to Suicide* (New York: Maidenhead, 1963), 99-110.
[66] A. Alvaraz, *The Savage God*, 131-32.

Jacqueline: *My father killed himself when I was 10.*

Sandy: *My father killed himself when I was 11. My hopes and dreams died with him.*

Remington: *My mother died of cancer when I was 14.*

Mary: *My brother died of cancer when I was 17.*

Freud further thought that the death instinct took over as a kind of "disease of the super-ego." The more virulent the disease, the more suicidal the person. The more fragile the ego (for whatever historical reason) the more vulnerable it is to the raging super-ego.[67] In other words, fragile (traumatized) people tend to beat themselves up with deep-seated wishes to die by suicide.

---

[67] *Ibid.*, 136.

Freud outlined his theory of the death instinct in his *Beyond the Pleasure Principle*, completed in 1920.[68] According to Alvarez,

...since that time the theory of a death instinct...has gathered considerable power as a kind of historical metaphor. Sixty-odd years of genocide and intermittent war between super-powers which, like Freud's diseased super-ego, have become progressively harsher, more repressive and totalitarian, have made the modified ego gratifications of civilization more fragile...

As the pleasure principle becomes less pleasurable and more manic, so the death instinct seems more powerful and ubiquitous: every perspective closes with the possibility of international suicide by nuclear warfare. It is as though the discontents of civilization itself have now reached that point of extreme suicidal melancholia which Freud so eloquently described: "What is now holding sway in the super-ego is, as it were, a pure culture of the death instinct and in fact it often enough succeeds in driving the ego into death!"[69]

---

[68] S. Freud, "Beyond the Pleasure Principle" (1920) in J. Strachey, tr. and ed., *The Standard Edition of the Complete Psychological Works of Sigmund Freud*, (London: Hogarth, 1959.)
[69] A. Alvarez, *The Savage God*, 138-9.

It may be, therefore, that we were also driven by powerful cultural forces of suicide, well beyond our own understanding and control. Cultural forces, superimposed on our childhood trauma wounds, pushed us deathward long before we even knew what the word "suicide" meant.

Jacqueline's Story

I was born in Australia to Austrian and Hungarian parents and raised in a Roman Catholic atmosphere. We spoke Hungarian at home. There wasn't much expression of love in my family. No one hugged or showed affection. It just wasn't done. It was understood that you were loved, I suppose. We never asked.

My father was an alcoholic. As the years went by, his drinking got worse. I knew something had to give. When we went to a dance, he got drunk in front of people, which was embarrassing. But he wouldn't let anyone else drive; he would take us home, driving at high speeds around corners. We were terrified. My mother always expressed her fear that he would kill us all. One night, she even took all the guns in the house away.

I went to a grade school with only three classrooms. There were about 60 of us. One family of seven had a child in every grade, and these kids were the bosses of the school. Whatever they wanted me to do, I did, because if I didn't, they'd physically threaten me. They punched me in the nose and forced me into fistfights. They told me they'd beat me up if I didn't go to the back of the school bus, where the oldest brother and another boy always tried to take my panties off. One time, they tied me to a tree. After six years, they finally moved to another school. I never told my parents about any of this because I was afraid the brothers would get wind of my tattling and come after me.

It was rough at home, and it got worse. I was sexually abused as a child. I would escape by riding my bike far away into the woods or by drawing pictures. I remember telling myself, *even if nobody loves me, I know that God is there.* That's what kept me going. Everyone else in the world could be against me, but I knew God was there.

When I was 10 years old, my father didn't come in one evening. Four weeks before that night, my aunt had died of a massive heart attack. She was only 39. My father took her death very hard. I

185

remember my father taking my hand into her coffin and his saying "Feel how cold she is? She'll never have life again." He cried and he drank and he didn't work for a whole week. Then, the first week in June, he took us fishing. He was very calm and quiet. Whatever we wanted, he gave us. (Now I think I understand why he was so calm and peaceful.) That night, with a storm coming, my father disappeared off into the woods. My mother, brother, uncle and I all looked for him near a neighbor's irrigation pond. None of us could swim. The police divers finally found his body. He had drowned himself. The priest came to our house and told us that my father was dead. Four weeks after my aunt's death, my father too was lying cold in his coffin.

For about three years after that, I don't remember much. I thought about suicide a lot. I thought it was normal; after all, it's what my father had done. But part of me didn't believe my father had died; I thought he would come back some day. In secret, I waited for him. I remember going into the bushes a lot at night, roaming all by myself. My mother and brother carried on with life, but I was in my own world. Slowly I realized he was not going to come back.

When I was 13,we left the farm. Mom decided to sell out. That was a big thing. I started high school, and that was another big thing. I kept to myself and didn't talk to anyone. Thinking I must be depressed, my family sent me to see a psychiatrist. He did psychological testing and concluded that I was not only very depressed, but that I had thoughts of suicide. I was afraid they'd hospitalize me. I didn't want that. So when he asked, "Do you really want to kill yourself?" I said "No, I don't, I really don't." I lied. I wasn't hospitalized.

I didn't like high school. I felt that I wasn't capable of doing anything. Everyone else seemed to be happy, but I couldn't laugh at things. I felt as if I didn't belong anywhere. I remember riding my bike to a railroad bridge, sitting on the bridge and thinking about jumping off into the ravine. At times I was really depressed and didn't know what to do, but I didn't let my mother know. Who knows what she saw or thought? I hoped things would get better.

At college, I didn't get close to anyone. I thought I couldn't connect with anybody. At the university, I got very depressed. I went to a counselor and expressed some suicidal thoughts. There were times when I looked down from a big building and felt the urge to jump. But I never told anyone what I was going through. I wanted good grades, and I wanted to get into medical school. I knew I needed help, but I didn't want it on my record.

Finally, I got into med school in Florida. I started to feel depressed again, and I ended up in an abusive, physically violent relationship. Once, he and another man both punched me in the face. In a rage, one of them choked me and wouldn't let me out of the room.

I drank. My favorite was Scotch. When I drank, I could forget everything. The rest of the time, I felt trapped. My grades were poor. Other students made fun of me because unlike them, I wouldn't cheat and steal exams. They got high marks; I got low marks. Whoever was lowest on the totem pole had to pay money. I paid up. I had a professor who regularly made sexual advances at me; when I refused, he failed me, twice.

One night I sat on the beach under a tree and drank. I didn't care what happened to me. Somebody could come by and rape me; I didn't care. I went into the ocean, with all my clothes on, and tried to drown myself, like my father. But I couldn't do it. Instead, I sat there in the moonlight, in the ocean.

There was a song by Bryan Adams, called "Never Surrender". I played that song over and over again on my Walkman, whenever I walked the beach alone. That was med school. I finally got out of that hellhole.

Into residency—and depression. I couldn't think straight; nothing was getting into my brain. Suicide kept rushing into my mind more and more. My team realized that I had a problem. They took me off call. I wasn't sleeping, so I got some pills for that. My depression got worse and worse. When we were on call, we residents lived on the fifth floor of the hospital, and the fifth floor led to the roof. I went out there many, many times and felt the urge to jump. The roof had a tower with a big clock in it, and the door to the tower was open a few times. I had the urge to go in there, and did. Finally, my team said, "Either you go to intensive therapy twice a week or we're going to admit you to the hospital." I didn't want anyone to know about my depression, so I did what they said. That whole year was useless. I just couldn't function. I felt like a failure. Things got worse, but I still didn't tell anyone.

Since I had enjoyed my surgical rotation in med school, I thought surgery would be a good choice. So off I went to the South to a residency in surgery. The work came easy to me, and I liked what I was doing. For a year, it all went well. I wasn't depressed; I could concentrate. I had no friends, but I was used to that. I was afraid of dating, but somehow that was okay too. I thought, *I can see someone for therapy. I can do that on my own.* So I got a psychologist, and I got a psychiatrist for medication. But then, for some reason, I started having more thoughts of suicide. They came up more and more often. I thought, *oh no, this can't be happening to me again! Am I going to lose my residency again? Will I ever be able to function?* If I lost it again, I could be totally out of my career. That really scared me. I went to my psychiatrist, and he told me I was in another depression. I thought it was the end of my career.

I said to my psychologist, "I'm really having trouble at night. I'm starting to think more and more about suicide." And he said, "You'll be okay. Just get more sleep." So I handled it by sleeping more. I had a box with pills from years before—Ativan, Valium, and other stuff that doctors had given me in Australia. They were always prescribing drugs for me, without any therapy. I'd thought, *that's not what I want; I want to talk to someone.* But they'd only give me pills. So I'd take one or two of the pills and save the rest.

One night, feeling suicidal, I pulled out the box of pills for the first time. I quickly put it away again, but my suicidal urges increased. The next day I told my psychologist that I really felt I might do something. The next night, I took out the box and poured the pills into my hand—actually looked at them. I said out loud, "No, I can't do this", put the pills back, capped the box, and put it away. I poured myself a glass of wine and cried a lot. I hoped the wine would calm me down. Then I thought, *what the heck, I'm depressed; I'll have another glass.* So I had another glass, and felt more depressed. Out came the pills. I didn't take many, only a few Ativan, with a whole bottle of Irish Cream.

I called the crisis team. When I hung up, my phone rang. It was 911: "Are you okay?" I answered automatically, "Yes, I'm okay," and slammed the phone down. Then it came to me: *oh my God, they know my number and probably my address!* I changed into jeans, grabbed all the alcohol bottles and the pills and got out of my apartment. I don't know how I got to the hospital where I worked, but I did. Once inside, I called the resident and told him I was sorry for everything. I hung up. I remember going to the bathroom and throwing up. I don't remember how long I was there, because I had a blackout—only my second one. When I came out, one of the residents put his arm around me and said "Thank God we found you." I spent that night in emergency getting my stomach pumped.

The next day, my program director took me out for breakfast and asked me, "If someone did what you did, what would you say to them? What would you do?" I said, "Well, I guess I'd hospitalize them." And he said, "Right." So I went to the hospital for the first time in my life. That was 1992, in Virginia.

I couldn't believe it was me walking down that hospital corridor. It hurt so much, thinking I'd finally ended up there. After two weeks, I'd have done anything to get out. The ward was full of people with multiple personalities; people were running around in the hallway, always loud. Any noise made me want to jump ten feet. I was always on edge. I thought about suicide a number of times. I wanted to run, to get away. But they kept an eye on me all the time. I tried wandering off into the bushes, but they fetched me back. I tried putting a plastic bag over my head. I tried hanging myself with my shoelaces in the shower. When another girl tried to escape, I was on the roof trying to help her. It took me back to searching for my father, that night.

After three weeks, however, everything seemed fine, until that October. I was back at work, preparing to go on a trip for the first time, an educational leave. They had me on antidepressants and Ritalin, because I was very depressed, psychomotor retarded, and they wanted to give me a boost. I was working about 12 hour days, badly overstressed. My attending physician on the last day said, "You can't leave; you still don't have those prescriptions done." I blew up and said to a med student next to me, "I might as well get drunk and kill myself." I went home, paced, the floor, and got through it. The next day I headed to the airport. People from my department called me at the airport, concerned: "Are you okay? What's going on?" I told them I was just fine, no problem, but they sent me off to a little hospital in

Pennsylvania. I stayed there five days; they shipped me off to a hospital in Little Rock—16 hours by bus.

It was pure hell. I was a day and a half in group, and I didn't want to hug anyone. It felt very uncomfortable. Another person in group said, "Well, if you don't want to do that, you might as well not be in this group." I fled to my room and cried. My first thought was to hang myself—I had a belt, and I tried out how I could use it in that room. But I thought, *No, calm down, go to lunch.* So I went to lunch and came back to my room afterwards, to wash my face and hands. Before I knew what had happened, the nurses came and escorted me to the locked seclusion room. I spent six straight days there, thinking of every possible way to kill myself. I tried to test out a number of routes—hanging, electrocution, even eating nicotine from a cigarette I found. I just didn't care. I didn't want to talk to anybody. I just wanted them to leave me alone. I wanted them to hate me so that they would get rid of me, like people in my past. I kept looking out the window and seeing the lake. I wanted to go there and drown myself— I almost managed it once; I got out, and people came running after me.

When they told me I'd suffered trauma, I didn't know what they were talking about. I thought it was just my father's death that I couldn't deal with after all those years.

Finally, I got out and went for extended treatment—I'd been a month in the hospital and was in treatment for a total of six months. I had constant thoughts of suicide. I thought about ropes, checked out where I could hang myself. I took half a day off from my treatment, wrote a suicide note, and started to walk to another hospital. I saw broken bottles; they made me think of cutting myself. I saw a pond, and I wanted to drown myself in it. That time, I ended up sitting in a chapel, thinking about God, and felt quieted. But other times, I drove past high-power transformer stations and dreamed of electrocution. I'd stop at bridges and try to jump off them. I drove at high speed, hoping for a crash, so out of it that I didn't know where I was going—and didn't care if I never got back. I drank liquid detergent and had to go back to the hospital. I was in and out of that locked unit 15 times.

Finally, I got back to the hospital where I worked and got outpatient treatment for my depression. One day, I came out of a treatment session and felt there was nothing anyone could do for me.

Kevin Taylor M.D.

It was hopeless. I went to a store and bought rope. I went to a special cemetery, with a pond. There was a particular tree there that I'd dreamed of; I knew the very branch I wanted to hang myself from. I'd been there many times. But it was still daylight; there were too many cars around. I thought *okay, I'll go home and hang myself in the back yard.* I'd wait till three in the morning and do it then. I took my medication and slept right through until morning. That's when the police came and found the rope. I tried to escape; I didn't want to go to the ER where I worked as a resident, but they took me there, handcuffed in the back of a cruiser. My supervisor cleared everyone out, so no one would know. They sent me back to the hospital in Little Rock. This happened several times.

I used to hide in a bush. Don't ask me why, but I felt comfortable, knowing nobody knew I was there. Once I sat in a bush near the hospital for hours, after a session, until night fell. I'd sit there crying for hours and then pretend everything was okay. Nobody knew.

Somehow I finished my residency in general surgery—in fact, I did very well.

Today, I don't think of suicide as often, but I can't lie—it does come into my mind, especially at difficult times, like now. It's a month till the anniversary of my father's death, and this year it's on a Thursday, the same day of the week; and this year I'm the same age he was when he died. I have to admit—there are ponds near where I live, and I think about it. But I know if I just work at it, I can get through.

I thought I'd never do mutilation, but in January, I was frustrated or angry or whatever, thinking about suicide. I took a knife and poked my arm with it. That was the first time I tried that. I've also tried to cut my scalp, in a place where nobody could see. I don't like to talk about it or admit it, though.

Other people may think I'm crazy, but I'm not. I just have strange feelings sometimes and don't know how to cope with life. Some people try alcohol, drugs, sex, whatever. I jump to thinking of suicide. It's an instant sort of thing, an impulse to do something. It passes quickly. Afterwards, I think *thank goodness I didn't do it. I don't want to die.* After that, I can focus on being a surgeon, a good one.

Chapter 5:

What Else is Wrong with Us?

"Death by suicide may be the final common pathway of
expression for patients with a variety of diagnoses.—"
Goldblatt and Schatzberg,[70]

Trauma was only one of the things that we, as a group, had in common. Many of us suffered from other psychiatric illnesses. Most of us had mood disorders—dysthymia (chronic low-grade depression), acute depression, or bipolar II disorder (cycles of depression and elevated mood). Some of us suffered from panic disorder. Many of the women among us met some of the criteria for borderline personality disorder. Most of us suffered from other addictions—to chemicals or sex—or eating disorders.

But treating these psychiatric illnesses had little effect on our suicide problem. We might blame our suicide attempts on depression,

---

[70] M. Goldblatt and A. Schatzberg, "Medication and the Suicidal Patient," in D. Jacobs, ed., *Suicide and Clinical Practice* (Washington: American Psychiatric Press, 1992), 23.

anxiety, or other addictions, but after these were treated and resolved, the suicidal flame burned bright as ever.

Raquel: *I thought my suicide problem would go away once I got sober. I blamed it on my drinking and drugging, plus my depression. I was wrong.*

Kevin: *After the best treatment available for nine months, I woke up chemically sober, not depressed, but ready to hang or shoot myself. I couldn't blame it on drugs or depression any more.*

Other Addictions

Those of us with other addictions continued to relapse until we surrendered *all* addictions. Many of us were alcoholics; some of us were addicted to narcotics or other drugs. We were using these substances to try to numb the pain of our childhood trauma and to dampen our suicidal impulses, both of which long predated our substance abuse. But these additional addictions only drove us further and further into hopelessness. We couldn't succeed at sobriety, and that left us feeling like failures. For others, our periods of chemical sobriety were interrupted by the suicide cycle, with its fantasies, rituals, and behaviors. Our inability to stop that cycle triggered more drinking or drugging. And so *both* vicious cycles continued until both were treated.

Chemical dependence and suicide do, in fact, have much in common. Alcoholism was called "slow suicide" long before the American Medical Association termed it a disease, in 1956.[71] Suicide and chemical addiction are both shameful. Both are secretive; both are deadly; both are progressive. Both may have a biological basis. And both are devastating for the people who have to live with us. We know now that alcoholism has a genetic predisposition, although no specific gene "for" alcoholism has been identified.[72] Suicide tends to run in families and may have a genetic basis, although again, no specific gene has been identified.[73]

---

[71] E. Marcus, *Why Suicide?* (New York: Harper Collins, 1996), 2.

[72] M. Schuckit, *Drug and Alcohol Abuse* (New York: Plenum, 1995), 86.

[73] E. Marcus, *Why Suicide?*, 11, 44.

The link probably lies in brain biochemistry. Certain brain receptors are activated by opiate-like substances produced by the brain itself as a pain control mechanism. It's these compounds that produce what we call "runner's high". When a compound activates these brain receptors, the individual feels a sense of peace and happiness. These brain receptors can be activated by narcotic substances—that's the mechanism by which narcotics give people a "high", relieve pain, and create addiction. Drinking alcohol leads to the production of a compound, THIQ, which binds to and activates these receptors.[74] Some suicidal behaviors such as wrist cutting, and possibly other types of cutting or stabbing, may lead to the release of beta-metenkephalins, endogenous opioids that also bind to and activate these receptors.[75] This seems to be one possible link between substance abuse and suicide.

Medical specialists in addiction know from experience and from their understanding of brain receptor chemistry that addicts in recovery from narcotics cannot safely drink alcohol, and alcoholics in

---

[74] M Schukit, *Drug and Alcohol Abuse,* 69.
[75] J. Coid, B. Allolio, and L. Rees, "Raised Plasma Metenkephalin in Patients who Habitually Mutilate Themselves," *Lancet* 2 (1983): 545-46.

recovery cannot safely use narcotics. Cross-addiction is well known. It may also extend to suicide. Specialists in suicide treatment know that 90 percent of alcoholic suicides and 30 percent of non-alcoholic suicides involve alcohol consumption.[76] Most of us had been drinking or taking narcotics before trying to kill ourselves.

> **Remington:** *Whenever I got my gun out to kill myself, I had been drinking.*

> **Raquel:** *I always had to get high on something—alcohol or drugs—before my suicide attempts.*

What about sexual addiction? A large number of us were sexual addicts. We kept relapsing into both behaviors, a terrible source of shame and distress for ourselves and our families. We felt like failures. Each lapse in sexual sobriety left us feeling more hopeless and trapped—feelings that triggered more suicide attempts.

---

[76] E. Marcus, *Why Suicide?*, 42.

Kevin: *After my first overdose, my sexual addiction increased a lot. It seemed to distract me from suicide for a while. Later on, I would leave my mistress and go try to hang myself. Then I would swear off both the affairs and the suicide—just like an alcoholic trying to go on the wagon.*

For others, the struggle against sexual addiction kept being interrupted by suicidal preoccupations, which left us feeling trapped and hopeless—and triggered more sexual acting-out. Whichever way, the two addictions were closely intertwined and stayed that way until both problems were dealt with in treatment. Again, it looks like classic cross-addiction.

Suicide and sexual addiction were, if anything, even more shameful than alcoholism—more secretive, more devastating for those who had to live with us. Both started early in life, as a response to childhood traumas. Both were fantasy-based, with possible biological links. Sexual addiction also runs in families and may have a genetic link.[77] Some researchers suggest that repeated sexual behaviors, including ejaculation, also bind and activate the same brain receptors that are involved in narcotics, brain-made opioids, and alcoholism.[78] Sex, narcotics, drinking, suicide—all may involve a common biological pathway.

Sexual addicts often describe their acting out as suicidal. They talk about "living on the edge", knowing that their sexual behavior is dangerous but unable to stop it. In the age of AIDS, sex-addicted men and women continue to have unprotected sex with many partners, fully aware that they are playing Russian roulette, but unable to help themselves. The riskier the sex, the greater the high. Sex in cars at high speed, sex with complete strangers who might hurt or kill them, cruising dangerous bars and parks alone—all are signs of the suicidal tinge of sex addiction.

---

[77] P. Carnes, *Don't Call It Love* (New York: Bantam, 1991), 71-72.
[78] H. Milkman and S. Sunderwirth, *Craving for Ecstasy: The Consciousness and Chemistry of Escape* (Lexington, MA.: Lexington Books, 1986), 45.

Remington: *The ultimate was sex in a swimming pool during a thunderstorm, which I found immensely stimulating and dangerous as hell.*

Thelma: *I kept hanging out in bikers' clubs in a rough part of town. I used to think I went to bars for companionship. As long as that companionship had Old Charter in his hand, I was all right.*

This "cruising for trouble" attitude paralleled one aspect of suicidal behavior: the suicide set-up. Many of us, unable to act out suicide attempts directly—either because we were too scared or because we wanted to conceal the suicide—fantasized about situations in which we would be "accidentally" killed. We dreamed of stand-off shootouts with police (the so-called "suicide by cop") or hoped an 18-wheeler would run us off the road. We fantasized about being caught in bed with a lover by a murderously enraged spouse.

These high-thrill high-danger fantasies and situations were powerfully mood-altering, probably through adrenaline production.[79]

Sasha: *When I was suicidal, I drove in the blind spot of an 18-wheeler on a narrow expressway with no shoulders—drove for hours in a trance, hoping he would forget about me, turn over on me, and crush me to death. It was a rush, just like drugs or a jolt of adrenaline.*

Eating disorders—especially bulimia and compulsive overeating—were also common among us. Most of the bulimics were survivors of childhood sexual abuse. We usually started binging and purging as teenagers, to try to keep ourselves thin. Saying "we'd rather die than be fat," we went to life-threatening lengths to keep our weight down. Purging lead to dangerous electrolyte imbalances, coupled with the addictive use of large daily doses of diuretics and laxatives. Unable to manage our weight or to stop the bulimia, many of us turned to suicide as "the way out". We relapsed over and over

---

[79] P. Carnes, *Out of the Shadows* (Minneapolis: Comp Care, 1983), 10.

until we felt like failures, hopeless and trapped, and these feelings triggered more suicide attempts. For others, suicidal thoughts triggered overeating. The wheel could spin in either direction. But when, for a brief time, we managed to stop both the bulimic and suicidal behaviors, the old pain of abuse surfaced, driving us back into self-destructive behavior.

Mary: *I ate the food and felt relief—no more pain. Next came the remorse. I threw up, took laxatives, diuretics, whatever it took. I felt so ugly. I just hated myself. Then came the suicidal thoughts.*

To kick both bulimia and suicide, we needed to deal with the underlying unresolved trauma of sexual abuse, usually through a prolonged treatment program.

Many of us suffered from compulsive overeating—a much less secretive behavior. Many of us had had weight problems since childhood. We knew we were eating ourselves to death and struggled year in, year out, to get our weight under control, invariably failing.

Failure meant hopelessness and feeling trapped—which triggered suicidal impulses. For others, obesity in childhood had got us ridiculed and shamed by other children and adults. Unable to handle the pain, we retreated into suicidal fantasies. The same pattern: until both patterns were treated, neither could be resolved.

> **Joe:** *As a child, I was fat. The other kids made fun of me,*
> *constantly called me names. I hated it. I wanted to die.*
> *That's when the suicidal thoughts started. When I look*
> *in the mirror today, the suicidal thoughts are still there.*

Mood Disorders

Many of us suffered from mood disorders as well as suicidal impulses. Trying to treat the mood disorder without first resolving all addictions—including suicide—almost never worked. Addictions seriously complicate the diagnosis and treatment of mood disorders, and suicide appears to be no exception to this rule. Repeated antidepressant trials, as noted above, produced only brief improvements that never lasted. The rebound effect—the sense of failure, hopelessness, and being trapped—pushed us deeper into suicidal thoughts and behaviors.

Once we had been treated for addiction, it became possible to diagnose and treat several different types of mood disorder:

Dysthymia, chronic low-grade depression, was very common among us. It usually responded well to SSRIs or other new antidepressants. Even those of us who had previously seemed not to benefit from antidepressants usually responded well once our addictions were treated. By making careful use of daily mood charts, we could monitor subtle signs and symptoms of depression. Once we could escape relapsing into our addictions, we became more compliant and persistent with antidepressant trials. We also grew more realistic in our expectations. One pill was *not* going to "fix everything."

Paula: *For years I fixed everything with pills or booze. Then I wanted psychiatrists to fix me with pills. When I got suicidal, I just figured their pills had failed. Once I* *accepted my suicide problem, I understood what the medication could do—and not do.*

During treatment for our addictions, some of us (especially the women) were accurately diagnosed for the first time as having **bipolar II disorder** (major depression with small manic attacks). Bipolar II disorder is more common among cocaine addicts and alcoholics, possibly as the result of a "kindling" process in the brain, initiated by cocaine or alcohol.[80] It is also more common among women than men.[81] Some studies find that it also carries a higher suicide rate than bipolar I disorder. It is difficult to diagnose bipolar II disorder in the presence of active addictions because the addictions create fluctuations in mood, with euphoric episodes that mimic small manic episodes.[82] When the patient is sober, it can be diagnosed through a daily mood chart.

---

[80] F. Goodwin, *Improved Treatment for Depression and Bipolar Disorders 1995* (Atlanta: Continuing Medical Education, Dec. 1, 1995)

[81] *Diagnostic and Statistical Manual of Mental Disorders,* 4th ed., ed. M. First (Washington: American Psychiatric Association, 1994), 360.

[82] H. Kaplan, B. Sadock, and J. Grebb, *Synopsis of Psychiatry* (Baltimore: Williams and Wilkins, 1994), 567.

Most of us with bipolar II disorder were also chemically dependent and victims of childhood abuse. Once sober, we found that mood-stabilizing drugs like lithium or Depakote could stabilize our moods. We learned that the bipolar disorder had helped trigger suicidal impulses. It took time, however, for some of us to understand that our suicide problem was separate from the bipolar II disorder.

Jacqueline: *My psychiatrist made me keep a daily mood chart for years. I finally began to see my rapid mood cycles and started accepting them. Then I went into denial of my suicide addiction—decided it was due to my bipolar cycles. It took years for me to accept that I had suicide cycles even when I was **not** in a depression.*

The remainder of us suffered from recurrent **major depression**. As with the others, we could make little progress recovering from this disorder until we had been treated for all other addictions, including suicide. Until then, antidepressants had little effect on our suicide cycles. Once sober, we found SSRIs effective, for a number of reasons. First, they have few side effects and are well-tolerated.[83] We often had a stormy history of non-compliance with medication, but SSRIs were easy to take. Second, they are harder to overdose on than tricyclic antidepressants.[84] It was important to both us and our psychiatrists to use a different drug because so many of us had tried to kill ourselves with antidepressants.

> **Kevin:** *Elavil was my drug of choice for suicide. It should have worked, and almost did.*

> **Jacqueline:** *For years, I kept only a week's supply of medication at home. Any more felt like hoarding and triggered my suicide addiction.*

Third, SSRIs are mood elevating, not mood altering. They could be prescribed safely for those of us with addictions. Many of us had sought drugs only for their mood-altering properties and were scared

---

[83] *Ibid.*, 548-49.
[84] *Ibid.*

of "drugs", especially drugs prescribed by psychiatrists. SSRIs were safe. Fourth, SSRIs act on serotonin metabolism.[85] Impaired serotonin metabolism has been directly linked with suicidal behavior,[86] while high levels of serotonin and its precursor tryptophan correlate with social behavior in humans.[87]

Many of us were not merely suicidal, but strongly impulsive about our suicidal tendencies. For all our planning and fantasizing, we rarely premeditated our suicide attempts. In addition, we tended to isolate ourselves, becoming almost like hermits. SSRIs, by stabilizing serotonin metabolism, helped to reduce our isolation and depression. They may have played a small role in directly stabilizing our impulsive suicide cycles.

Personality Disorders

Many of the women in our group met DSM IV criteria for borderline personality disorder, which includes problems in mood

---

[85] *Ibid.*

[86] G. Brown *et al.*, "Aggression, Suicide, and Serotonin," *American Journal of Psychiatry* 134 (1982): 741-45.

[87] D. Klein, "Anxiety Reconceptualized," *Comprehensive Psychiatry* 6 (1980): 411-27.

regulation, impulse control, reality testing, interpersonal relationships, and self-concept.[88] According to this diagnosis, some of our behaviors—chemical dependence, risk-taking, sexual promiscuity, violent outbursts, self-mutilation, and suicide attempts—resulted from the problems with impulse control and self-care that are part of this disorder.[89]

But was it the right diagnosis? Or was the problem really suicide addiction? The evidence was inconclusive. We responded well to a Twelve-Step approach—and female alcoholics with borderline personality disorder do improve with this approach and proper treatment. The Twelve Steps apparently give them an external structure that helps to compensate for their lack of internal boundaries. But as we went through the Twelve Steps, the diagnosis became less and less certain.

Raquel: *Once I surrendered and gave it all to God, I stopped*

all the crazy stuff, one day at a time. No more drinking

---

[88] B. van der Kolk, *Psychological Trauma* (Washington: American Psychiatric Press, 1987), 111.
[89] *Ibid.*, 116

and drugging, no more running off with other men, no more explosions, and no more suicide attempts. Some days it hurts real bad. I just go to a meeting and talk about it.

Van der Kolk suggests that childhood trauma, especially sexual abuse, plays a significant role in the development of borderline personality disorder.[90] Clinical studies of borderline children describe their extreme sensitivity and physical reactivity to stimulation, their preoccupation with themes of mutilation and death, and their fear of annihilation.[91] Bowlby found the same characteristics in studies of abused children, and Green observed self-mutilating behavior in abused children.[92] Childhood abuse, then, seems to predispose children to suicidal preoccupations and other characteristics also found in borderline personality disorder.

---

[90] *Ibid.*
[91] *Ibid.*, 117.
[92] A. Green, "Child Abuse: Dimensions of Psychological Trauma in Abused Children," *Journal of the American Academy of Child Psychology* 22 (1983): 231-37.

Our group was full of victims of childhood abuse, especially sexual and spiritual trauma. We had been extremely sensitive and physically reactive to stimulation since childhood. Like the children described in these studies, we were preoccupied with themes of mutilation or death and feared becoming psychologically trapped or annihilated. Many of us exhibited self-mutilation—anything from smashing our fingers or piercing body parts to slashing our own wrists or abdomens. Almost all of us were suicidal when we started self-mutilating; we were trying to get up the nerve to go all the way. And in fact, we did go all the way to serious suicide attacks, even if sometimes we were labeled "pseudosuicidal."

Joyce: *For years, I dug my nails into my thighs or cut my abdomen with sharp objects. Then I started smashing my fingers. My fantasies and preoccupation with death and suicide went wild when I started getting close to deep emotional stuff in treatment—especially without my other addictions. I felt trapped, desperate.*

Akiskal suggests that some borderlines may suffer from variants of mood disorder, including bipolar II disorder.[93] Some women with a previous diagnosis of borderline personality disorder respond to Depakote with fewer symptoms of the disorder. This raises two possibilities: that Depakote could treat borderline personality disorder; or that these women were misdiagnosed.

Some experts believe that "borderline personality disorder" is a hodgepodge of different difficult-to-classify disorders. Some have gone so far as to call it a "diagnostic waste basket." Bipolar II disorder, which is a relatively new diagnostic entity, may be a new term for one of these disorders. On the other hand, other psychiatrists hold firm that borderline personality disorder is a definite, consistent psychological diagnosis. If Depakote and Twelve Step programs bring about improvement, it does not invalidate the diagnosis; it means they are valid treatments for this problem. The debate is ongoing.

"Borderline personality disorder" clearly aroused strongly negative images in us and in our therapists. When we were given this

---

[93] H. Akiskal, "Sub-affective Disorders, Dysthymic, Cyclothymic, and Bipolar II Disorders in the Borderline Realm," *Psychiatric Clinics of North America* 4 (1981): 24-46.

diagnosis, it left us feeling hopeless, angry, humiliated, and frightened. It felt like a permanent stamp of disapproval. It said we were not treatable. The diagnosis felt more like a badge of shame than a name for what ailed us. Our therapists also felt angry, ashamed, and scared that they had so little to offer us. They too felt helpless and hopeless.

> **Jacqueline:** *Every time I heard the diagnosis "borderline", I got angry and defensive. It seemed so shaming, so hopeless—like nothing could be done about it. I heard it as a judgment or a sentence. Then I argued with my therapist about it.*

Whatever the diagnostic rights or wrongs, it is more hopeful to believe that at least some of us who had been diagnosed as "borderline" were, in fact, addicted to suicide, as well as having other addictions, all with underlying childhood traumas. Addictions cannot be cured, but people can live in daily recovery, with strong Twelve Step support. This approach brings hope to millions of people who need hope, from millions of people who have found hope. We needed that hope.

Childhood wounds can be treated. Trauma work is rewarding. The field is developing rapidly and giving hope for healing to millions of survivors. Again, we needed this hope, for, remember, we were survivors of trauma.

Thelma's Story

I'm a registered nurse, the oldest of four children, the mother of a daughter and two sons. I don't remember my natural mother before I was five. I lived with my aunt until then.

Even as a young child of two or three, I remember having thoughts of death and hopelessness. I had a great-grandmother, who I loved very much. One day I accidentally stepped on her foot and got whipped really hard. I felt ashamed, as though I had meant to hurt her foot. That day, I wanted to die.

One day when I was five, a man I didn't know walked into our house and told me it was time I came home. I looked at my aunt. She wasn't fighting to keep me. When I got into the car with the man, I recognized the woman in the back seat. Somehow, I knew this was my mother. She had my younger brother at her breast. I've been angry with him from that day forward; we fight like cats and dogs. As part of my recovery, I've had to let go of him.

My natural mother could be loving and nurturing. I remember her brushing my hair and doing all those girls-together things. But nobody understood how traumatic it was for me to be taken from my aunt. My aunt made it worse by teasing me, telling me that she really *was* my mother and that this strange woman had taken me away from her. One night when I was six, while my parents were at a neighbor's house, I loaded the car with my clothes. When they came home, I told them my real mother had called and said that I was supposed to come home right now. I got the beating of my life. My parents told me that I was home and I'd better get used to it. I never trusted my aunt after that.

When I was about seven, my natural mother became severely abusive, physically and emotionally. That's when my depression started. I started school around that time. I felt awkward there, as though I was inferior to everyone. I felt like an outcast; I didn't fit in, and I was scared of people. I was also a very angry child. My grades were good, but I was a tomboy, a real fighter.

One day a boy and his little sister climbed in the drainage ditch by our house, right before a storm. The boy got out, but his little sister drowned. Later, when we were walking home from school, I was walking behind the boy, poking him and accusing him of killing his sister. I thought I had power, and that I was hurting this boy because my parents were hurting me.

When I was 11, my baby brother was born. He was the first real ray of light in my life. My mother was tired of having kids, so I got to be his mother. I raised him and nurtured him, and we were very close. My life got better, until my teens, but I was still depressed deep down inside.

My parents were very protective. I wasn't allowed to go to concerts or on a date until I was 16, and even that was a double date. I still managed to get pregnant at 18, before I was married. I thought I loved the guy, and I was afraid that I'd lose his love and attention if I didn't give him sex. I was pregnant and suicidal the last half of my senior year. My boyfriend and I broke up once, and I overdosed on aspirin.

We got married, and the marriage lasted a year and a half. Feeling like a loser, I struggled hard, but my Roman Catholic family and his Roman Catholic family swooped down and scooped me up, telling me that I wasn't the one at fault and that I could go on. With their emotional support, I put myself through nursing school and raised my son while living with my parents.

I met my second husband at a bar; we partied a lot. The two years after we married were the happiest of my life. But then his drug addiction and alcoholism flared up. I turned into the Ice Queen and stayed that way for another three years, through his addiction. After another year of hearing him say he didn't love me any more, I turned against God, him, my family, my values, and my upbringing, and left him. By then, we had a two-year-old daughter.

Within two months I was partying every night, all night, from six or seven in the evening until six in the morning, while working 12-hour day shifts at the hospital. My family tried to intervene. My father

SEDUCTION OF SUICIDE
Understanding and Recovering From Addiction to Suicide

was kind, my mother abrupt. I wouldn't listen to anybody. I was spiraling downward into self-pity, loneliness, and a broken heart.

I was screwing up as a mother. My son got into trouble in nursery school at age three. He was going up the little girls' skirts with one hand and punching out the boys with the other. As a scout leader, I failed to show up for a big camping trip, which was canceled because of me. When my brother asked if he could help, I agreed. He offered to take my son to live with him, and I said "Yes." My daughter ended up with my in-laws. My real motive wasn't their welfare; it was to get them out of my way so I could drink and drug the way I wanted to. I abandoned them for four years.

During the second year I was on my own, I had a sexual identity crisis and became suicidal again. I thought I was homosexual. I'd had two marriages fail and had no clue how to make a relationship work. But I didn't want to be homosexual; I wanted a successful relationship with a man.

The first night I tried to kill myself—it was in 1980—I was trying to force myself to have a homosexual experience. Rather than carry through with it, I tried to kill myself. There was so much about me that wasn't acceptable, and with a load of alcohol and drugs on board, I couldn't live with myself. I was obsessed with sex. I was obsessed with getting power over men and hurting them. I was obsessed with becoming a stripper, and I was obsessed with homosexuality. These were all ways in which I could have power over men.

At that time, I was living with an ex-biker. I believe God put this man in my life when I was drinking and drugging to keep me from going places where I could have been killed. He had done a lot of the things I wanted to try. I was desperately running from God and my own sense of what was right. If the good girl couldn't cut it, I would become the baddest girl I could be. I hung out at bars, played sad country-and-western songs on the jukebox all night, and got drunk on Old Charter and Tab.

My suicidal thoughts were becoming more frequent and much stronger. I got involved with heavy drugs. One night, at a party, I smoked a joint laced with PCP and took the trip of my life. I thought I was going to die. I managed to get to the emergency room where I worked as head nurse. My friend and partying buddy was on duty and managed to talk me down—it took about 12 hours. That was just God-awful. It probably led to my psychotic break the following year.

But I kept running, hanging out in bikers' clubs in a rough part of town. Things were getting so bad that I was starting to risk the safety of my friends and family to keep my addiction going. I took my daughter to bars. I took my kid sister, who was very naive and virginal, to a bikers club for her birthday. We both got wasted and ended up back in that same emergency room.

After three years, my mind started racing all the time. I was obsessing so badly that I couldn't manage a coherent thought. I could not make a decision without going back on it. Over a period of three weeks I got three hours of sleep. I was becoming psychotic. When I looked in the mirror, I didn't know the woman I saw—this woman with the empty eyes. I was smoking one joint after another, hallucinating wildly. In one hallucination, I had gone to heaven. There were a couple of angels sitting around on clouds, and my two children were running around. The angels told me not to worry about my children; they would be fine, and I would be forgiven.

One day, my boyfriend walked in the house, took one look at me, and phoned my dad, saying "Something's wrong with her. Get over here." My dad was there in three minutes. They had me admitted to the hospital's psychiatric ward, where they did a lot of testing. For the first time, I acknowledged feeling suicidal. They were concerned about this and wanted to give me shock treatments. I would have done anything to fix me. Life wasn't supposed to hurt this much; if God was real and good, He wouldn't allow anyone to be in this much pain.

I agreed to shock treatments. I did run into Alcoholics Anonymous meetings while I was on the psych ward, but nobody paid any attention to my drinking and drugging. I found that disappointing. Nor did anyone mention manic-depressive illness. I stayed there for six weeks, taking the shock treatments, and then got out.

Three weeks after, I surprised myself by driving up to my old bar. In my head I could hear some of the things they said in AA meetings, but I went back anyway. I started drinking again and taking drugs, to change the way I felt. I wanted that escape and that euphoria. I used to think that I went to bars for companionship, but as long as that companionship had Old Charter in his hand, I was all right.

Things got worse. I was very sick, psychotic, talking about suicide all the time, and obsessed with homosexual issues. I was seeing a therapist two or three times a week and a psychiatrist once a week. He had me on high doses of Thorazine, and the side effects were awful. My tongue kept pulling over to the right and my face was contorted for days. My nursing mind was looking at me and saying "I can't believe this is you." I'd look in the mirror and think, with disbelief, of all the things I'd done. I hated myself for all I was worth.

My boyfriend was afraid that the AA meetings I was going to were brainwashing me. They didn't help. The suicidal urges were getting stronger; the homosexual urges were getting stronger; the urge to strip and the fear of doing it were getting stronger. All of them went against my basic beliefs.

I started going to a women's treatment center to talk to some of the people there. I'd leave the center and go to work in the emergency room—and oh, that was hard! I'd rescue other people from death when all I wanted to do was to die myself. Resuscitations would roll in and I couldn't remember what the hell I was supposed to give them. I didn't want to revive them. I wanted them to have what I wanted—peace. Why would anyone want to be brought back to life when life hurt so much?

There were two men who I identified with in the AA meetings. I used to talk to one of them when I was on duty at the emergency room. I'd slip back to the pay phone and call him, telling him how I felt—not wanting to save people because I wanted so badly to die.

One day, all of a sudden, I decided I'd fought as long as I could. It was the anniversary of my second marriage. I just gave up. I thought of shooting myself in the head with a gun, but once I'd nursed a patient who'd done that and lived. I didn't want to be left with one eye and a horribly mangled face. I thought about driving my car under an 18-wheeler, or stepping out in front of one, but again, I'd nursed a patient once who'd done that and survived. He'd had to be in a body cast for ages and he still had to live.

I came up with the perfect method: I'd inject myself with a respiratory paralytic drug—one that would stop my breathing. I knew it took only a dab of this drug to work on ventilated patients, so I'd take three times that dosage. I went home and wrote a suicide note to my ex-husband, asking him to leave the kids where they were—I figured we'd already screwed up their lives enough by giving them no attention. I parked my car two blocks from home, drew up the shot, and gave myself the injection. Within three minutes I could hardly move. I grabbed a bottle of Thorazine and slammed a bunch of pills down my throat. I wanted to go out painlessly. I managed to crawl into my bed. I wanted a cigarette, but I was worried about setting fire to the bed. I didn't want to burn—that was too painful.

My last thoughts were about Medusa—the woman who had snakes for hair. I dreamed that I was Medusa and the snakes were biting my face. I started spiraling down. Suddenly I was terrified: the Baptists were right! I was bound for Hell. *Please don't send me to Hell, God. I've already been there. I'm trying to get out of Hell now, God.* I couldn't move a finger. I went under.

I woke up 14 hours later to the ring of the telephone. It was my boyfriend. He could tell by the tone of my voice that I'd done something. He told me to get up and throw out the drug. When I did that, I had my first spiritual experience. As I was flushing the medicine down the toilet, looking at the syringe, I heard a voice in my head saying *You know, I'm not writing the book. I don't know how*

229

this story is supposed to end. Before, I'd always known how it ended: in death. Things were too bad; the pain was too great. I'd destroyed my children. I couldn't face the guilt. But I had lived through all this shit. So I didn't know how it was supposed to end anymore.

I called my psychiatrist and he put me back in the hospital. There I came across a minister who started telling me parables. The parables said that good things were happening in my life, even if I couldn't see them—nor did I have to see them. I looked at my psychologist one day and said "I need for you to tell me how to live when all I want to do is to die." He looked at me very lovingly and said, "How about this? It's your duty." A lot of lights came on inside my head. I had a purpose!

I got out and started going to three or four AA meetings a day. I didn't go right back to work. God put me in the path of a woman at another treatment center. She tried to get me to do the Fourth Step, but I was stuck—I was obsessed with my suicide attempt. I couldn't get anything done. This woman turned to me one day and said, "Knock it off. I've tried to commit suicide nine times. You're just an amateur." When she told me that, I knew that she knew what she was talking about. She took my thunder away and brought be back to earth. About two months later, in the summer of 1980, my suicidal thoughts disappeared.

Life didn't get easier, in some ways. I went through many traumatic events during the next 15 years. I was diagnosed with manic-depressive illness in 1985. I chose to give up sex and stayed celibate for nine years. I went into a deep depression, but suicide never crossed my mind. I swore I'd never take that path again.

I was stunned when, in November 1994, the thoughts came back—my first "mixed state" break. I was almost catatonic. I couldn't walk or talk or write or eat. My whole immune system crashed. I had infections in every orifice. I lost 30 pounds in two weeks and my hair started to fall out. I was bombarded by suicidal thoughts.

For two months, I hung in there with God's help and the help of friends in the program. I stayed on the phone all day. I kept calling people and trying everything they told me to do. I did everything—I made gratitude lists, wrote out inventories, called people, prayed my butt off. I lived for when I could sleep, because only then was I at peace.

One day I called a friend I hadn't talked to in years. She mentioned a hospital that had saved her life. I went there the next day. It was a miracle: the place specialized in alcohol/drug addictions and psychiatric problems. They knew what was wrong with me and what needed to be done.

* * *

Today I roll out of bed, and before I get to my feet I take Step One and beg for another day of sobriety and the courage to do whatever's in front of me. Then I say Step Two. I'm starting to see God restore me to sanity again. I feel the anxiety lift as I take Step Three. I just turn it all over to Him, and whatever happens is what happens that day.

It's been several years since my "break." I'm stabilized, going to Alcoholics Anonymous and Suicide Anonymous meetings, and mostly free of suicidal thoughts and urges. The program *has* worked for me again. It's taken me different medicine, a new doctor, the right treatment center, a new minister, and a better definition of who God is. I've had to face some scary things about myself. I'm taking it one day at a time, staying in close touch with people, trying to hang onto my courage to let them know what's going on with me.

I've had to rethink things about sex and love. I started doing this in 1984, but I still feel like a novice. It's sort of like a sexual anorexia—I'd starve myself until I was too hungry, then eat too much of the wrong kind of food.

Recovery goes slowly, but the light has never gone out. It was lit inside me that night when I flushed the drug down the toilet and realized that I don't know the end of my own story. I learned then that there is a Something in the universe that does give a damn whether I live or die. That's crucial to my recovery. It took a lot of help from a lot of people, but that light has never died. That's crucial to my recovery. I can't tell you how grateful I am for that light.

And yet I think I always knew that I'd find something that worked, if I tried long enough—if I fished until I caught something.

People in despair ask me how I've made it through. I'm open with them: I share the story—the surrender, the asking, the seeking God and professional help, and the willingness to go to any lengths until it works. These people are my purpose in life today. I am deeply at home with them. We are one.

Chapter 6

Families: Oh, What Have We Done to You?

> "Suicide is not a single, quiet thing you do
> only to yourself. Rather, it is like pulling
> the pin on a hand grenade while you are
> surrounded by everyone who knows you."
> —P. Quinnett[94]

Until our first suicide attempts, our families were confused—in the dark, shut out by our secretiveness. Our preoccupation with suicide made honesty and intimacy and real communication with them impossible. The people who loved us had no idea of our fantasies and obsessions. Instead, they excused our distance as just a phase we were going through, or blamed it on overwork.

Sometimes, they confronted us, wanting to know what was wrong. We'd brush them off with pat answers— "Nothing's wrong" or "I'm busy with work" or "I'm worried about money". Our coverups only added to the distance and the lack of real closeness. Communication

---

[94] P. Quinnett, *Suicide: The Forever Decision* (New York: Continuum, 1992), 129.

suffered from our efforts to look good. We tried to brighten up and do more with the family, and maybe for a while, things seemed to go better.

Morgan: *When Kevin dropped out of med school six months after we married, I knew nothing about his suicidal thoughts. I got the message that there was a secret and I wasn't to ask questions. I felt scared, alone, without my own mother, who had died the year before. I began to feel like an inadequate new bride. Then he started teaching high school and things seemed wonderful, with both of us teaching and traveling. I forgot about the crisis. I thought Kevin just wasn't meant to be a doctor, that medical school was the problem—it was too tough for him, trying to follow in his dad's footsteps as a doctor.*

Cindy: *I had no idea Remington was an alcoholic when we married. In the first couple of months of our marriage,* *he seemed erratic at times, difficult to get along with, and demanding.*

Sooner or later, though, the problem deepened. Suicide fantasies and rituals took up more of our time and energy, shutting out our families even more and further blocking communication. Not knowing what was in our minds, the people close to us found themselves feeling confused and shocked. They questioned not us, but themselves.

Morgan: *Moving away to start medical school, Kevin seemed driven to fulfill his father's dream and be a physician. It seemed like a chance to start anew, just the two of us. I loved it. I was teaching school, and I made many friends. But something was missing. There was an emptiness. I felt left out—I just didn't know all the truth. Something was wrong, but what? Our first child, Kevin Jr., was born, and we were both scared. We were fearful about trying to provide for him while Kevin was* *still in medical school. Little did I know that Kevin was "fixing" his anxiety with drugs and his first extramarital affair. I was shut out even more, and I started to doubt myself. I figured I had to be the problem. My life became centered on my child and my teaching—the start of my super-mom and super-teacher roles.*

Spouses

Our obsession with suicide hurt our spouses deeply. They went through a wide range of painful feelings and decisions before we hit bottom and made the choice between death and recovery. Our secretiveness threw them into a morass of self-doubt and self-blame. They asked "What's wrong?" but they could not get an honest answer from us. We were deep in denial, to them and to ourselves. The truth was simply beyond us. And this strained the intimacy that they deserved, until in the end, it snapped.

Morgan: *After Kevin received his M.D., I could tell that he was very ambivalent about being a physician. But he never shared his desperation about finding a specialization and his suicidal thoughts with me. Down deep, I knew there was trouble. I felt scared and lonely, without support. Kevin was drinking more, hiding his affair, shutting me out more and more. When I tried to ask what was going on, he would tell me that there was no way I could understand the pressures of practicing medicine. He tried to change me—the way I wore my hair, the way I dressed. He said I had to lose weight, be more intelligent—then he would be okay, and we would be okay. I didn't know he was trying to make me be more like his mistress.*

The First Attempt

Our first suicide attempts shocked our spouses. They felt a crushing sense of abandonment. Nothing cuts deeper or causes more betrayal than the realization that a spouse has chosen death over the marriage. "Devastating", "incomprehensible" —these were the words they found, as they reeled in shock. They were initially relieved that we were still alive after coming so close to death. But then they were flooded by overwhelming and conflicting feelings:

Morgan: *I remember Kevin's first overdose. It happened on Friday, August 13, 1976—I remember it as though it were yesterday. I sat expecting it all day. I'd had too many warning signs. But at the same time, I was shocked and devastated. My emotional clock stopped that day; I went into robot mode until 1982, when Kevin went into Woodlawn. I felt betrayed, abandoned, and ashamed. I realized I could not make Kevin choose me and life over death. He was choosing drugs, other women, and suicide over me. When I looked at him, I didn't see the man I had married. But he was still the father of our children, and I had made a covenant "for better, for worse".*

Shock gave way to intense anger. Sometimes our spouses could express this anger directly, sometimes only indirectly, sometimes not at all. *How could you do this to me?* our spouses screamed at the empty walls or into the loneliness of their own minds. There were no answers. They felt alone, with nowhere to turn and no safe place to go. It's hard to find someone you can talk to about suicide; it makes people too uncomfortable. Nobody wants to hear. In their isolation, our spouses had nowhere to take their anger and began to feel guilty about feeling it.

So anger gave way to guilt, which gave way to fear and mistrust as time passed. Our spouses asked themselves *How do I know it won't happen again?* Waiting for the next time, they felt like victims—but victims of what? Of suicide? Well, we'd survived, hadn't we? Of abandonment? But we were still there, on the other side of the bed, across the kitchen table. Of embarrassment and shame? Yes, certainly. Of others' judgment? Absolutely. Somewhere deep inside themselves, our spouses were on watch, never able to relax fully and let their guard down. They could never really trust us again.

Morgan: *From 1976 until Kevin hit bottom in 1982, I never uttered the "s" word. But I was on watch constantly, waiting in fear until it happened again. Kevin was in his third love affair, and somehow I knew that his womanizing kept his suicidal thoughts alive. He started therapy briefly, and for a short time, we agreed to blame his problem on depression, the stress of a new practice, and childhood issues with his mother. But I knew in my heart of hearts that these were excuses. They gave me no real relief. I was constantly on guard, hearing the clock ticking, waiting for his next attempt.*

Like spouses of alcoholics, waiting for the next binge, our spouses became hypervigilant. They turned emotionally numb to protect themselves. But the pain of living with a suicidal person is much greater than the pain of living with an alcoholic. There's the same sense of anger, fear, and mistrust, but the wounds are sharper and go deeper when a spouse attempts suicide. The pain is closer to that reported by the spouses of sexual addicts: intense anger, fear, mistrust, and a sense of deep betrayal. Extra-marital affairs do damage to sexuality and intimacy—areas closely linked to our identity as people. A spouse's love affair with death is potentially even more damaging, because life is at our very core.

Suicide defies explanation. It confounds experts. There *are* no answers. Our spouses tried desperately to make some sense of our suicide attempts. They looked for something or someone to blame, because to blame is to explain. They found a transient relief in blaming our suicide attempts on depression, stress, childhood issues, spiritual problems, or sheer bad judgment ("it was just a mistake"). These "answers" —denial, by any other name—let life get back to something like normal. But they did nothing to repair the deep damage to trust and intimacy.

Our spouses began The Watch. We knew, and they knew, that the clock was ticking. We knew that they were watching and waiting for signs that it would happen again. Denial might let our families operate as though nothing was wrong. But we knew better. And so did they.

Children

Our children were especially wounded by our first suicide attempts. Often we and our spouses tried to keep them in the dark about what was going on. We and our spouses were so preoccupied with the unspoken struggle between life and death that we had nowhere near enough interest or energy for our children's needs, and they suffered a sense of abandonment. We made up lies or half-truths, or simply ducked their questions. But truth has a way of surfacing, and when our children learned or suspected that we were lying to them, it did deep harm to their sense of trust in us.

If adults can't explain suicide to each other, how on earth can they hope to explain it to a child?

Kevin Jr.: *When Dad first attempted suicide in 1976, I was just eight. I was mostly in the dark about what was going on. I remember a lot of people in the house. Mom said that Dad was in the hospital for an illness or surgery. I didn't figure that something was going on until about '78 or '79, when I noticed his mood swings. We got into a big fight. One day, I found his little blue* *pill case and wondered why the hell he was taking all those pills.*

Their sense of shock gave way to fear and shame. *Will my dad try it again? What made my mother do this? Can I do something to keep this from happening again?* Their minds were full of questions. But if they found the courage to ask us, we lacked the courage to answer them. Or they were too frightened to ask and turned inward—a setup for intense shame.

Kevin Jr.: *After Dad's last suicide attempt in '82, I kept waiting for it to happen again, all the way till '89, when I got some help. I didn't trust anyone except Rosie and her husband.*

Parents and Siblings

Our birth families too were wounded by our suicide attempts. No parent ever expects a child to kill him- or herself, just as no parent ever expects a child to die before the parent. It seems all wrong, against the natural order of things. Their natural response was shock and denial—attempts to push back this unwelcome knowledge. Some simply refused to believe what had happened; it was a nightmare, a bad dream, with no reality. Or we kept our parents completely in the dark.

If our parents knew about our suicide attempts, they felt at first shocked, then relieved that we'd survived, and then angry, fearful, and ashamed. Their emotions were powerful and contradictory. Their anger at us was mixed with guilt about feeling angry at all. *How could my child do this to me?* they screamed inside their own minds. There were no easy answers. *Where did I go wrong? Will it happen again?* Too afraid of what the answers might be, they kept their questions to themselves, and blamed themselves for our problems. Our siblings, like our parents, were shocked and disbelieving. Shock gave way to anger; anger gave way to guilt; guilt gave way to fear and mistrust. They too wondered if they were to blame.

So: each one harboring fear and a sense of wrongdoing, each one struggling to make sense of the senseless, each one struggling with a wild mixture of emotions, our family members tried to find ways to cope. The easy way was to assign the blame for our suicide attempt, as our spouses and children did: to depression, to stress, to an error in judgment. Denial lets a family get on with being "normal". It's the easiest trap to fall into...

Bottoming Out

Between our first and second suicide attempts, denial seemed to work. We'd found a reason for the problem; we were "working on" the problem (depression or stress); for our families, life had gotten back to what passed for normal. We knew they were watching us, and we redoubled our efforts to hide our suicidal thoughts, fantasies, and rituals. In preserving our secrecy, of course, we simply shut everyone else out of our lives, more and more effectively, increasing the distance between ourselves and our spouses, children, parents, and siblings. And not surprisingly, this distance further affected our relationships. Our spouses struggled with loneliness and depression. Our children felt parentless.

And yet, nobody knew what hell there was to come. We and they all hoped the problem was over. *Maybe if we don't look too closely, maybe if we don't talk about it, we won't waken the dragon...*

But the thoughts and fantasies and rituals spun out of control. We tried suicide again. And this time, everybody's worst nightmare came true. None of the old explanations would work any longer.

The second attempt put the end to many of our marriages. Our spouses were too devastated and demoralized to go on. They just wanted out.

Morgan: *With Kevin's last suicide attempt on January 6, 1982, I knew it was over one way or the other. I wasn't going to live like that any more. The rationalizations had to go. His drugs, the other women, the suicide attempts—they had to go, or the marriage was over. I was panicked, angry, and terrified. I gave up trying to make any sense of it. I just wanted it to **stop**. Or I wanted out.*

If the marriage survived the second suicide attempt, our spouses went through hell. Since the old "reasons" wouldn't hold, we needed new scapegoats to blame our suicidal impulses on—anything other than the truth! And so we began to blame those closest to us. We told our spouses that it was all their fault. We needed someone to strike out at, and they were the closest targets—and the most vulnerable.

Cindy: *Remington came home one weekend, and it was obvious to me that he was drunk or on drugs. By Sunday, he had passed out. When he woke up, he was disoriented and unaware of his surroundings. Monday morning, I was sitting at the word processor with my back to him. I could hear the click of his gun as he checked the clip and then cocked it. I wanted to turn around and grab the gun, but I knew I wasn't strong enough. Hoping he was just doing it to get a rise out of me, I left the room.*

The next ten minutes were the longest and most wrenching of my life. I lay down and listened. I heard him cock the gun—and then silence. I felt myself getting frantic and wishing he would just get it over with. I felt a pang of guilt for having such a thought, and for not being able just to jump up, grab the gun, and take all the pain away.

After all was quiet, I went back in the room. Remington lay on the couch, passed out, cocked gun in hand. I called the sheriff and paramedics. They took him to the emergency room. I sat there wondering what to do, how to feel.

We abused our spouses verbally and sometimes physically, loading them with guilt and doing terrible things to their self-esteem. They felt confused, depressed, isolated, self-doubting, emotionally torn apart, and raw from having to cope with our illness.

Morgan: *When Kevin woke up in the neurotrauma unit in 1982, he totally blamed me. He lashed out at me* *verbally, making me out to be the whole problem. He wanted a divorce so that he would be okay. By that time, I had accepted the fact that he needed serious help. I kept supporting his plan to go to Woodlawn. I was hoping for a miracle. Those first five months of treatment were hell. No matter what I did or said, Kevin attacked and shamed me. He continued to blame me. I was emotionally battered and bruised. I became numb and depressed. Even so, I had to run the household, take care of three children, and go on teaching school.*

Often, it was our spouses who found us after a suicide attempt. They had to deal with calls to 911, EMTs, ambulances, blood, vomit, and coma—experiences of sight, hearing, or smell that would leave lifelong traces. The exposure to trauma left them scarred forever.

Morgan: *I thought Kevin was dead when the paramedics rolled him into the ER in 1976. He was white as a sheet, just like a corpse. I could only see the whites of his eyes* *because they had rolled back in his head. I'll never forget it. That sight is burned into my brain forever.*

Cindy: *The sound of that gun being cocked will never leave me.*

Our spouses' illness mirrored our own illness, ending in its own painful bottoming-out. They usually hit bottom before we did— something that could later be an important key to our recovery.

Our children, deeply wounded by our first suicide attempts, were further traumatized by subsequent attempts. The explanations we had fed them no longer made sense. No theory could make the deep hurt better. They had no answers and no hope. And often, they had to cope with the breakup of their parents' marriage and their families. Not surprisingly, many of our children began their own pattern of suicidal behavior. We'd passed the torch to the next generation.

Kevin Jr.: *In 1982, Mom told me that Dad had attempted suicide. It took her several days to tell me. Then I* *figured out what had happened in 1976. I realized what*

I'd been told then was just a cover-up. I felt anger—lots

of anger!—rising almost to rage.

Our parents and siblings were stunned by our second attempts. They could no longer write off our behavior as a "big mistake". They searched desperately for answers, but none were forthcoming. Secretly fearing that they were part of the problem, they increased their search for something or someone to blame—because to blame is to explain. They blamed our psychiatrists, our spouses, our careers, our responsibilities, any possible cause. Usually they kept their blame to themselves. With hidden anger piled on top of fear, family relationships came under overwhelming strain.

Suicide took its toll on everyone in our lives. No one was spared. Everyone went through living hell.

Recovery

No two of our family members took the same path to recovery, but in all cases, the paths were difficult.

Our spouses took their first steps back from hell by resigning responsibility for us. Unable either to explain our suicide attempts or to stop them, they had to turn us over to God's care and get on with their own lives. They faced defeat and admitted that they were powerless. They still loved us; they still remembered their marriage vows ('in sickness and health, until death do us part"). But they had no choice but to detach themselves from our illness. As painful as the decision was, it was absolutely necessary.

Morgan: *In many ways, I hit bottom in 1976, even though Kevin didn't hit bottom until 1982. I cried a lot. I prayed a lot and asked God to take care of him. I loved him and didn't want a divorce, but I also realized I had to make a life of my own and give up my dream of sharing my life with my spouse.*

Cindy: *While Remington was in treatment, I felt surprisingly relieved and calm. I made good friends, was introduced* *to Twelve Step support, and began to understand what*

had happened.

In some cases, our spouses started therapy when they hit bottom. In other cases, they didn't. The critical step, however, was getting on with life. No more blaming themselves; no more letting us or other family members blame them. Regardless of our outcomes, life or death, our spouses decided not to take the rap. They weren't the problem, and they weren't the answer for us. They found new jobs, new interests, new friends. Slowly they reached out. Concentrating on their own well-being and the well-being of their children, they lived one day at a time, holding the family together, even though one member of it was seriously—perhaps fatally—ill.

The road to recovery was long; often it took years. Eventually most of our spouses turned to therapy to work through their traumas. But the healing could not be full and complete until the war was over.

Morgan: *It finally became obvious to me that I had to start therapy, even though I resisted it. I had put the pain in a* *closet. I noticed that I could talk openly about the issues and suicide attempts with compassion—and then I would have no recollection of what I'd said. I thought I was going crazy. Finally, I realized that I was a trauma victim, that I had needed to "forget" in order to protect myself.*

Therapy has been a slow, painful process. I get angry if people say I exaggerated the whole suicide thing. Actually, I forgot most of it and I have to work to remember and feel it.

But there was also a sense of blessed relief. They had left the landscape of hell.

Cindy: *Life is so much more sane now.*

Children are resilient. Often, our children healed more quickly. In other cases, however, they fell into depression and became suicidal, needing hospitalization. But if our sickness seemed to leave them a legacy of pain and problems, so our recovery gave them an inheritance of hope. Since there seems to be a genetic component to suicide and addictions, our children will have to watch out for these traps. Some will fall into them and will need to find their own breaking points and their own path to recovery. Perhaps, though, they will be able to learn from our experience.

Our parents and siblings had to begin their recovery by letting go of their anger, their fear, and their guilt. Few of them went into formal therapy, although most participated in family therapy sessions. They also often had their own support systems—church, friends, social groups—and used them in their own ways to make peace with the past.

Each person touched by suicide has to find his or her own answers, not for others, but for him- or herself. Since suicide has no real explanation or answer, it has to be "every man for himself." People have to find their own answers, inwardly, in the heart and soul—and in their relationship to God, from whom the healing really comes.

Quick and easy answers are no use. In fact, they're worse than useless: they only obscure or delay the truth. Far better to let go of the need for quick and easy answers, and to let the answer happen in God's own good time and God's own good way.

> **Morgan:** *The miracle I prayed for all those years finally came true, not overnight, but steadily over Kevin's last three months at Woodlawn, and during the two years after that. Kevin and I worked hard in couples therapy. As he got to be more honest with himself and others, he stopped blaming me. We agreed to stay married one day at a time. Now those days have grown into more than 20 years, and we are again best friends and lovers. I'm reminded of the quotation, "Let no man put asunder…"*

Morgan's Story: Till Death Us Do Part

As the wife of a suicide addict, let me never forget the power and pain of suicide.

For me to tell my story again after all these years of recovery, I have to go back down into the deep darkness, where all the hurt is. I do this as a gift, so that others might not have to go there or, if they do, so that they may have some company.

My father was 56 when I was born. He was born only one generation after the end of the Civil War, when Reconstruction was still a very big deal. He was a farm boy from Kansas, with eight brothers and sisters. My mother came from Oklahoma, and was the baby of 10 children, including one set of twins, who died. She was a direct descendent of Sequoyah, the Cherokee chief. My great-grandfather, a missionary, brought his family across the Trail of Tears to help establish the Oklahoma Territory. Mother was 44 when I was born.

I come from strong rural roots and from a family of unconditional love. My parents thought they would never have a child, so they educated two nieces and one nephew as their children. All three were part of my family when I was a child, and we are like brothers and sisters.

The day I was born, my dad's friends were ragging him, calling him "Stud Winfred". When he saw my mother, he gave her 12 dozen red roses. The hospital room was filled with flowers. Later that day, he went to the country club to play a round of golf, and he hit a hole-in-one on the #1 tee. The next day, the local newspaper's sports page read, "Ed Winfred gave birth to baby daughter, Morgan. Hit hole in one today. Miracle Man!"

I had a nanny named Mamie. We also had a yard man named Brown and a housekeeper, Ella. They were given instructions to train me properly. When it came to picking up my clothes, changing my bed, or doing yard work, they were the teachers and I was the pupil.

I was no little princess, with no chores or responsibilities. When it was time to change the sheets, I changed them. When it was time to clean the gutters, Dad and Brown sat in chairs in the yard, drinking root beer (the only thing to drink when doing yard work!) and giving me directions while I was up on the ladder. When I asked, "Why do I have to do this?" my father would say, "Well, there are no guarantees in life, and I'm training you so that you will always be able to do something."

My mother was a hands-on woman, a cuddly teddy bear. I could tell her my most horrible secrets and she'd take me in her arms and listen. But when it came to protocol, she was very well schooled.

There was a proper way to set the dinner table and a proper way to dress.

Dad was a junior CEO. He had a swing set built for me in the back yard, high-grade steel poles and all. Uncle Marvin, a contractor, built me a playhouse tall enough for a grown man to walk in. My dad would come home in the afternoon, immaculate in his coat, tie, and starched shirt. We would have mud tea and mud cakes with leaves and berries in the playhouse. He would say, "Honey, this is the best tea I ever had in my life." I played a lot as a child. I guess that's why there's still so much of the child in me, even after 50.

With older parents, I learned how to manage money, and I knew about sickness and hospitals. My dad had a bleeding ulcer, and one night he was hauled off to the hospital in an ambulance. I was absolutely terrified that my daddy would die.

Even though I had staff to take care of me, I learned to be in charge. My parents prepared me carefully because they knew they wouldn't be around for me forever. I learned how to buy groceries, make meals, organize things, and run a household. They told me I could do it. They believed in me. I am eternally grateful for that gift.

When I was 8, I went to camp for six weeks in the hill country of Texas. It was beautiful country, on the Guadalupe river, probably the greenest river I've ever seen. I went there from the time I was 8 until I was 16 and learned about leadership. If I could run a house, I could run a cabin. In fact, I tried to run the whole camp.

I made many friends in Savannah and at camp. There were 16 of us whose parents were friends. We grew up together, and our nannies were friends as well. We still get together. I was popular in high school, but I was also naive. I believed that when someone met me, they would always like me. I was always delighted to meet new people, and it never made any difference to me who they were.

When I graduated from high school, I went to Rollins College. I drove to the airport, got on a plane, and landed in Monroe, a place I knew nothing about. Mother had told me to get a yellow cab—they were the safest, she said—and to ask for the price up-front. Fortunately, I had traveled on my own before. My parents had made a reservation for me at the old Parkview Hotel. I checked in at 7 PM. I didn't know a soul in Monroe.

The next morning, I took a cab over to the college. That was rough. Everyone else's parents were unloading their things and helping move them into their rooms, but my parents weren't there. They hadn't been able to drive me to school. My trunk had arrived, and everything had been taken care of, but I still felt lonely and scared. Fortunately, I could talk to people. Soon I had other kids and their parents helping me.

Then, in the library, I saw this young man—he looked to be about 7'5", with blond hair and blue eyes, very Ivy League. I thought, *That's a neat guy. I think I'd like to meet him.* His last name was Taylor and mine was Winfred, and we were in alphabetical order in groups. Sure enough, standing in line to get our shots, he was right behind me. I hate shots and told everyone, "I'm going to faint." Kevin said, "It's going to be okay. It's going to be okay. My father's a doctor." I felt very calm. His father had just retired as campus physician. Everybody knew Kevin. I thought I'd made a good move.

Soon we were busy with freshman rush. I was invited to a dance at his fraternity, but I was too outgoing for him. He was reserved. I was going out with Bill in Savannah and also dating Kevin in college, and Kevin had trouble with that. I couldn't understand why; it seemed perfectly reasonable to me. We fought about that.

By the summer after our freshman year, Kevin and I were pinned. He came to Savannah and sat at our antique dining table and tried to explain to my mother why I should not go to parties unless he could escort me. My mother told him that he could either stay at the house and escort me, or he could stop trying to control her daughter. Kevin didn't like that much. Mother and Dad were strong-minded people; I inherited that from them.

My mother died in 1965, the February before Kevin and I were married. My parents and I had planned the wedding before her death because we agreed that the worst thing would be for me to stay at home taking care of my father, who was 77.

We got married in 1965, in Savannah. I was 21. I had gotten to know Kevin's family fairly well by then. They were emotionally reserved people, while I tended to bound up to people and give them a hug. Kevin started medical school that September, and I started teaching. Everything was going really well, I thought. I enjoyed teaching, and Kevin was studying hard.

In January, I came home from work one day to find Kevin sitting in the apartment. He said he had dropped out of med school. I said, "Oh, really?" He had gone to see a friend of the family, a psychiatrist, and had talked with his dad. They decided that we needed to spend the night at his family's home. I agreed, and we went. I didn't know what was going on. Nobody was talking about it. There had to be a reason why he dropped out of school, but I didn't push for an explanation. I was scared; I didn't know what to do. I got up the next morning, taught school, and went home to our apartment that evening.

A couple of weeks later, Kevin got a teaching job. We were both teaching, and that was fun. He was coaching volleyball at one school and I was coaching volleyball at another school. The kids on our teams knew each other, and we took them on trips. There was a fun rivalry between the two schools. The students enjoyed having a married couple as rival coaches. We had more money than we'd ever had.

That summer, we took a trip up the East Coast to look at schools, because Kevin was investigating law school, seminary, and architectural school. We also took a trip to Cozumel and played. We were the best of friends, the best of lovers, and the best of fighters. We were really solid. We did it all.

Kevin decided that he wanted to go back to medical school. By that time, I was more introverted, less proactive. I sat in our Volkswagen for five hours while he had his interview—just sitting. He was accepted, and we moved. I went on teaching school. I got pregnant in December 1967, and Kevin Jr. was born the following summer. Kevin Sr. was going into second year med school and was finding the going emotionally rough.

Things started to go bad that year; I could feel it. Something had shifted; something was wrong, but I couldn't tell what it was. Our safety was gone. Looking back, when a man has had a doting wife and she has her first baby, it's bound to be difficult, but this was different. Kevin was drinking, but then we all were; everyone drank back then, and nobody thought much of it.

We'd been very close to another couple; she was my best friend. She and Kevin had planned for the four of us to get away together for a weekend. That was when I realized that she and Kevin had been having an affair. I was absolutely devastated. I cried and cried; I couldn't stop. I had no mother to turn to, and I couldn't tell my dad. All I could do was to cry and pray, and then turn numb. I'd do a lot of numbness in the years to come...Then, on top of everything else, my "friend" tried to kill herself with an overdose of aspirin. Kevin phoned me, asking me—me!—to go take care of her. I read about the affair in the suicide note she'd left. I wanted to kill her. I wanted to kill Kevin too, and nearly did. I had a royal fit. I'm part Cherokee and I have a hot temper.

Kevin finished medical school. As an intern, he had trouble with internal medicine (probably because his dad was an internist) and switched to pathology. Things were worse than I thought. One night, he got a call. He knew that a child had been very sick and that they'd probably have to do an autopsy on him that night. The child was a blond 2-year-old who looked like our son. Kevin didn't go to the hospital that night. Instead, he drove off and took his first overdose and drove all night. Nobody could find him. The Chief Resident and attending physician were calling me, and I didn't have a clue where he was. I was terrified.

I called Kevin's parents in Monroe, and they came up with Kevin's younger brother and sister. We lived in a two-bedroom house with a couch and a pull-out bed. I gave his parents our room and put his brother and sister on the couch and the pull-out bed. That left me with no place to sleep. I took a pillow and blanket and curled up, comfortless and crying, in the back seat of the old Mercedes that Kevin and I had restored together. About 6 AM, his parents realized I wasn't in the house and came out to ask why I was sleeping in the car. Something about that moment made me realize, painfully, that I wasn't really part of the family—that I didn't matter at all. At noon, Kevin drove into our driveway as though nothing had happened. That was in the summer of 1971.

We moved back to Monroe in December. I was 28 and was pregnant with the twins. Kevin was a resident in psychiatry. Two weeks after I had the girls, Kevin Jr. developed Legge-Perthes disease, a disintegration of the hip joints. He was just turning 4. For the next two years, he had to be non-weight-bearing in a wheelchair. Kevin was on call every third night and was moonlighting as well. That left the burden squarely on my shoulders—caring for this sick little boy and two newborns, plus running the house. Things were very bad.

Another painful memory: Kevin had promised to take Kevin Jr., who was still in his wheelchair, out turkey hunting. Our little boy was so excited; he adored his father and was really looking forward to going hunting with his dad. The day came for the hunt, and Kevin came home from work. He refused to take our son out. He didn't feel like it. Kevin Jr. was devastated. It hurt so much to see him suffering. I was furious: how could Kevin do that to his own child? I wondered.

If you've got a problem and you don't want to admit it or deal with it, it's easy to give the problem to someone else to hold for you. Kevin and his parents didn't want to admit that there was anything wrong with him. So it had to be all my fault. I can't tell you how emotionally abusive this was, being made to feel that *he* was just fine and *I* was the problem person. If I changed this, fixed that, I could make it all better…If I was supermom and superwife, if the house was spotless and everything was in perfect order, maybe we'd be okay. If I made sure everything was in perfect order, I could head whatever-it-was off at the pass. I changed my hair style and the way I dressed—it was only long afterwards that I realized I was trying to make myself look more like his mistress.

I know now that what I was doing was taking on the responsibility for his illness, when that really belonged to him. Kevin had me going to psychiatrists all the time to find out what "my problem" was. I bought the notion that I was the screwed-up one. That was *my* share of the problem. Instead of accepting that I was the person who needed to change, I should have been saying "Honey, this is *your* problem" and just getting on with my life. Taking on that wrongful responsibility almost crushed me—almost, but not quite, because I had my strength and my faith from my parents. But oh, did I have the blinders on for a long time!

I know (and this still grieves me terribly) that because of our family situation, I wasn't the mom I should have been. I was hyperprotective of the kids, but I was also half-crazy a lot of the time. I've always been an energetic person, full of vim and vigor; now I was crazy-busy. I was hypervigilent, buzzing with nervous energy, off the wall. I had to play tennis three times a day to get myself tired out so that I'd be able to sleep. I was the ultimate high achiever, teaching and running the household and raising the kids single-handed. I learned to be emotionally numb most of the time. It was that, or facing up to the huge and growing pile of hurt from Kevin's affairs. I just couldn't face that kind of pain.

His second affair was purely sexual—actually, the woman grew to be fond of me and the kids. Now, one of the ways in which I stayed sane was by keeping my sense of humor. I can be *quite* wicked sometimes. I made it my business to get to know this woman, and I started to get innovative. I asked her over to dinner, got the kids all cleaned up, had a nice fire in the fireplace, and served her spaghetti, with small individual bowls of sauce. I'd dosed her sauce with Ex Lax. I could see her getting greener and greener. She said, "I'm really not feeling very well." I answered, "Honey, don't worry about it. If you have to leave, I understand." That's terrible, but I did it. It was part of surviving. Sometimes I'd screw up Kevin's pills, so that he'd take the downers when he needed the uppers and the other way around. I kept a tube of Crazy Glue in my bedside table and fantasized about which parts of him I'd glue together as he slept.

Little bits of insubordination and mischief—they can be empowering, when you're stuck in this sort of situation.

Oh, 1976 was a bumper crop…That year, we moved to our present home. Kevin's mother had a massive heart attack in April. No one could find his father after he'd taken her to the hospital. I found him in a depressive stupor, and we had to ship him off to Woodlawn Hospital. Kevin's sister went to North Carolina to live with their younger brother. I helped move her out of the apartment. I thought I was doing a good job. I was running everybody's family and home, including my own.

The crowner came on August 13, a Friday. I got the call at 4:30 in the afternoon, but I had known since about noon that Kevin was out somewhere trying to kill himself. The call came from a farmer. He hated to tell me, but Kevin was on the way into Monroe in an ambulance. I felt so angry and so scared. I didn't know what to do. I felt so alone. I went to the hospital and saw him in the Emergency Room. He looked like a corpse, dead white, with his eyes rolled back in his head. He went into respiratory arrest several times and was in a coma for days. When he finally came out of it, he hated me. Oh, the verbal abuse was stunning…According to him, I'd ruined his whole life—but I didn't have a clue what I had done wrong. I came home to a house full of people, but no one asked me how I was doing. All the concern was for Kevin. I remember feeling abandoned and very alone.

Rosie, the maid who had raised Kevin and later our children, was the one person I could trust. She was my refuge and strength. I knew that she loved Kevin, but she also loved me. She might not approve of what was going on, but she was there, and she wasn't making any snap judgments. At least I had one safe person.

That's when I bottomed out myself. I realized I had to get on with my own program. I had the children to look after, and I had to take care of myself, and to do that, I would have to be tough. I started finding my own way step by step. It still took six years before I finally got my head on straight. I had to insist on normality, whatever Kevin got up to; I couldn't let his illness run me and our family.

I realized that I couldn't let Kevin pull my chains any longer. If he could get my attention with his obsession with suicide, he could feed on the high it gave him. "Oh, I'm so sorry—what can I do to help?"

All the "compassion" I'd given him had done no good at all. I'd invented managed care, and it wasn't working. Codependency? I'd written the book. He'd taken my greatest strengths—my love and devotion—and turned them to protect his own demons from discovery and to scapegoat me. Now, if the kids and I were going to survive, I had to take back these gifts and use them for better ends.

I had no intention of divorcing him. That was never in my wildest plans. When I married Kevin, I made two covenants, one with him and one with God. My covenant with God mattered more even than my covenant with Kevin. I was going to see this thing through until I had done everything I could. I might ask God "*Why* does it have to be this hard?" I might pray to be spared more suffering. But I couldn't give up on him.

The next six years were hell. I never knew what to expect when I came home from picking the kids up at school. Some days his car would be there, and he'd be in bed. I'd leave the kids in the car, saying "Just wait out here until I go see" —as though that was normal! I didn't want them to walk in and find their father hanging from the ceiling or blown up in the bed. A side of me started thinking that this was just normal life, something lots of people go through. But it wasn't. It was crazy.

By January 1982, I decided enough was enough and went back to teaching. I remember the morning of Kevin's last suicide attempt. It was hectic; he was trying to get ready for work, and I was trying to get ready for my first day at school and to get the kids ready as well. I said, "Kevin, this is the way it's going to be." I went off to my job and met a friend for lunch, at Grisanti's. I told my friend that Kevin was going to try to kill himself.

Sure enough, that afternoon, Kevin wasn't at his tennis group. I found him behind the couch in his office, in a coma. I remember kicking him in the ass as hard as I could. It was after that that he went to Woodlawn. It was his choice. We had to agree to disagree for months. And finally, we had to agree to be married one day at a time—a choice to be repeated over and over again.

After Woodlawn, I put all this stuff away. I didn't want to look at it. I'd spent too much time looking at it in the past. Until the Oprah Winfrey show came along, I was able to keep the past in a closet and not think about it. Kevin seemed fine, and everything seemed to be going well. But the Oprah show, and the book with Kevin's story of suicide attempts, came right together. I guess God was trying to tell me that it was time to clean out that closet. I couldn't run from the past any longer.

I can tell you now that I'm not afraid of suicide. I think I understand how it works. And I hate it. Those of us who have had to live with this problem have to walk the finest of fine lines. We want to do everything in the world to help and protect our loved ones—but we know our protection might smother them. We have to let them go *and* love them, and trust me, that's the hardest work in the world. It can be very painful and frightening for us. But we have to accept that whatever will be, will be, and that we aren't in control. It can be a lonely road.

So few of these marriages survive. I can't blame the husbands and wives who gave up—who didn't follow the road I took. I don't think it's a road that many *can* take, or should. It was my road. I was fitted for it better than most, by my solid childhood, my faith, my own strong sense of integrity—that's my personal core.

Through it all, my faith never wavered—never so much as flickered. I trusted God's purposes for me, even when I didn't understand why I had to go through such hell. I know now that God has turned all that suffering into gold. I have a powerful drive towards healing and wholeness. I know now how strong I truly am, and I know that I have a deeply non-judgmental heart and a passion to help others who are where I once was.

If you see someone in this situation, give that person quiet support. Don't try to intervene, to rescue, or to force the person out of the marriage; that's a choice that the person has to make in his or her own good time, and you can't make it for another.

If you are in this situation, never forget that God is with you every moment of every day. Insist on normalcy. Don't let yourself get drawn into the toxicity. You aren't the problem here; the addiction is the problem. God bless and keep you and bring you out safe, into the sunlight of healing and recovery.

Chapter 7

The Solution

"Part of the recovery is to give up the suicide fantasies and threats
and make a commitment to live, for better or worse. In essence,
one has to close that back door, seal of the escape hatch, and
get married to life with all its pain, paradox, and struggle."
—C. Kasl[95]

Surrender: The Awakening

Recovery from suicide addiction is difficult. In fact, it requires a
miracle.

We who suffered from suicide addiction—at least those of us who
survived to share our stories for this book—described the beginning
of our recovery as a profound spiritual experience. We underwent a
deep psychological change, usually involving a sudden, new, dramatic
awareness that God was in charge of our lives and deaths. While this
may seem obvious to some people, to us, this was a stunning
revelation, highly personal, felt more than thought, remembered in

---

[95] C. Kasl, *Women, Sex and Addiction* (New York: Harper and Row, 1989),
205.

exquisite detail. Our lives were redefined, or perhaps defined for the first time. This was the breakpoint of our lives.

Kevin: *I remember it like it was yesterday—still can feel it. My life is divided into "before that day" and "after that day". Something snapped inside me, and my life all made sense for an instant. I've lived a "second" life on borrowed time from that day forward. I can't explain it.*

As we came to consciousness after our last suicide attempt, many of us described a sense of "coming to", as if we'd been roused from a trance or altered state. We'd wakened before, but not like this: before, we had come from unconsciousness into a sense of enormous pain, cursing God, feeling punished by our very survival, cursed by our failure. But this was different. This was a wholly new reality. We realized, all of a sudden, that our best efforts had failed. God *wanted* us to live. All at once we had a new outlook on life, a changed mindset.

Alcoholics Anonymous's Big Book describes the experience of alcoholics who hit bottom and begin recovering from their addiction.[96] These experiences tend to be dramatic Saul-to-Paul "knock you off your donkey" conversions, sent by God. We went through the same sort of experience. We came face to face with the stark reality that we were powerless over our suicidal fantasies, rituals, and compulsions. We could do nothing that would fix ourselves. It was over. We had to surrender, and surrender without any reservation whatsoever.

Raquel: *There was no one to ask for help anymore. I was licked. My life was totally unmanageable. I surrendered. The nurse in white heard me crying and talked to me about God for a long time. I felt a hope that I had not felt for a long time. Then I prayed a simple prayer and asked God to take control of my life. That was the turning point for me.*

---

[96] *Alcoholics Anonymous* (New York: AA World Services, 1976), 171-561.

It was a frightening point for many of us. Up to that moment, we'd been consumed by our craving for control and power—for they were all we really believed in. We'd thought of ourselves as the center of the universe; no one but ourselves truly existed. Now we stood revealed and naked, shivering in the light of recognition and self-knowledge. If our spiritual experience had stopped right there, we would have fled straight back into suicide.

But for those of us who went on to recover, this moment of awareness came coupled with another revelation: we understood, suddenly and completely, that God had saved our lives for God's own purposes. This was not a sustained thought or a deep moral conviction; it was an abrupt childlike "reborn" feeling that came out of nowhere and was highly personal.

Kevin: *Walking by the nurses' station on the locked psychiatric ward after my last overdose, I stopped dead in my tracks. It hit me like a bolt from above. I realized that my best efforts to die had failed, that some Force had been in charge during each suicide attempt. There*

was no doubt that I was alive for some reason, but I
had no clue what the reason was.

Early Recovery: The Spiritual Awakening

The first part of recovering from suicide addiction is spiritual. The cognitive and emotional work comes later. Trying to reverse this order—looking for mental and emotional healing first—simply does not work. God knows, we'd tried psychiatry, many of us, but no matter how hard we and our therapists worked or how sincere were our efforts, therapy hadn't budged the problem. Doomed as we were, no human intervention could help us.

The Big Book goes on to say, "And God could and would if He were sought."[97] That's all it took: seeking. It didn't matter that we didn't know who or what we were seeking for. All that mattered was that we had started to look for something outside ourselves. Minute by minute, then hour by hour, then day by day, we willingly stayed *alive*, and we did so by staying in conscious contact with this new

---

[97] *Ibid.*, 60.

awareness—this knowledge both of surrender and of the Someone outside ourselves who loves and protects us.

Step 3 of the Twelve Steps says, "Made a decision to turn our will and our lives over to the care of God as we understood him."[98] We'd handed over our lives to God: *here, you look after this. I can't.* Our wills had been turned toward death, like moths to a flame. That impulse could come back at any time. The only help was to open our wills to God's gentle probing—no secrets, no hold-outs, no reservations, no game-playing—only surrender.

Kevin: *In September 1982, I admitted to my friend Steve and my therapist Tom that I was suicidal again—that I wanted to hang or shoot myself, cold sober. I admitted it in my AA group. Then I glanced up at Step 3 on the wall. It jumped right out at me—almost jumped off the wall: "Turn our will and our lives over to the care of God..." Wow! Nothing in that step about alcohol or drugs. I had turned my alcohol and drugs over to God,*

---

[98] *Ibid.*, 59.

*but **not** my will and life. "If the Twelve Steps don't*

work, I can still kill myself" —that had been my motto.

I suddenly realized that it just couldn't work that way. I

*had to give it **all** to God. Nothing less.*

Nothing worked better for this process of surrender than the Twelve Steps. Our Twelve Step meetings provided us with a safe, non-shaming place for disclosure and healing.

What about church? After all, we'd just come through a profound spiritual conversion. Surely we should want to be involved in active church life? The answer was usually "not yet". Remember: we were deeply wounded children, and many of our wounds were spiritual. Too many of us carried religious baggage from the past and needed time and healing before we could learn to trust the church again. A few of us did return to church in the early phase of recovery, and some came with "new eyes", suddenly hearing things differently, understanding them in new ways. When this went well, it helped confirm us in our spiritual transformation.

But for most of us, the moment of change occurred outside of church, as we came through our final suicide attempt—in a hotel room, alone at home, in a hospital, in a car. We found God in the most unlikely locations, not on consecrated ground. And most of us continued our spiritual healing outside church, at least for a time.

Paula: *My moment of surrender happened that day, in the hotel room, as I lay bleeding.*

Raquel: *It happened in a hospital, while I was all alone, with no one to turn to. I cried. I just gave up and surrendered.*

Turning our will to God was like turning a battleship: it can't be done on a dime. We were, after all, very strong-willed people—look at the devotion and energy we'd put into our addiction. We'd teetered on the brink of death and survived; we'd spent years and years obsessed with suicide. It wasn't all going to change overnight. In early recovery, we continued to be plagued by fantasies, thoughts, and impulses of suicide. These could be very strong—strong enough almost to pull us back into the old cycle. For this reason, it was essential to "share the secret" —to draw the power out of our thoughts by talking about them with others.

Sharing the Secret

The most effective tool for many of us, in blocking the power of the addiction, was sharing our thoughts and fantasies immediately with another person. We chose to tell on ourselves, to be honest about our thoughts and impulses *as they occurred*. Previously, we'd hugged our secret thoughts to ourselves, savoring the sense of power they gave us. Now we had to give them up. Then, and only then, did the addiction's power diminish.

Time and again, we chose to turn away from the seduction of the trance state and to expose the fantasy to the light of day. And each time we did this, we took one step further into recovery. It was immensely hard work. We were, after all, running directly counter to years and years of past practice. Our addiction had fed on secrecy and total silence. It wouldn't die all at once. We had to starve it to death.

Jacqueline: *I kept the suicidal fantasies to myself. No one knew. To start talking about them, actually telling someone—that was agony. I struggled to tell my therapist a little of it at first. But to call someone on the phone and tell them my suicidal struggle—to get current with them—that seemed impossible. It took everything I had to do it.*

Reaching out to another human being required three things: immediacy; honesty; and no expectations of the other person.

Immediacy meant telling the suicidal thoughts as soon as they happened. A fellow Twelve Stepper or a trusted friend would do as confidante, as long as the other person didn't shame us or over-react. Family members usually couldn't help because they were too emotionally caught up in the problem and often shamed or frightened us. A therapist could help, as long as the therapist understood the nature of the addiction and could listen without making any attempt to fix the problem or to force hospitalization. The therapist also had to be immediately available.

It was essential to have that sense of being in touch with God until we could find a person to talk to—but it did *not* work to tell God and then not tell another human being. The power of the suicidal thoughts did not diminish until we disclosed them to another person.

> **Jacqueline:** *At first I wanted to cheat. I figured God already knew my suicidal fantasies and rituals, so I didn't have to tell Him. And I certainly didn't have to tell another person, if God already knew! But it didn't work that way.*

Honesty was essential when we reached out. There could be no half measures, no window-dressing, and no holding back. Probably the most difficult part of being honest was staying in the present, in this particular moment, as we were reaching out. It was tempting to say "I was thinking about killing myself, but that's over and now I'm okay." That wouldn't do. Pushing the thoughts into the past suggested that the addiction was in the past tense, and that was denial. We had to keep remembering, "I *am* powerless over suicide," not "I used to be powerless over suicide." We had to be very specific, to the point—no hinting around, or being vague, or hoping our listener would fill in the blanks and let us off the hook. Healing required the most rigorous honesty possible.

We could have **no expectations** of the listener except mere listening. The purpose of our disclosure wasn't to get the other person to rescue us; it was to make ourselves accountable for our thoughts and actions. The person doing the listening was only a listener, no more—a link to reality, not a person whose magical powers could somehow fix or salvage us. If, when we called, we had rescue fantasies in mind, then both parties became first frustrated and then angry. The resulting sense of rejection and abandonment was apt to trigger our suicidal cycle again. The sole purpose of reaching out was disclosure, nothing else.

Kevin: *That morning in '82 when I called Steve at 5 AM and was suicidal, I was terrified. It was the hardest phone* *call I ever made. I knew I couldn't hide it or I would*

die.

Sharing in Twelve Step meetings was equally essential, because it reduced our sense of shame. Addictions are shame-based, and nothing is more deeply shaming than suicide. Facing a group took courage, because it increased our vulnerability and exposed our sense of shame. But hard as it was to stand there feeling emotionally naked, it helped as we started to unload the secret life of our addiction. Each disclosure released another piece of shame. Little by little, we started to learn to be honest with ourselves and others about the extent of our addiction. The group listened, identified with us, and accepted us as we were, openly addicts.

Sasha: *At first I was in a lot of denial—I saw myself as just a survivor of suicide, not an addict. One day in a Suicide Anonymous meeting, I was defending my belief and started remembering the truth about my suicidal*

*preoccupations. It went 'way back! I broke through my
denial that day.*

This process healed us in ways that defy explanation. Being accepted as suicide addicts by a group of suicide addicts allowed us to integrate parts of ourselves that we had hated and hidden deep away from consciousness and God. As we could bring that darkness up into the light, it lost its power. Moreover, the group provided enormous support, a sense of *not being all alone*. As we spoke the truth about our struggles with suicide addiction, we became living examples of hope for each other. We weren't the only people in the world with these thoughts, fantasies, and behaviors.

Remington: *I thought I was the only one in the world with these fantasies of suicide.*

Sasha: *I thought I was hopeless, all alone, that no one else understood.*

Kevin Taylor M.D.

Kevin: *Hearing other people speak my private thoughts about suicide confirmed my own experience. I began to heal, somehow.*

Other Addictions

With basic tools in place, we began to tackle recovery with increasing enthusiasm. We could now face our other addictions with hope. And there was much to tackle. Most of us had problems with sex, drugs, or alcohol, and those who did not were at high risk of switching from suicide to another addiction.

Those of us who were chemically dependent learned that chemical sobriety was essential for our ongoing recovery from suicide addiction. Half-measures were useless. We needed detoxification, treatment, honest involvement in Twelve Step programs—whatever it took. We had, in fact, usually tried to tackle our chemical addictions in the past, with varying degrees of success. Some of us managed to stay chemically sober for longer or shorter time periods, but we would invariably suffer relapses triggered by our suicide addiction. The problem was that in our previous Twelve Step programs, we had withheld the essential truth: that we were suicide addicts. But this only triggered a rapid descent into both addictions. Both had to be dealt with, not one or the other. Both required honest self-disclosure. But now that we could be honest about our addiction to suicide, we could also acknowledge the other secret: that we'd used alcohol or drugs to numb the pain of our suicide addiction.

Paula: *I would become suicidal and would numb the pain with alcohol and drugs. When I went back to AA meetings, I couldn't tell them the truth about my suicide attempts. I was too ashamed.*

For us newly recovering suicide addicts, chemical abstinence was, for the first time, a strange and frightening experience. Giving up alcohol, tranquilizers, marijuana, narcotics, or other drugs is hard enough for most addicted people. For suicide addicts, it is overwhelming. The prospect of living without mood-altering chemicals was terrifying, and our fear only intensified our craving for chemical relief or for the old comfort of suicide fantasies. We were extremely vulnerable to relapse in those first few months, as we stepped gingerly between our twin addictions. To drink or take drugs would only lead us back to that particular hell. But to be sober meant facing our suicide addiction feeling naked and helpless.

> **Thelma:** *Only two people seemed to understand where I was coming from. I would run to the phone at work and call one of them just to keep going for a few more minutes.*

> **Kevin:** *During that first year of recovery, I felt like a child, a 4- or 5-year old in a white coat, taking care of very sick patients.   I would call Steve from work, just to talk, wishing he could make it all okay.*

Some of us were sexual addicts. We'd turned early in life to sexual fantasies and acting out, to numb deep childhood pain and traumas. Sex was powerfully mood-altering, deeply rooted in shame. Like our suicide addiction, it seemed to start earlier in life than chemical dependency. But because it started earlier, it was also more deeply embedded in our lives. Fantasy was a core element in our sexual addiction, just as it was in our suicide addiction. Sex numbed the pain and shame of the suicide addiction. The two addictions fit each other hand and glove. Inevitably, we couldn't free ourselves from one without tackling the other. There was no easy way out, no shortcut.

Recovering from sexual addiction was extremely difficult. We had to give up our "drug of choice" —a lover, often, or "paper sex" through masturbation—long enough to experience and work our way through emotional withdrawal. And the withdrawal was no picnic. We went through enormous anger, fear, and loneliness not once, but time and time again over months. We started to realize that we'd used sex, especially sex with another person, to hold our suicidal thoughts and fantasies at bay—for a while. Sex had become literally a life-or-death matter for us, and now recovery was life-and-death as well.

Giving up a lover or sex-with-self felt like a death. We had to mourn deeply personal losses, as real to us as deaths in the family. Each goodbye triggered painful feelings of abandonment, often stirring up both sexual and suicidal fantasies. During this time, we were extremely vulnerable to relapse. But until we'd started the recovery process for both addictions, we could not get to our deeper trauma issues and so had little chance of stable long-term recovery.

Paula: *I didn't want to be a sex addict. I hated it when they told me in treatment that I needed to look at it. I hated it, too, when they made me look at my suicide addiction. As long as I acted out sexually, I kept trying to kill myself; then I'd try to fix the pain by drinking or drugging. It was like a huge merry-go-round that I couldn't get off.*

Remington: *I thought the treatment team was nuts for calling me a sex addict. Then I developed a conflict with a female patient who reminded me of one of my affairs. It was confusing. I wanted to get drunk or kill myself.*

Raquel: *Along with my suicide addiction, I have serious problems with alcoholism, drug addiction, sex addiction, food addiction, and gambling addiction. Basically I am* *compelled to repeat any action that alters my mood, no matter what the consequences.*

Withdrawal

Nobody said that abstinence would come easy…With programs in place, we plunged into withdrawal. The experience, while painful, is absolutely necessary for emotional and spiritual growth and recovery. Denial gave way to waves of anger as we slowly came back to life, as though from a deep sleep or nightmare. For the first time, we saw our addiction as it really had been: that we had been victims of a horrible illness, a grand diabolical hoax.

What before had looked like the solution, we now saw clearly as the problem. Suicide had always seemed so alluring, so attractive and soothing—a permanent, peaceful relief. Now as our sanity started to return, we could see that suicide had only masked the deep pain and hidden trauma that had been there all along. The real damage lay down deep; suicide was "but a symptom of our illness."[99]

---

[99] *Ibid.*, 64.

Little by little, one bit of awareness at a time, we started to delve into our past, but with fresh insight. Pieces began to fall into place. Freed from the web that had caught and held us, we could begin to see for the first time, honestly and with conviction, that we were not bad people, but that we had been sick people—very sick, and for a very long time.

As denial gave way to anger, so anger gave way to grief—the true beginning of the healing process. For some, it was like opening a floodgate of tears as years of bottled-up sadness surfaced abruptly. For others, it was a more controlled process—great bubbles of grief rising slowly, breaking and dispersing, over years of therapy and meetings.

Many of us started individual therapy, both for immediate support and to get professional help through the long grieving process that lay ahead of us. Therapists who understood the nature of addiction, childhood trauma, and grief stages were especially helpful; they gave us a safe place to stand while we worked through our pain. They helped move us gently through the stage of grief toward healing and wholeness.

Slowly facing our addiction head on, we broke through layer after layer of denial and found all of the anger that we could never before experience and express. We needed permission to feel such anger about our addictions—about the damage to our own lives and the people we loved at home and work. We fought our way back to sanity inch by inch, session by session, meeting by meeting.

The work could be discouraging. Sometimes we wondered if we would ever stop hurting so much. What helped the most was the validation we got from therapists and other members of our Twelve Step groups. We needed to hear we were making progress, especially since we couldn't always see the progress ourselves.

Kevin: *That first year sober was tough. I made a bunch of AA meetings and saw Tom weekly. I felt like Rip Van Winkle waking up to a strange world after a long nap. Some days the pain was almost unbearable without the drugs, the women, and the suicidal fantasies.*

Some took naturally to sorrow, finding relief in learning to *feel* again after years of numbness, addiction, and acting out. But for others, the sadness was new and unnerving; it seemed like a loss of control. We instinctively resisted expressing these feelings, fearing the unknown, afraid that we might fall apart in the process. It took much support and reassurance as we moved forward, finding a little more relief with each tentative small step into this new world.

Jacqueline: *I often wanted to quit therapy. Some days, it just didn't seem to be worth it. I thought nothing could fix me. Then I would throw a fit, cry my way through it, and get back on track. I am getting better, but it has been very difficult.*

Raquel: *Each time I reach out, talk in a meeting or call someone, it hurts. But I feel better later. I can tell that I'm healing.*

Mood Disorders

As deep emotions surfaced—especially grief and sadness—many of us could finally recognize for the first time that we suffered from mood disorders (*see* Chapter 5). With our addictions in remission, we and our therapists could see the depressive episodes, mood swings, and unstable mood disorders that had previously been masked by our addictions. We needed careful evaluation by psychiatrists familiar both with mood disorders and addictions. Often they diagnosed dysthymia (chronic low-grade depression), recurrent major depression, and bipolar II disorder (major depressions with small manic episodes).

We were taught to keep accurate daily mood charts, while at the same time reconstructing life mood charts. The process helped us discover new truths about ourselves. We found that we'd been in denial about our mood disorders as well as about our addictions. It took much work—education, reading, and careful journaling of the past—together with feedback from family members and people we trusted and were close to, but we began to learn the truth. And as always, it is the truth that sets us free...

Medication often helped. Some of us were reluctant to consider psychotropic drugs after struggling free from drug addiction. Again, education helped, as did the realization that antidepressants could help prevent relapses into addiction. With support, we learned to accept our mood disorders and our need for antidepressants or mood stabilizers. With appropriate trials, we found that drugs such as Depakote or lithium could make a real difference, helping to level out and stabilize our mood swings.

Jacqueline: *I had tried antidepressants in the past and they didn't help. I refused lithium or Depakote for a long time—refused to believe I had bipolar illness. Finally I tried Depakote and the mood swings got better.*

Later Recovery

Sooner or later, we had to come face to face with the ultimate source of our addiction: childhood trauma. As we were freed from our addictions, our wounds finally began to surface, rapidly or slowly. All of us had deep childhood shadows and wounds, physical, emotional, sexual, or spiritual. Memories of these traumas were often repressed and usually minimized. Sexual and spiritual traumas were especially common, although few of us realized the true extent and nature of our wounds at first.

Starting trauma work was extremely painful and frightening for us all—a time of high risk of relapsing into addiction. As we began to rediscover old memories and feelings that had been buried beneath our addictions, our old suicidal fantasies threatened to return, blocking the full emergence of traumatic memories and the feelings that went with them.

As these memories and feelings surfaced, we "took on the shame of the abusers", as Bradshaw puts it.[100] We had to own these shameful feelings, take a good long look at them—and hand them right back to their rightful owners. This required a long, deep grief process, moving through anger and sadness to full acceptance. The process took months and years of extremely hard work, often two steps forward and one back.

---

[100] J. Bradshaw, *Homecoming* (New York: Bantam Books, 1990), 47-48.

Slowly but surely we began to piece together the puzzle of our lives. Two or three pieces together over here, four or five over there, the odd bit that didn't seem to fit anywhere (but finally fell into place)...As the process continued, we moved away from being the victims of abuse and addiction and began to take charge of our lives, with a touch of God's constant love and the help of our support systems.

Treating the Trauma

We found the best treatment for the underlying trauma in a combination of individual and group therapy and (possibly) Eye Movement Desensitization and Reprocessing (EMDR). The goal of treatment was to help us reintegrate the repressed memory of the traumas into our psyches, without dissociation.[101] In the past, we'd coped with a painful experience by putting the memory of what happened over *here* and our actual emotions over *there*, because the totality was too overwhelming to bear. Under stress, we'd vanish off

---

[101] B. van der Kolk, *Psychological Trauma* (Washington: American Psychiatric Press, 1987), 7.

into a safe place inside our heads—a trance state, where nothing could really get to us. Now we had to bring the two halves together again and re-experience the whole. Once we found we could make the connections between the events and our emotional experience, our intrusive symptoms—nightmares, flashbacks, re-enactments, and bouts of anxiety—diminished both in frequency and intensity. We no longer went into trance states, and the compulsion towards suicide either stopped or became very much weaker.

Individual therapy gave us a sense of safety. There, we could hope that, with a therapist's help, we could regain a sense of control[102]—something that was of great importance, especially in the early stages of our therapy.

Kevin: *Tom was a lifeline for me during the first few years of recovery. He listened unconditionally and helped me make sense of my life and struggle. I hung on his every word.*

---

[102] *Ibid.*, 163.

Jacqueline: *For several years, I saw my therapist every week. Life was a struggle, sometimes minute by minute. Without him, I wouldn't have made it. At first, he was the only one who understood my struggle with suicide.*

Group therapy provided mutual support. It let us be flexible, taking part actively or passively, talking or listening, sharing or supporting, being victim or helper. It was the best treatment in the later stages of our therapy, usually in conjunction with individual therapy.[103] Group therapy helped us to get over our sense of shame and stigma, the forces that had driven us deeper into secrecy and denial—all forces that had driven the suicide cycle.

Kevin: *I've been in group therapy for years. Facing other people, looking them in the eye, and telling my suicide story really helps me let go of the shame. I know they love me in spite of my suicide attempts.*

---

[103] *Ibid.*, 164.

Remington: *More and more, I see what a big part suicide played in my addiction. I find myself taking risks in meetings and sharing my story. It helps me heal.*

For us, suicide was a compound trauma. That is, we were survivors not only of the childhood traumas that had set us up for suicide, but of our own suicide attempts as well. We'd had near-death experiences that were profoundly traumatic in and of themselves, and they had marked us with a deep sense of shame. Each attempt compounded the trauma and did further damage. Making peace with this reality was extremely difficult; it needed its own healing process, and the more attempts we made, the more complex the healing process had to be. For some of us, the process took well over 10 years.

Kevin: *It's been 20 years. That's how long I've been in therapy and recovery. Only in the last few years have I touched the really deep pain around suicide.*

Thelma: *For 18 years I've been in Twelve-Step recovery, plus a lot of therapy. I don't believe I'll ever be fully cured— just more comfortable in my own skin, without alcohol, drugs, sex, or suicide for a fix.*

Those who work with us have reached consensus about the best way of treatment. They believe that psychotherapy should not proceed directly to work on our own painful material. Instead, it should proceed in three stages: (1) establishing a sense of safety; (2) remembrance and mourning; and (3) reconnection. These states are beautifully outlined in Judith Herman's book *Trauma and Recovery.*[104]

Finding Safety

The first task of recovery, establishing safety, is an essential precondition for any other work.[105] We had to be sure the war was over. We had to have a sense of having someplace safe to stand.

---

[104] J. Herman, *Trauma and Recovery* (New York: Basic Books, 1992), 155.
[105] *Ibid.*

Without that sense, no real therapy was possible. Our previous attempts at power and control had only reflected our underlying sense of being powerless and out of control; now, we had to establish a healthy sense of empowerment and solidity.

Especially for those of us who had been victims of chronic abuse, establishing safety could take months or years. How long it took depended largely on our own histories: the earlier and more severe the abuse, the longer it took to establish a sense of safety. Since most of us had suffered abuse at very early ages and had lacked any sense of having safe places or safe people in our lives, simply establishing a sense of safety could take years of therapy.

We started by focusing on the safety of our bodies and moved gradually towards having a sense of control over our environments.[106] To establish a sense of body safety and control, we had to deal with such basic health issues as proper sleep, health care, adequate nutrition, and exercise. We also had to build up a sense of mental, emotional, and spiritual safety. We had to *know* that we were free of any further threat of abuse. For some of us, that meant divorce or

---

[106] *Ibid.*, 156.

moving away to a new place. For others, it meant eliminating all contact with previously abusive people or setting strict boundaries to ensure our physical safety. Whatever it took!

> **Raquel:** *Slowly I realized that I would never heal unless I stopped my abuse of myself—the sex, the booze, the drugs, the suicide attempts, even some contact with my family. I was willing to do it one day at a time, with a lot of help.*

Body safety also required us to abstain from self-destructive behaviors, including suicidal behaviors, self-mutilation, alcohol, drugs, sex, or compulsive eating. These addictions blocked our trauma recovery process. Sometimes it took years of Twelve Step recovery to establish our sobriety solidly enough that we could get on with the work of trauma recovery.

> **Paula:** *For years, I kept trying to hold onto part of it—the sex or some of the secrets around suicide. It didn't work. I*

just kept re-traumatizing myself and ended up drinking

and drugging again. It was awful.

Our therapists' work was to give us a sense of internal safety; they were our safe place, spiritually, mentally, and emotionally, where we could do our trauma work, with all its pain and sense of deep fragility. Regardless of their own personal beliefs or values, they always respected our own thoughts, feelings, and spiritual values. EMDR also helped to provide a sense of inner safety by teaching us how to focus on targeted high-anxiety material that we found particularly threatening.[107] In several simple sessions, we discovered how to use eye movements to help us discuss trauma material without feeling re-traumatized.

Laura: *For a long time, I could barely talk about my abuse without trancing, actually becoming a child, holding myself and rocking. I first had to feel safe with my*

---

[107] F. Shapiro, *Eye Movement and Desensitization and Reprocessing: Basic Principles, Protocols, and Procedures* (New York: Guilford, 1994).

> *therapist—had to know I wouldn't get hurt or shamed.*
> *He suggested EMDR. It worked immediately. I could*
> *talk. I felt safe. I can't explain it.*

We needed years of patient support and acceptance by our therapists in order to establish and consolidate this internal sense of safety. Trying to get to the second stage too quickly, before we had established this sense of mental, emotional and spiritual trust, usually failed. We'd simply relapse into addiction.

Sasha: *I have been able to share intimate events and feelings*
with my doctor—details I've never heard myself say
before. It took me a long time. I trust him, but that trust
still scares me.

The Work of Mourning

With that sense of safety, we could afford to turn back and revisit the trauma.[108] We had to return to it and retell it to ourselves and our therapists—both the facts and the feelings, whole and integrated. Janet described normal memory as "the action of telling a story."[109] But our traumatic memories were wordless and static. The work of therapy was to provide the color, the music, the words, the feelings.

But this was deeply frightening. We felt we could not manage it. Getting past that fear meant trusting our therapists to help us negotiate a safe passage between the two extremes: shutting down (trancing, dissociating) and emotional flooding (pain so intense we could not handle it).

Jacqueline: *Sometimes I would talk about my childhood without feeling anything at all. Other times, I could hardly discuss it without overwhelming pain. The*

---

[108] J. Herman, *Trauma and Recovery*, 175.
[109] *Ibid.*, 175.

> *mention of my father's name, or of his suicide, brought*
>
> *on enormous sadness and guilt.*

To reconstruct our trauma stories, first we had to review our lives before the trauma happened, to restore a sense of continuity with the past.[110] Next, we had to reconstruct the trauma as a recitation of the facts, including the traumatic imagery and our memory of physical and emotional sensations. Simply reciting what had happened, without emotional content, did no good. As Breuer and Freud noted almost a century ago, "recollection without affect almost invariably produces no result."[111]

Slowly but surely, we reconstructed our experience of trauma, at first a sterile, disconnected narrative, but later with intense feeling and meaning.

---

[110] *Ibid.*, 176.

[111] J. Breuer and S. Freud, "Studies on Hysteria" (1893-95) in J. Strachey, tr. and ed., *The Standard Edition of the Complete Psychological Works of Sigmund Freud* (London: Hogarth, 1953).

Elizabeth: *At first I didn't think I had experienced much trauma. I couldn't understand what others had gone through. Then I told my suicide story. I guess my brain had been free of alcohol and narcotics long enough. The pain started. It was intense.*

Chastity: *I never stopped to see all my illnesses and hospitalizations as trauma. I just got through them with the drug addiction and suicidal fantasies. For years, I talked about it all matter-of-factly, with no feelings.*

Trauma brought loss. The telling of our trauma stories pitched us into profound grief.[112] The plunge into mourning was what we most feared in recovery, and since it was so difficult, we sometimes stalled, unable to go forward. Resistence to this stage was probably the most common cause of stagnation in the recovery process.[113]

---

[112] J. Herman, *Trauma and Recovery*, 188.
[113] *Ibid.*, 189.

Talk about the horns of a dilemma…to go back meant returning to the hellhole of suicide; to go forward meant struggling with intense grief and mourning, a terrifying prospect. We were apt, at this stage, to entertain dreams of a magical resolution. We fantasized taking revenge on those who had hurt us; we dreamed of their humiliation and punishment. Or we hoped, through "cheap forgiveness", to bypass our own anger. We clung to the hope that those who harmed us would acknowledge what they'd done, ask our forgiveness, and make restitution. But none of these worked. On this particular journey, there are no shortcuts.

Jacqueline: *During the first couple of years, I wanted to quit therapy. I actually fired my therapist several times, only to come back the next week. I would go in and out of denial, argue with him that I was not a trauma victim, then try to convince him that I had already worked through he pain. Finally I would do some work—really painful work—and it felt like a death.*

We had not only to grieve for what we had actually lost, but for what had never been ours to lose in the first place. In grieving our lost childhood, we mourned the loss of our foundation of basic trust, the belief in a good parent.[114] We confronted the existential despair that we, as children, had been unable to understand and accept. Leonard Shengold posed the central question of this stage of mourning: "Without the inner picture of caring parents, how can one survive?...Every soul-murder victim will be wracked by the question, 'Is there life without father and mother?'"[115] This confrontation with despair brought with it an increased risk of suicide.

As we came through the mourning and the confrontation with despair, we made a discovery. We could survive. And we did feel something else coming back, a renewal of hope and energy.

Kevin: *God does indeed know what he's doing. I was sober for*
many years before I was ready to explore the deep pain
around my suicide attempts. It hurt a lot. Appearing on

---

[114] *Ibid.*, 193.
[115] L. Shengold, *Soul Murder: The Effects of Childhood Abuse and Deprivation* (New Haven: Yale University Press, 1989), 315.

the Oprah Show opened me up and started the process.

I had mourned my drug addiction and sex addiction over a number of years. I figured I was almost finished with therapy. The sadness and despair I had to go through about my suicide attempts was intense. Yet week by week, I felt a new strength, a new hope for recovery. My life, including all the suicide attempts, began to take on new meaning.

Reconnection[116]

Once we'd come to terms with the past, we could start looking at the future. We needed to challenge old beliefs and relationships and to develop new faith and interconnections. With a new sense of safety, we could afford to engage more actively in the world.

It felt a little as Rip Van Winkle must have felt, facing the wonder and uncertainty of a new world. We might be adults in body, but we felt like children facing life for the first time—and so we were, because for the first time we were facing life as whole, feeling people.

---

[116] J. Herman, *Trauma and Recovery*, 196.

We were exquisitely aware of our vulnerability to threats and reminders of our trauma. But we chose to engage with life, with all our fears, rather than to hold back from it. We challenged ourselves: with vision quests, with reconnecting with other people. Each time we mastered a situation, we gained something and took another step toward healing.

Most survivors just want to get on with their own lives,[117] but others feel called upon to witness to the world. We felt we could best redeem our own experience by helping others.

Kevin: *For 10 years, I had the basic ideas for a book on suicide addiction, but I could not write the first few words. I tried several times, but it just wouldn't be put down on paper. One of my deepest wounds went back to the time I got an F in Latin class—that's when I had my first suicidal thoughts. I call it my academic wound: a fear of academic ridicule, rejection, or failure. Once I started mourning the wound, I started writing the book.*

---

[117] *Ibid.*, 196.

It was clear to me that writing the book was my way to face my fears, confront my academic wound, and declare a survivor mission for myself.

The Lasting Scar

Healing our trauma did *not* cure our suicide addiction. While the addiction had grown out of the trauma, like all other addictions it had become a progressive illness. It had left deep tracks in our psyches and changes to our brains, and these could not be fully undone. What we were given was a "daily reprieve contingent on the maintenance of our spiritual condition."[118]

Working through our trauma wounds, although it could not fully cure us, did make sobriety easier and more comfortable, and it also made us more aware of our relapse issues and triggers. That let us take precautions against potential slips, which in turn helped to make our recovery easier and more stable.

Such triggers were usually related to our deepest trauma wounds. These usually stemmed from abandonment in one form or another,

---

[118] *Alcoholics Anonymous*, 85.

usually in early childhood. Sexual abuse by a parent, suicide of a family member, repeated emotional or spiritual shaming by a parent—these were the common patterns we remembered. They had left us feeling abandoned, with no safe place to turn.

Triggers could take many forms. Anniversaries, for example: maybe we remembered the event as though it had happened yesterday, or maybe we'd forgotten it even existed, but on the anniversary date, we found ourselves triggered into old behavior:

Raquel: *I was sexually abused by a family member, then molested by my friends father and brother, date raped at 16, physically abused by a man from 17 to 22, then beaten up by another man in 1995. Each time I was abused, I turned suicidal; the fantasies and rituals kicked in. Later on, anything that reminded me of my abuse triggered my suicidal fantasies.*

Other triggers were less obvious and more symbolic or disguised. We could identify them only after processing more of our childhood

321

trauma. These "shame triggers" —daily reminders of conflict—took on larger-than-life reality for us, because the trigger mimicked something in our original trauma. A harsh word from a male boss could trigger memories of a father's angry suicide. A conversation overheard in the grocery store could trigger the buried memory of a mother's coldly shaming criticism—even if we couldn't remember where or when.

> **Remington:** *I remember violent arguments between my father and mother when I was four. I dreaded weekends, felt alone and afraid, and watched my mother look for his pistol. He was so abusive. He raged a lot. When I rage today, I want to get my pistol out and stroke it or use it on myself.*

A Second Chance

Slowly, surely, we started to get back our sense of self-esteem. On a spiritual level, we began at last to reconnect to family, friends, and co-workers. We had been trapped in the web of addiction; now we finally had the energy to give and receive love.

It wasn't overnight. Family members who had been devastated by our suicide attempts were very slow to trust us in the beginning—how can we blame them? They held themselves aloof, waiting for the next attempt. But as they sensed a change in our lives, they came to believe that the attempts were finally over. Little by little, they learned to trust us again, and our relationships began to heal.

We truly did have a second chance. Thank God.

Mary's Story

There were six other children in my family, four girls, two boys, and then me. I hung out with the boys a lot and was closer to them than I was to my sisters. I always felt weird because I was the last girl. I was "special", but I also felt different from everyone else.

My parents raised us on a farm. My dad was a workaholic. After a day on the job, he'd come home and work on the farm, coming in only briefly for supper. That's when we'd see him, before he went back to his chores.

So Momma raised us on her own. She was a workaholic too, but then, with seven kids, she didn't have much choice. When I was in third grade, she went back to work as a schoolteacher.

People say I had a "Leave it to Beaver" life. Our family looked good. That's what we were all about, looking good. If anything unacceptable happened in our family, we didn't talk about it. We shut down. We were never allowed to be angry, and if we displayed any anger, we were shamed for it. We weren't allowed to show feelings because we didn't know what to do with them.

So I held my feelings inside. "I'm just not right," "something's wrong with me," "I can't do this!", "I just don't measure up." These were the sorts of things that ran through my mind constantly during high school.

All of us became overachievers. I was in 4H and Girl Scouts, I was Junior Class president, I was in student council and I was the volleyball manager. I did everything. I kept achieving more and more, hoping that one day I'd come home and my dad would say, "Gosh, Mary, that was great. You did a good job." But that too was unacceptable in my family. They called it bragging. The best I ever heard was "Good job!" from my mother. My father, I learned later, hadn't a clue what I'd accomplished.

I started to look to other people for approval. My feelings about me had to come from someone else; I couldn't feel good about who I was. I had to achieve something—make another A—to feel good. A B wasn't good enough.

When I was 14, my brother got lung cancer. My parents did the best they could, but I was forgotten. They didn't mean to; it just happened. They had to take care of him. He suffered from cancer until I was 17, and then he died.

During those years, the message I got was *take care of yourself. Do your own thing. Dad and Momma have their hands full. Help them, please them, don't get in their way, don't have any needs of them.* So I withdrew more and more from my family. I went to school, went to work, did all my extracurricular activities. I was a "little adult". By spring, I had my driver's license and my car. And the message was, *Be as independent as possible, because we can't handle you right now.* But I still felt, deep down, like a little girl. I needed love, and I needed my parents. However much I achieved, I never felt good enough. I kept comparing myself to my sisters, who were in college. My achievements seemed so much less than theirs. I felt I wasn't a good person.

When my brother died, my first question was "Why him?" Everybody loved him. He was bright, quick, and funny. I hadn't done anything of worth. I was slower than he was. Deep down, I knew I was worse than he was, that I was the bad one. I prayed at night, "Why not me?" I was angry. I knew I was the one who didn't deserve to be here, that my brother should have stayed. I was also angry because my dad hadn't been there for me, but my brother had. He was the one who had given me unconditional love. When I did something wrong, our parents would shame me, but my brother would put his arms around my shoulders and say, "Oh Mary, it's okay." I can still feel his arms around me today. I loved being with him. He was my friend. So I was really pissed off at God for taking him instead of me.

I had become a Christian and was trying to be the best Christian there was. I'd see all these other Christians, and they all looked happy. They looked like they had it all together. I thought they were having perfect lives, and I was the only one with these terrible feelings. It had been drilled into my head that I was supposed to accept God's will. And it was God's will for my brother to die, and for me to be left behind, for some reason. So I must accept what God wanted and never be angry with God. I was, but I never admitted it.

My brother died in February. That summer, I worked at a Young Life camp, and then went on to college. I went on working for Young Life and trained to be a leader in my freshman year. The harder I tried, the more I felt like the biggest mess-up ever. I asked God to help me keep from messing up. I worked for another Christian camp the next summer and was even more miserable.

During high school and college, I was dating the man I later married. He was a shy guy, someone who needed taking care of. I was good at taking care of people, and I was good at taking care of him. But at the same time, I resented having to take care of him.

I drank some in high school. When I had my first drink, I thought "This will take care of how I feel inside." Most of the time, if I drank, I'd be sure to do so when I was with Stu. He was a good caretaker himself, and he would get me home when I got drunk.

After my brother died, I went on a food binge: I ate and ate and ate. He died in February, and by the end of summer I had put on 20 pounds. I went on eating, but when I got to college I learned how to vomit the food back up. All the girls in the dorm did it. I'd eat to make the pain go away, and then the remorse would hit: *you're just so stupid, you can't get it right.* I'd make myself throw up, or I'd take laxatives or diuretics—whatever it took. I continued that pattern throughout my freshman year. I felt ugly. I hated myself. I couldn't see how anyone could ever love me. Convinced that I was unlovable, that's when I started having suicidal thoughts.

Stu asked me to marry him. I thought, *Stu loves me. He must, because he's put up with so much already. If I don't marry him, no one will ever ask me again.* So I agreed. I married Stu before my senior year. I had to hide my bulimia from him. I'd study till late at night, take my diuretics and then throw up. Eventually he found out about it and I had to stop.

And then I found alcohol. It became a substitute for bulimia. I didn't like beer, but it was all we could afford. In Food Science, I'd learned that all of our sense of taste is on the top and sides of the tongue; the back of the tongue has no sense of taste. So I'd take a cup of beer, stick out my tongue, put the lip of the cup on the back of my tongue, and down the hatch with the beer. Beer became my drug of choice.

And my god was Stu. When I married, I gave up on God and turned my will and life over to Stu. That was our relationship: me and Stu, each other's gods. That's how we lived. Eventually I got tired of taking care of him, and I'm sure he got just as tired of taking care of me. He was so shy, though. I'd make all his phone calls for him. I tried so hard to be the Perfect Little Wife for him.

I got my bachelor's degree and we moved to Texas. I was working full time and working on my master's degree part-time, but I'd still fix Stu's lunch every day. And of course I was trying to do all of it perfectly, at the same time feeling that I wasn't doing anything right—and I was getting angrier and angrier at Stu. He was getting angrier and angrier at me, too.

I started "talking" to other men, and that caused problems too. Stu got so upset about it that they had to put him in the hospital for anxiety. They gave him tranquilizers—which meant I had a supply of tranqs.

The day I defended my master's thesis, I defended at two o'clock. I came home from work at noon and ate lunch. I was a nervous wreck. So I took a tranquilizer, drank a beer, and defended my thesis.

When I got to West Virginia and started my PhD, I started drinking more heavily and hiding it from Stu. I started having anxiety attacks at night so badly that I couldn't study. I'd drink and pass out. And then I would wake up and think, *I haven't studied at all.* So I'd get up at two or three o'clock in the morning and study until six. I'd take a shower, go to my classes, work part time, come home, and start all over again.

Finally there was a point when I looked at the bottle of tranquilizers and thought, *I'm going to take that bottle…*My sister had come for a visit, and she found the bottle and said, "What are you doing with these?" I said, "Oh, they're Stu's." She said, "He should be careful. These are the same type the Quinlin girl took with beer before she went into a coma." I thought *That would be my luck—a coma!*

My suicidal thoughts increased and I felt more and more trapped. I kept having anxiety attacks. Finally I went to a psychiatrist; I'd decided I was going crazy. He immediately identified me as an alcoholic. I got to AA and started working my program. I had a wonderful sponsor, but there were still times when I was suicidal. I still meant to take those tranquilizers. I confessed to Stu, and he threw them away. My sponsor helped me through it.

After I finished school, we moved to Florida. I got a big industry job down there. I was a brand new little be-boppin' female in the middle of five 55-year-old men who had been at the plant since forever. I had a tough time. In addition, Stu had never forgiven me for "talking" to other men in Texas. He grew more and more insecure about our relationship. The more he wondered if I was misbehaving, the more he'd cling to me, and the more he'd cling, the more I'd push him away. I felt trapped. Finally I got him to go to a counselor, and that helped for a while. Then he said, "I'm fine, I'm fine, I'm fine." He never would work on his part of the problem. (Today, he's in recovery, and that's made a world of difference in him.)

I was getting sick from thinking *It's all me. I'm the alcoholic, I'm the whole problem in this marriage.* Our relationship was pretty poor. I almost got involved with another man, but I called it off—I didn't want to repeat the same behavior. Instead, I got pregnant, and six months into my pregnancy, the plant laid me off.

There I was: six months pregnant, felt like dirt, felt worthless. I felt suicidal a lot of the time, but I knew it would mean killing two people, and I couldn't do that. I was struggling, going to a new meeting every day. When my baby was born, he had hip problems, and he had to spend three months in a body cast. It was awful, watching him suffer. Having a baby didn't fix the marriage.

We moved home. I started teaching college and absolutely loved it. I taught for six months—and then Stu got cancer. I went back into that box and I couldn't get out. I kept telling people, "It's not going to be the same. I'm going to *do* something this time. He won't end up like my brother did." But deep down, I saw Stu dead. As he went through chemotherapy, I turned into a robot, feelings turned off. We made it through the summer; I started teaching again in the fall, and things were better.

The next December, the first anniversary of his cancer—and bingo! The college laid me off. I got very depressed. February, the anniversary of my brother's death: it was turning into a daily battle not to kill myself. Finally, in late April, I hunted for the guns and couldn't find them. On the way to work that morning, I almost pulled in front of a tractor-trailer, but when I saw the car with a little baby in it, I just couldn't do it. That night I thought, *I'll slit my wrists. That way, I'll be dead before Stu gets home.*

At that point, I had a God-given thought: *I need some help.* All this time, I'd been seeing a therapist. I went to her office and told her, "You've got to do something with me! Please help me!" She saw at once that I needed hospitalization. I stayed in hospital for four days. Then they put me in extended care; I lived in an apartment with other recovering people. What an experience that was!

It was intense therapy. They helped me to express my anger at God, who had taken my brother; at my father, who hadn't been there for me; at my mother. I had shut out my brother so thoroughly that I couldn't remember anything about our childhood. I couldn't remember the good times. I couldn't even go back and look at his pictures.

Now I can go back and look at pictures. It's a whole new feeling, a new life. While I was there, I came clean about my struggle with suicide. I realized that I've got to talk about my feelings. If I'm thinking about suicide, I have to tell someone.

It's interesting that during that time—especially the last few years—I didn't think about drinking. Every time I started feeling trapped and desperate, I'd think *I want to die! I want to die!* But I didn't want to drink. I knew if I drank, I'd die anyway. I didn't want to live through that again. Getting sober once had been hard enough.

When I thought *I want to die*, I'd start to think about how I would kill myself, and when I did that, I would get a rush—just as though I'd had a drink. I'd get a powerful feeling sweeping over me: *I can do this, you know. Yeah, that's the answer.* It would give me a sense of relief. That's why I call myself a suicide addict.

Everyone says that suicide's a selfish thing to do. But when I was in that frame of mind, I truly believed that I was so worthless, so terrible at everything I did in life, that anyone could replace me and do a better job than I had done. What about my four-year-old boy? He's the most wonderful kid in the whole world. But when I was in that state of mind, I thought any stepmother would be better for him than the mother he had.

My mother gave me a wonderful gift the day before I went into treatment. She said, "Think about it this way. Do you want your son growing up thinking that his mother didn't love him enough to stick around?" That was my first glimpse into how crazy my thinking was. It was all about me and what people were doing to me. In that sense, I suppose it was selfish.

I've been a victim long enough. I had approached my last job thinking, *what are the kids going to do to me?* Now I'm learning that I am worth something. I have something to give. Whatever I have, I can give it away, and I'm trying to do that. It makes me feel worthwhile. When I work with another alcoholic or suicide addict, I feel better about me.

I think the same thing now when I walk into class: not *what are they going to do to me?* but *how can I help someone here?* Maybe it's only one student, but maybe I can make a little difference in that person's life. I'd never grasped that before. I thought I had to do big things to make a difference. But I've learned that I can do things one day at a time, and that's important.

Whenever I feel trapped now, I call someone and talk about it. I find if I tell someone whatever's going on, it loses its power over me. I don't want to kill myself the way I used to, but the thought does still sometimes come out of the blue, and I think, *well, now, where'd you come from?* I realize then that I'm feeling trapped. But I find that feeling trapped is something I can do something about. The trapped-feeling is me, not life, and I do have some control over what's going on—especially with God as my partner.

The truth is, I hate having to admit I'm human and not perfect. I'm afraid you're going to find out I'm human. But the person who needs the most to learn that is me. That's got to be my discovery. And if I'm not perfect—well, that's okay.

Chapter 8

The Hope

> "...and you will know the truth,
> and the truth will make you free."
> John 8.32, NRSV[119]

In the Beginning...

On May 13, 1996, 15 scared souls, borrowing heavily on the strength of the Twelve Steps of Alcoholics Anonymous, met for the first time, in order to "share our experience, strength, and hope with each other that we may solve our common problem and help others recover".[120] What scared us most was that the program might not work—that we'd be stuck in the trap of suicidal preoccupation and behavior. That fear drove us forward instead of causing us to hang back. Somehow we found courage to step out, still terrified, but

---

[119] The Holy Bible, Revised Standard Version, The New Testament (New York: Thomas Nelson and Sons, 1946) 114
[120] Alcoholics Anonymous, *Preamble New York: AA Grapevine, 1947).*

finally able to tell someone that we were suicide addicts or survivors of suicide. And then we began to tell our stories.

The story-telling didn't come easily. A small part of each one of us wondered whether talking about suicide might make something bad happen—that it would set the thoughts going once more, or push us into doing something stupid yet again. But oddly, what happened was the opposite. Sharing our preoccupation stripped it of its power. We realized quickly that we finally had a safe place—the one thing no one else had been able to give us. Psychologists and psychiatrists might lock us up; our nearest and dearest were hurt or incredulous or angry if we spoke honestly, and the church warned us we were damned. But here, in this circle, we were finally, truly, completely safe. We had come home.

Slowly the truth came out of us, the *whole* truth, for the first time. We could speak freely, sharing the thoughts and fantasies that we'd locked away from everyone's sight for years. It was a deep relief to realize that others had similar thoughts—to see the nods and smiles of recognition: *yes, I've been there too*. They drew more truth out of us. It got easier to talk.

The greatest comfort was our new awareness that none of us was alone. We had company. We bonded with each other swiftly and deeply. We began to see that we could do together what none of us could do alone. There were times when we wanted to avoid the meeting, but something always drew us back. We owned up to our ambivalence and kept returning. Something was happening. We all sensed that.

We found ourselves engaging in lively but deadly serious discussions. The more serious the subject was, the louder the laughter. We found our own group expressions: "Just hang in there!" was our watchword. As we began to speak more freely, we finally saw how ludicrously insane our addiction had been; for the first time, we saw it as it really was. We learned to take the addiction seriously, but also to take ourselves less seriously. As this happened, we started to become detached from our illness. Safe in the group, we could admit how powerless we were over suicide—sometimes with relief and laughter, sometimes with enormous pain and tears.

One by one, we stepped forward to tell each other how the disease had begun, how it had progressed over time, what our individual experiences were. As we grew stronger and more confident, and as we recognized the part that secrecy had played in the progression of our disease, we found ourselves willing and able to speak to outsiders. No more holding back! We opened our meetings to the public.

With no other sources than the Twelve Steps of Alcoholics Anonymous (see appendix) and a beginner's faith in God, we started to write our way to recovery. Writing out our truth wasn't easy, but putting it down on paper made it more real, more concrete. The more we found we could verbalize the addiction, the better we understood it and the weaker its power over us. With each word, each sentence, the past began to make more and more sense.

We found that we had business issues to deal with. What about putting together a phone list? But what should we do if someone called a number on the list and claimed to be suicidal? For the first time, really, we tried to walk in someone else's shoes, to imagine what the person might want or need. Should we just listen, or should we try to get help for the person? People were unsure and nervous. In the end, we decided to trust God to do the right thing and went ahead with the phone list. It proved to be a powerful tool.

This is how Suicide Anonymous got off the ground—the first Twelve—Step program for people addicted to suicide. It has proved to be, quite literally, a life-saver.

Suicide Anonymous

Suicide Anonymous was a fresh start, with no condemnatory history. The purpose of the program is to provide a truly safe environment for suicidal people, to give us a chance to share our struggles with each other, to prevent suicides, and to develop strategies for support and healing from the devastating effects of suicidal preoccupation and behavior. Unlike religious organizations, Suicide Anonymous does not judge suicide as a sin; members can share their stories without fearing condemnation. Unlike mental health professionals, Suicide Anonymous has no obligation to commit suicidal people to psychiatric hospitals. Suicidal people can safely come to meetings without the fear of being "thrown in a mental hospital".

The power of Suicide Anonymous is not easy to describe; it has to be experienced.

Those of us who were in on it from the beginning are still dumbfounded by its strength. Many of us had years of experience with the Twelve Steps in other settings, but we found a fresh and vital energy within Suicide Anonymous. Did the power come from ourselves or our subject matter, or was it a gift of God? The answer really doesn't matter. For us, our hope is in the meetings of Suicide Anonymous.

From the beginning, Suicide Anonymous agreed to adopt the traditions of Alcoholics Anonymous, especially the principles of anonymity, non-professional status, no dues or fees. (Please see the appendix for the traditions.)

For our safety, **anonymity** is of utmost importance. Suicidal people need a totally safe place to get honest about their struggle with suicide; knowing that others will keep their confidence is the cornerstone of such safety. Anonymity provides safety for suicidal people, allowing us to attend meetings without fear of disclosure.

Non-professional status means that we have no professional leader. Members of the group volunteer to lead meetings as trusted servants who do not govern. Having professional leaders would mean we'd be stuck with the problem of professional codes and the need for possible commitments to psychiatric facilities. As such, Suicide Anonymous would become a form of professional group therapy, and the professional leader would be forced (at times) to invoke commitment laws or face liability. Non-professional status, therefore, ensures that we can tell the whole truth at meetings without fear of being committed to a psychiatric hospital.

No dues or fees means that meetings are free for those of us who need it. There are no financial or medical records kept. In fact, no contractual relationship exists. Following the custom of Alcoholics Anonymous, a basket is passed at meetings and members are free to give a dollar. Free meetings ensure that we can get help under all economic conditions without fear of having a medical record. In this era of shrinking budgets for mental health issues, we think such a resource is invaluable.

SA's Resources and Tools

To counter the destructive consequences of suicidal ideations and behavior Suicide Anonymous draws on four major resources:

- our willingness to set "bottom lines" for ourselves (see below) and to observe them every day;

- our capacity to reach out for supportive fellowship within Suicide Anonymous;

- our reliance on the Twelve Step program to achieve sobriety; and

- our development of a relationship with a power greater than ourselves which can guide and sustain us in recovery.

In a little over six years, Suicide Anonymous has developed five important tools for hope and healing from the devastating effects of suicide addiction:

Discussion meetings: During our hour-long weekly meetings, the volunteer chairperson presents different topics and members share their experience or simply listen. Members are encouraged to present their own feelings and ideas instead of responding to others' statements, in order to foster free discussion without criticism. The last fifteen minutes are reserved for members to "get current" about how they are dealing with suicide. Experience has shown that talking openly about suicide with people who understand the problem lessens the shame and stigma, combats isolation, and teaches the suicidal person that it is safe to reach out for support in a crisis.

Phone lists: The exchange of members' phone numbers provides a valuable resource for dealing with crises between meetings, especially late at night. Initially reluctant to bother others, most members learn to reach out to fellow members for support in a suicidal crisis. Members receiving calls feel useful and learn how it feels to be on the receiving end of a suicidal crisis.

Sponsorship: New members pick existing members to guide them through crisis and through the Twelve Steps. Both individuals benefit enormously from the experience and learn that they are not alone in their struggle with suicide.

Kevin Taylor M.D.

Speaker meetings: At regular intervals one member shares his or her life story and experience with suicide at a meeting open both to group members and to the public. In sharing his or her story, the teller overcomes the shame and stigma of a life of struggle with suicide. The listener, meanwhile, has the opportunity to identify with the story, to break through denial, and to start understanding the full extent of his or her own struggle with suicide.

Bottom Lines: A bottom line is a line an individual draws, saying "I will never do this again." Some examples: "I will not attempt suicide; I will call a group member before acting on suicidal impulses." "I will not stockpile drugs, weapons, ropes or any other tools for suicide. I will call a group member if I feel the need to do so." "I will not allow myself to fantasize about the relief I believe suicide will give me: I will call for support." "I will call for support if I find myself starting to make a plan." "I will call for support of I find I start to feel trapped, angry or afraid." Keeping our bottom line is what defines sobriety. We celebrate sobriety by handing out colored chips that mark the length of time that an individual has managed to stick to his or her bottom line: White at the start, red after three months, blue after six months; and then a new medallion on each annual anniversary.

What We've Learned

Those of us who have been actively involved in Suicide Anonymous from the beginning have discovered several important things about ourselves and about our suicide addiction.

First, **denial runs deep within us**: Many of us were shocked to learn that our suicide addiction started much earlier in life than we first remembered, consumed far more energy than we realized, and "hooked" us more powerfully than we initially admitted to ourselves and others. Some of us attended numerous Suicide Anonymous meetings before our denial began to lift and our real stories began to emerge. At first, we could only see our recent struggles with suicide, not the years of addiction. In time, as fragments of memory became a whole in our minds, we realized that we were truly addicted to suicide.

Second, **there is no cure**: Most of us realize that there is no "magic-bullet cure" for our addiction to suicide. Instead we will get a daily reprieve from it, contingent upon maintenance of our spiritual condition. We have good days and we have bad days, and some of us have progressed farther in recovery than others. But the good news is that almost all of us have reduced our suicidal preoccupation and behavior, and a few of us have even been free of suicidal thoughts for some time. None of us, thankfully, has committed suicide, though several of us have made attempts. Each of us who made an attempt, or came close to suicide, returned to Suicide Anonymous, got honest about it and picked up a white chip. We felt love and support within Suicide Anonymous and credited the program with saving our lives.

Third, **we need all the help we can get**: Almost all of us discovered that we needed professional help as well as Suicide Anonymous. Many of us needed antidepressant medication or mood stabilizers for depression or bipolar illness. We sought out psychiatrists who understand mood disorders, addictions, and psychological trauma. Those of us who chose to get psychiatric help found our psychiatrists have aided in our recovery, especially when they supported our involvement in Suicide Anonymous. They have arranged hospitalization when we needed it. In addition to psychiatrists, individual therapists have been helpful to our recovery and allow us to explore the roots of our suicide addiction, especially our trauma wounds. Suicide Anonymous meetings often trigger memories and help us break though denial; we then need to process the reemerging trauma with our therapists. Many of our therapists have been grateful for the support of Suicide Anonymous.

Fourth, **we must be rigorously honest in real time**: All of us learned that we had to "get honest" about each suicidal thought with someone the moment the thought occurred. This someone could be a sponsor, a therapist, a psychiatrist or a group member. In addition, we found the last fifteen minutes of our Suicide Anonymous meetings, our "getting current period", to be an important place to unload our suicidal thoughts so that they did not progress to plans or attempts. Some of us learned from experience that bypassing this step leads to later problems. Generally, we learned to call someone on the phone list immediately, usually our sponsor or a trusted friend, later to update our therapist, and finally to get current at the next Suicide

Anonymous meeting. If we are open to suggestions offered to us, this takes care of most suicidal thoughts. For tougher times, we learned to stay with each other for a while for support and protection—a "buddy system" for suicide prevention. This step promotes trust for both members and strengthens Suicide Anonymous.

Fifth, **we must give it away to keep it**: Most of us learned that helping others in Suicide Anonymous helps *us* even more. At first we were "takers", desperately trying to grab any lifeline we could. Over time, however, we began to watch others, to see their needs and to reach out to them. At first we doubted that we had anything to offer others, but in time we discovered that we had our own experiences to share as well as ears to listen. And the more we shared ourselves and listened to someone else, the more we healed.

Start Your Own!

Do suicidal thoughts cross your mind often? Does the idea of suicide seem to dominate your life? Do you want what we have? Are you willing to go to any length to get it? Then start your own Suicide Anonymous group. Get together with others in the same boat and talk honestly about suicide. Listen to others; receive them, and let them receive you. Share your story and your pain. We all have stories to tell.

And may God's blessing be with you and keep you safe.

SUICIDE ANONYMOUS

Phone: (901) 763-3693

Website:
www.geocities.com/samemphis

Email:
samemphis@hotmail.com

Chastity's Story

From what my family tells me, I showed addictive behavior from the time I was born. I cried through the first year of my life. The doctor prescribed knock-out drops for my first three months. I guess I took one look at this world and decided that I'd rather be somewhere else.

Both my parents were strict fundamentalists. My father was the church choir director, as his father had been before him. All the girls in my family had to learn to play piano. We were at church every time the door to the place opened. I heard conflicting stories at church: how God loves little children, but struck Egypt's first-born dead; that Jesus loves you if you're good, but if you're bad he'll burn you forever in hell. It just didn't make any sense, somehow.

I was abused in early childhood. I have some strong memories, as well as vaguer ones that pop into my head now and again. And I was a very angry child; I always wanted what I didn't have. I wanted my sister's dolls. I wanted anything that wasn't already mine. I used to throw fits when we went places. Some of my sister's favorite stories were about my childhood temper tantrums. Once I locked a little girl in my bedroom and held onto the doorknob and told her I wouldn't let her out until she turned into a skeleton. That's the kind of kid I was.

I was fascinated with death. My friend's dog died when I was about four or five, and I went into his backyard just to look at that dead dog. I couldn't imagine what was going on with him. Dracula was my favorite character. On Saturday evenings, my parents went skating, and my sisters and I pulled the curtains and watched Fantastic Features. I loved vampires and wanted to be one. They seemed so powerful, so exotic. Vampires were cool.

When I started school, my teeth were black from my having been given tetracycline as an infant. That physical defect made a big difference to me. I never felt good enough. I had to be the fastest runner, the very best; I had to prove myself over and over, and I did strange things for that reason. At seven or eight, I went to my grandparents' farm in Louisiana. They kept pigs. Nobody was supposed to go into the farrowing stall where the mother pig lay with her new piglets. I got into that stall and started to play with the baby pigs, and mama pig came after me like a freight train. I rolled under the fence and stood in the briars while that big pig stood there thinking *I'm going to kill you.* I asked myself, *why did you do that?* It was so dangerous, but it just seemed like the thing to do at the moment.

Death was an ordinary part of my life as a child. One time, my mother went to lay out a man who had died, bathing his body and putting his false teeth back in his mouth. I looked in through the door and watched her. My grandfather was very sick. We had to go over to visit him all the time; I hated going there, because he was always in his robe with his hair sticking up, pacing from the bed to the couch, saying "Oh Lordy, oh Jesus, help me. Oh Lord, take me home." That went on for years before he finally died. My grandmother sang old gospel songs. One of my favorites was "This World is Not My Home." The chorus went, "The angels beckon me from heaven's open door, and I can't feel at home in this world anymore." I felt like that too, always.

When I was 11, I developed Crohn's Disease and was out of school for three years. I was scheduled for exploratory surgery. I screamed at the doctor, that he just wanted to cut people open; I couldn't understand how people could survive that. I thought they were going to kill me. For three years, I had left my bedroom window open, waiting for Peter Pan to take me to Never Never Land, but I didn't want anyone else in on the act. I was sick for a long time and took Valium three times a day. I'd get a prescription for 100 Valium, with five refills. Painkillers? I could have any kind I wanted. I grew up like that.

In my teens, if anything hurt, I took something for the pain, and if it hurt badly enough, I learned to cover it up. One summer I went into hospital weighing 63 pounds and came out weighing 172 pounds. When I started back to school, the kids were not friendly. I had nicknames like Porky Pig. I hated the names. I hated school. I hated kids who were normal because I knew I was not. I knew there was something wrong with me. I knew that I had to be bad, because God had punished me with an illness that would leave me marked for the rest of my life.

By 1975, I was *really* sick. I put off going to the hospital because I wanted to die at home. I was taking 17 semester hours of pre-med courses and working at a dime store. I worked every day with a temperature of 103-105%F. As long as I stayed conscious, I put off going to the doctor because I knew he would put me in the hospital. I had told my sister to put my makeup on when I died and I had given instructions to my mother about my funeral. When I finally went into the hospital, I was not conscious enough to stop them from taking me. My uncle carried me in.

The day before I was discharged, my niece died. She was nine months old. I'd always pretended she was my own child. I couldn't understand her death. It should have been me. I just wanted to die. I lay in bed that night, thinking about all the pills I had and how I could take them and be out of this. I felt that if I'd died, she would have lived. It was all my fault. I was so angry with God...It seemed as if God had told me, "As long as you keep holding on, I'm taking away everything you love." Of course they told me that it was silly to feel that way, and that God didn't work like that. I didn't believe them. I was so confused about God anyway.

The day I got home from the hospital, I made coffee and heated up some food. I didn't go to the funeral home—hell, after six months in the hospital, I couldn't walk. But I felt as though a part of me had died. Afterwards, I immersed myself in reading science fiction and historical romances. I wanted a perfect world, an exciting place with nothing but happy endings. That's what I'd always wanted anyway, and that's why I never felt at home in this world—because it wasn't like that. Reality sucked. I wanted no part of it.

I went to nursing school because I had been sick and people had taken care of me, so I thought I owed it to the world to cure everybody. Also, part of me thought, *If I'm not the patient but the nurse, then I'm not the sick one anymore.* Nursing school was a liberating experience. I had finally gotten well enough to party, and I partied with a vengeance. I loved to drink and dance. I loved to flirt with strange men. I drank and drugged my way through nursing school. I still had all kinds of pain pills. All I ever had to do was to call my doctor, go by the pharmacy, say I was having a problem again, and I'd get my drugs.

We had some really wild times. Some of them, I can't remember at all. I remember waking up in the Hilton one morning, not knowing where I was or where I'd left my car. I had to take a cab to find my car. Once I woke up to find my apartment full of people I didn't know: *Who the hell are these people?*

I led a double life. I started working the 3-11 shift at the hospital, in surgical intensive care. It was an exciting place to work. We'd go in at 3 PM, work our shift, and then go party. I'd go to low dives by myself and pick up men. I was married by then, but I'd have a different man in a different bar, in different parts of town, at different times, for different purposes—and then go home to spend the night with my husband. I kept all these men in separate compartments, and that's where I wanted them to stay. *You belong to this part of my life, not this part. Don't cross those lines.* Saturday night, I didn't know where I would end up, but on Sunday morning I'd still go to church and play the piano.

I'd met my husband at work. I was drinking a lot, smoking a lot of hash, going out all the time, and he was available. He told me I was beautiful, that I was wonderful and a great lover. We drank and partied. One night we'd partied all night long. When we sobered up the next afternoon, I'd married him.

He had his problems too. He was bipolar, I think, and he'd decided that my love was going to cure him. So he stopped taking his medication. He was extremely abusive. I was afraid of what I might find myself doing next. I'd already crossed lines that I had never thought I would cross, and I was turning into someone I didn't know.

I was terrified, and excited, living from one adrenaline surge to the next with this guy.

He'd choke me until I passed out. One day he choked me, and the next thing I knew, I was sitting astride him with his penis in one hand and a butcher knife in the other. That really scared me. One wrong movement, one wrong gesture or word and I would have hurt him. There was no conscious thought involved; it was pure reflex. Something in me snapped, and I thought *fuck this!* I was so frightened, and so ashamed. I was scared of myself, scared of him, scared of what my parents would think of me if they ever found out. I thought no one could ever love me, as low as I'd got.

My brother and mother rescued me and took me back to my mother's house. I wasn't capable of making a rational decision at that point. That incident scared me so much that I stopped drinking. I thought, *it was the alcohol. That's what it was. Drugs didn't have anything to do with it. Everybody needs drugs, but I can get in trouble with alcohol.* After that, I was very cautious with alcohol. I never wanted to wake up and find myself married to someone like that, not ever again.

I started dating the man I'm now married to. I still kept things compartmentalized, though. I kept my work life over *here* and my dating over *there* and my home life in another pigeonhole. These things weren't supposed to mix. I still thought about dying a lot, and I still loved those sad songs. I still read a lot, always fantasies. I loved the fantasy world because it was perfect. It had just enough adventure, just enough excitement, and always a happy ending. That's the way life was supposed to be.

In 1987—I was working in the recovery room—I developed a pelvic ulcer that had to be drained. I thought that the Crohn's Disease had come back. I'd already made up my mind that I would never have abdominal surgery again. I was going to die at home. I had the ulcer drained, and then a few months later, I had to have a hysterectomy for a benign tumor. I'd always wanted kids, and now I could never have them. It was as though God had said, "I told you: you weren't good enough to have kids." Every time I saw a commercial with babies in it, I cried.

Then I developed a terrible cough. I needed cough syrup real badly. Terrible pain in my knees? I needed pain killers. Bad headaches? I needed instant relief. I took cough syrup for four or five months running; I'd get a prescription with three or four refills and keep coming back for more. Funny, how much cough syrup I needed to settle that cough...

Next, I started taking what we call waste drugs from the hospital. It started out small—just the dregs at the bottom of a bottle. But then I realized I could take whole bottles. I took more and more. At one point, I crossed a line: I stopped telling myself, *I'm going to take this to be high* or *I'm going to take this to have more energy.* I began to say, *I'm going to take this to be normal.* All I wanted was to feel normal, but I needed more and more drugs for me to feel that way. It got to the point where I had to empty out my pockets at work in order to have room for all the drugs I was taking home. I stopped counting when I dumped 30 empty vials out of my pockets at work and scooped up 30 or 35 full vials to take home. I don't know how much morphine I was taking—probably about 500-600 mgs. During the day, I took just enough to make me feel normal. Then at home, after my husband had gone to bed, I'd lock myself in the bathroom, fill up the bathtub, and while it was running, fill up a 10-cc syringe with morphine and inject as much as the vein would take. A soft tap on the door, and my husband's voice: "Honey, are you all right?" "Can't I have even a *little* privacy? I'm trying to take a long hot bath." "But you've been in there three hours." "Well, I fell asleep. I'm very tired. Okay?"

Of course, to get all those drugs, I had to work extremely long hours. Any call that was available, I'd volunteer for. I'd go in when there was nothing to do but paperwork. I got access to all kinds of different codes to get hold of drugs. And every day, I would take just enough to get me to work. At home, I'd try to take just enough to get me through the night. This went on day in, day out, for a very long time.

The intervention came on April 10, 1995. By then, I was still coping at work, but that was about all I could manage. At home, I lay in bed, doped up, angry and sad. I didn't want the real world to touch me. I didn't want any part of life with my family; when I was with them, all I could do was cry because I was so ashamed. I was too scared to tell anyone. I knew that nobody could possibly love me enough to want to help me, as worthless as I was. I'd given up trying to be good enough to live. I didn't like it here. I never wanted to be here in the first place. I just wanted to be somewhere else. That last weekend, I stole drugs and did nothing but shoot up. I don't know why I'm still alive.

During detox, I couldn't hear anything that anyone said to me. It took me a long time to tune in. I sat in my little groups, with my blanket wrapped around me, shaking, hoping that people would notice how very sick I was and feel sorry for me.

About a week before I went into treatment, I had prayed for God to help me. I didn't like the kind of help God was providing, but somehow, I still kept showing up. I stuck with it, even though I didn't want to be there. About every second day, I'd pack my bags and call my husband, saying "You have to come get me. I can't stand it here any more." But I'd end up staying that day, and another. After a while I gave up unpacking my bags. I was so angry at the people there. They couldn't seem to understand that I was *special*. I was different, I wasn't like everyone else. I needed special treatment. I needed my drugs. But still, in spite of everything, I managed to pray for willingness, and I started getting it, a bit at a time.

I was sitting in a lecture one day, and the lecture was on suicide. There was a test they gave us. I filled it in: *Shit! I scored almost 97 out of 100!* I'd long since lost the notion that suicide was taboo. I'd been jealous of the patients of mine who died. I'd hoped to get cancer. I'd given them extra narcotics, to make their dying easier. And now, I had to think about starting to choose to live.

Once I got into recovery, a light came on in my head. Nothing's been the same since.

My daughter and I went fishing, not long ago. We hiked through the woods, looking at baby badgers and raccoons. I realized how much that meant to me. Shortly afterwards, she got into an accident and called me: "Mom, I wrecked the car!" My instinctive response was "Baby, are you all right?" I realized later that in the old days, I would have said "Goddamn it! Can you still drive it? Are you going to have to take *my* car? Your insurance will go through the roof! What are we going to do?" I would have been so totally absorbed in my own reactions that I wouldn't have been there for her at all.

I am so grateful for my recovery. I'm grateful that I now know that I deserve *not* to have drugs in my life, and I deserve *not* to die. I am as valuable a human being as anyone else. That's a great gift to me. God has been there for me so many times: in big ways and little ways, in big gigantic miracles and tiny little miracles. Every day God is with me, holding my hand. I'm not alone any more. I'm no longer ashamed to cry, and I don't have to be perfect. That's a real relief. I don't have to handle everything all by myself.

My life is so much better than it ever was. I started reading a novel about three weeks ago, and I'm still not through it. I've been too busy living to finish the damned book. And that, for me, is a miracle.

It's a relief to know that when I go to the bathroom, I go there only to use the bathroom. If I'm out at a restaurant for dinner, I don't have to scope out which stall is the best one for shooting up, so I can stop feeling like hell. I can feel lousy today and know that the feeling will pass, and that I don't need to take anything to make it go away. That's one of my favorite gifts from God. I always thought *It's never going to feel better; I'm always going to be unhappy. I might as well be dead. I'm ready to go on to Heaven.* Now I know that when I have a bad day, it's just a bad day—not a bad week, or month, or year, or eternity. That's magical.

My life's good even when bad things happen. When my mother had a stroke, when my sister-in-law had open-heart surgery, when my daughter wrecked her car—it wasn't the end of the world. It was just the way things are sometimes. My attitude is completely different. I feel lucky to have been an addict: I've learned so many things that many people never do learn.

Yet I know it would be so easy to fall back into that black hole of suicide. I know it's still there. There's a little net over it, but it hasn't gone away. If I don't take care of myself, I could go back there. But I have friends I can call and say, "You know what? I think I'd be better off dead," and they're willing to listen and talk me through it without making me feel ashamed.

So many people out there are lost, without direction, the way I used to be. I didn't know how to live my life, or how to be happy. I didn't know I *could* be happy. I believed those old gospel songs that said "Life's a burden and then you die." I know better now. There is a spirit in me that makes me feel connected to God and other people. I'm not disconnected any more.

Chapter 9

Starting Your Own Recovery

"Easy Does It"
-Slogan of Alcoholics Anonymous

Let's say that you've finally come to understand that you have a problem with suicidal thoughts and behaviors. Perhaps you've hit rock bottom. You've decided that you don't want to do this any more. You really desire change; you long for healing and a fresh start. What things do you need to know to start your own recovery?

Talk about it! Silence is a killer. Fight that instinct that tells you to keep your struggle to yourself. Don't try to go it alone. Keeping this addiction a secret only makes it bigger. With silence, suicidal thoughts grow into plans for suicide, and these plans can too easily grow into attempts. It's like a snowball rolling down a mountain. By speaking out, you nip the process in the bud.

Many of us had terribly dangerous misconceptions to overcome to start our recovery. Here are some of the more common ones:

- "If I talk about suicide, they'll think I'm crazy."

- "If I talk about suicide, they'll lock me up."

- "If I talk about suicide, I'll kill myself."

- "God already knows what I'm thinking so I don't need to talk about suicide.

- "I'll talk about suicide later - after the urge has passed."

- "I'll just give little hints about my struggle with thoughts about suicide but I'll leave out what's really in my mind."

For us, these beliefs kept us sick. We did not get better until we corrected our misconceptions.

Safety first: You must feel safe to start talking about suicide addiction. Feeling trapped or judged, sensing there is no way out, or thinking that those around you do not understand - all of these perceptions make the problem worse. But the first step—to look for a safe place—is one you have to take for yourself. You have to *want* to reach out.

There are several safe places for you to talk about suicide addiction. Suicide Anonymous is one of them. Those of us who started Suicide Anonymous took great pains to make it a truly safe place for people to talk honestly about suicide addiction and to recover together. There is nothing you can say in a meeting that we haven't already heard. The more you talk, the faster you will recover.

Therapists who understand addictions, suicide, and psychological trauma are another safe place. Pick one carefully and tell your story! But first, establish a trusting relationship with your therapist. This trust is absolutely critical to your recovery. Go over ground rules for your relationship, including rules for hospitalization in the event of a suicidal crisis. Agree on the ground rules and stick to them. Remember: a good therapist is like the safest of safe friends.

Attack denial: Attack your denial as though your life depends on - because it does! You can't lick a problem you don't know you have. Denial is lying to yourself about what's really going on. Most of us spent years in denial, lost, unable to fix our problem because we didn't believe we had one.

Suicide Anonymous is an excellent place to combat your denial. Hearing other people share their struggle with suicide addiction will trigger memories tucked away in the crevices of your mind. Little by little, you find yourself able to break down denial and reconstruct your story of suicide addiction. But be patient. Rome wasn't built in a day.

A Suicide Anonymous sponsor is a must. Talking regularly to someone who has been there will help break denial and provide a safe person to call in a crisis. The more your sponsor knows about you the better. Remember your sponsor is only a phone call away.

Use your phone list. Find several people in Suicide Anonymous who you are willing to call in a crisis. Then call them. Don't wait; just do it. In time, calling someone gets easier. Many of us learned that calling someone takes care of little problems before they become big ones.

Set a bottom line and do your best to keep it. It's far more important to set a bottom line than to worry about setting the perfect bottom-line. You can change your bottom line later - when you understand more about your addiction. Let your sponsor help.

Work on denial in earnest. Once you have your support system in place, tell your suicide story to your therapist and sponsor. Go slow! It may shake up some very tough issues and leave you feeling shaky and vulnerable. And don't despair. It really does help.

Complete a suicide first step. (See Appendix.) Then discuss it with your therapist and sponsor. In your first step you will admit exactly how powerless you are over suicide addiction and how your life has become unmanageable. At first this may seem confusing, possibly frightening, even hopeless. Don't panic. Paradoxically, powerlessness is the key to finding a Power over the addiction. We have found an honest first step is the foundation of stable recovery.

Tackle the trauma: Trauma work is a necessity. When you feel more secure in your recovery, begin working through past traumas because these issues probably fuel your addiction. We discovered that our physical, sexual, emotional, or spiritual traumas fueled our suicide addiction. Cutting off the fuel supply through trauma work made the fire subside considerably.

A trauma inventory is an excellent tool for discovering the connections between your wounds and your current suicidal thoughts and behaviors. But please don't try to fill out an inventory by yourself. Trauma work can be scary at times. Don't go it alone. Use your therapist and your sponsor for guidance. And take your time.

Eye Movement Desensitization Reprocessing (EMDR) is helpful for processing trauma memories. EMDR-trained therapists are excellent, safe resources and can help you safely process painful memories. The technique is simple and gentle. There's nothing to fear in EMDR. Go for it when you are ready.

Deal with mood disorders: Be honest about your depression. Don't run from it, or from bipolar illness. Either one can block your recovery from suicide addiction. Talk honestly to your therapist about depression, and learn all you can about mood disorders. If you can, see a psychiatrist who understands mood disorders and addictions. Medications can help, but be careful about addictive drugs, especially benzodiazepines. Experience has taught us that these drugs block our recovery. On the other hand, antidepressants and mood stabilizers can be life savers. Don't hesitate to try one if your psychiatrist recommends it.

Face any other addictions: You may suffer from chemical dependence, sex addiction, an eating disorder or gambling addiction. If you do, tell your therapist or sponsor and get help. Addictions will block your recovery. There are many good treatment centers and Twelve Step programs. Join one.

Live the Twelve Steps for real: Don't just read them. Work them; live them on a daily basis. The Twelve Steps are God-inspired and will save your life. Meet with your sponsor and go through all the steps. Read all that you can. The Big Book of Alcoholics Anonymous and the Twelve Steps and the Twelve Traditions are excellent resources. Use them.

Remember, we get a daily reprieve contingent on maintenance of our spiritual condition. Good luck. You can do it. If we can do it, you can do it.

Remember H.A.L.T.: Avoid getting too hungry, angry, lonely or tired. Any of these states can trigger relapses. Check all four daily. Be careful to look after your own physical well-being: make sure that you get regular exercise, that you eat properly, and that you get enough sleep. You may need to consult a sleep clinic if you have problems with insomnia. It may be hard at first, but keep reaching out to people. Friendships need regular tending, but they're worth every bit of effort you put into them.

Handling hurt and anger can be difficult: it's all too easy to relapse into old behaviors when you're under emotional stress. Talk out these problems with people you trust, instead of trying to deny or repress your feelings.

Be patient! A final tip: be patient and gentle with yourself. Look for progress, not perfection. Your addiction did not start overnight. Learning new ways to think, feel and behave takes time. But with God's help and the help of others you will find a new happiness and a new freedom.

Chapter 10

Working the Steps [*]

> "It works if you work it"
> -Slogan of Alcoholics Anonymous

The Twelve Steps were originally formulated in 1938 by Bill W, the co-founder of Alcoholics Anonymous. They grew out of the principles of the Oxford Groups, a religious fellowship that sponsored the first AA meetings in Akron, Ohio. The steps were first published in Bill W's *Alcoholics Anonymous* (1939) and received a more detailed treatment in his *Twelve Steps and Twelve Traditions* (1953).

The Twelve Steps provide a comprehensive and thorough approach to the problem of addiction. Without them, recovering from suicide addiction may be impossible. Our debt to the pioneers of AA is incalculable.

---

[*] Adapted in part from *Alcoholics Anonymous* (1939), *Twelve Steps and Twelve Traditions* (1953), and *Sex and Love Addicts Anonymous* (1986).

These are the Twelve Steps: [121]

1 We admitted we were powerless over our suicidal preoccupation - that our lives had become unmanageable.

2 Came to believe that a Power greater than ourselves could restore us to sanity.

3 Made a decision to turn our will and our lives over to the care of God as we understood Him.

4 Made a searching and fearless moral inventory of ourselves.

5 Admitted to God, to ourselves, and to another human being the exact nature of our wrongs.

6 Were entirely ready to have God remove all these defects of character.

7 Humbly asked Him to remove our shortcomings.

---

[121] Reprinted with permission from Suicide Anonymous and Alcoholics Anonymous. The Twelve Steps and Twelve Traditions are reprinted with permission of Alcoholics Anonymous World Services, Inc. Permission to reprint and adapt the Twelve steps and Twelve Traditions does not mean that A.A. is in any way affiliated with this program. A.A. is a program of recovery from alcoholism only-use of the Steps and Traditions in connection with programs and activities which are patterned after A.A., but which address other problems, or in any other non-A.A. context, does not imply otherwise.

8 Made a list of all persons we had harmed, and became willing to make amends to them all.

9 Made direct amends to such people wherever possible, except when to do so would injure them or others.

10 Continued to take personal inventory, and when we were wrong promptly admitted it.

11 Sought through prayer and meditation to improve our conscious contact with God as we understood Him, praying only for knowledge of His will for us and the power to carry that out.

12 Having had a spiritual awakening as a result of these steps, we tried to carry this message to those who still suffer and to practice these principles in all our affairs.

Step 1: We admitted we were powerless over our suicidal preoccupation—that our lives had become unmanageable.

No one wants to admit defeat. Every instinct rebels against the idea of powerlessness. It is truly awful to admit that we have become so obsessed by the idea of suicide that only an act of Grace can set us right.

The word "powerlessness" sums up for us several ideas. It means that we ourselves lack the power to make sound choices for our own lives. We are enslaved to suicide. The fact that we became captive to suicide shows that there was something important and powerful in our suicidal patterns which gave us some kind of "payoff". Many of us were seeking, by trancing ourselves with suicidal activity, to shut off the world with all of its demands. Or we masked our fear of commitment to life by thinking of death. We made use of our suicidal preoccupations to lessen our pain or enhance our pleasure.

Soon our obsession became an addiction which destroyed our ability to concentrate on important things. One by one, all the things that make life worthwhile—satisfaction at work, family, friends, and social activities—dropped away as suicide absorbed all our time and attention. Some of us were caught up in the hypnotic intensity of suicidal trances. Such experiences, exuberant at first, became overwhelmingly compelling, carrying us along with them into prolonged bondage to our thoughts of suicide. The original quest for distraction from life's tensions now led us off into oblivion. Control over our lives no longer resided within us. We had lost control, whether we admitted it to ourselves or not.

Each of us, in his or her own time, finally experienced a sense of real desperation. We began to realize that living with our addictive patterns and being controlled by them meant that we risked losing our sanity. We stood on the edge of an abyss, and if we slipped into it, we would lose all possibility of stability or health, forever. We decided we had to stop.

Now we began to confront a paradox: accepting that we couldn't control our addiction is the first step towards recovery. Most of us had tried all sorts of strategies to control our behavior. These strategies, no matter how strong, were futile. If we had some initial success in controlling our addictive behavior, we would become smug and conclude that we could now manage things. This only lowered our defenses, so that we gave in to old patterns again, often within days or hours.

Our loss of control had become an established fact. Therefore we could approach the prospect of surrendering our suicide addiction with true humility, for we had no way of knowing if surrender was even possible. True surrender of our suicide addiction meant not only being willing to take ourselves out of the painful situation at hand; it also meant being ready to be free of the whole obsession with suicide. The resolve only to be rid of a *specific* painful situation, without the readiness to break the whole addictive pattern, amounted to "going on the wagon" without truly giving up the addiction.

When we were first challenged to admit total defeat, most of us revolted. We had approached Suicide Anonymous expecting to be taught the self-confidence to conquer our own suicide addiction. Then we were told that, so far as suicide was concerned, self-confidence was a liability. We were the victims of a mental obsession so powerful that no amount of human willpower could break it. There was no such thing as personal conquest of this addiction.

Finally, we reached a point of unconditional surrender. The proof of this surrender was that we refrained, one day at a time, from every form of behavior we saw as part of our addiction. We recognized that these were no-win situations. Each of us was now willing to go to any length, a day at a time, to stay sober. We were willing to be available to whatever might happen within ourselves. Paradoxically, this was not willingness coming from strength, but from the certainty of the consequences of continuing our addiction.

We were driven to Suicide Anonymous, and there we discovered the fatal nature of our situation. Then, and only then, did we become open-minded, to listen as only the dying can.

Step 2: Came to believe that a power greater than ourselves could restore us to sanity.

As we came to appreciate the magnitude and mind-altering nature of suicide addiction, we had to admit that we could not reshape our whole identity unaided. We felt the need for a Someone greater than ourselves, a Something at least one step ahead of our disease, to give us the guidance we could not provide for ourselves. But what might that Someone or Something be?

We found the best answer to this question of faith through other Suicide Anonymous members, people who had found faith themselves. As we listened to their stories, we could identify with their patterns of addiction. And we could see that they were now leading healthier lives. As living examples, they offered us the hope that the same Power who had helped them might be available to us as well.

Contact with other recovering suicide addicts also helped us sustain our day-to-day sobriety. As we realized how helpful this network of support was, we sensed that we didn't necessarily need organized religion. What we needed was the spiritual guidance we could receive from other Suicide Anonymous members. They helped us lay the foundation for building our own faith. We could even, if we wished, make Suicide Anonymous itself our "higher power". This was, after all, a group of people who together could solve their problem with suicide. In this respect they were certainly a power greater than we were. We could have faith in them. Many members crossed the threshold into faith this way. They told us that, once across, their faith grew wider and deeper. Relieved of the obsession with suicide, their lives transformed, their belief in a Higher Power grew stronger and more certain. And most of them began to call it God.

we found that true humility and an open mind will lead us to faith. Every Suicide Anonymous meeting was a fresh assurance that God would restore us to sanity.

Step 3: Made a decision to turn our will and our lives over to the care of God as we understood Him.

Like all the remaining steps, Step 3 called for affirmative action to cut away the self-will which blocked us from God. The question, as always, was "how?" There was only one answer: willingness.

Every man and woman who had joined Suicide Anonymous had, without realizing it, made a beginning on Step 3. Wasn't it true that in matters relating to suicide, each of them had decided to turn his or her life over to the care and protection of Suicide Anonymous? Each newcomer felt sure Suicide Anonymous was the only safe harbor for the sinking vessel that he or she had become. If this was not turning one's will and life over to a newfound Higher Power, then what was it?

What would it be like, if we were really to empty ourselves of diseases and refrain from refilling ourselves again with anything other than God's grace? We had no idea. All we knew was that we did not want to go back into active suicide addiction. We came to understand that if we were unable to prescribe our own treatment for suicide addiction, then we would be better off turning "our will and our lives over" to the God of our understanding even if we did not know what might happen.

Having made this decision, how could we now begin our new relationship with God? The answer was simple; what we added was prayer. We now began each day in communion with the God of our understanding, asking for help to stay free, for that one day, of addictive behavior. And if we were successful in not acting out by day's end, we thanked God for helping us live another day free from bottom-line suicide addiction.

And in all times of emotional disturbance we paused, asked for quiet and simply said: "Thy will, not mine be done."

Step 4: Made a searching and fearless moral inventory of ourselves.

To our surprise we found that there came a point where we approached the task of Step 4 without fear, because we had come to terms with Step 3. If God was helping us to manage our external lives, it was easier to be open to the idea of clearing up the debris.

But how were we to accomplish such an inventory? No two people would do it exactly alike; there was no single "right way". What we needed was to achieve some understanding of ourselves without fear, pride or secret reservations. Furthermore, we needed to understand the payoffs we had derived from our addictions.

Most of us found that writing down our inventory was helpful. Looking at what we had done in black and white was an invaluable aid to honesty and objectivity. As we read our version of what happened, we could see through our excuses and our need to blame others.

In writing down our inventory, some of us used the guidelines in the Big Book of Alcoholics Anonymous: resentments, fears and sex.

"Resentment is the 'number one' offender." So says the *Big Book* of Alcoholics Anonymous.[122] We also found this to be true for suicide addicts. In order to deal with our resentments, we set them down on paper, listing people, institutions or principles with which we were angry. When we took a hard look at why we were angry, we found that we had seen threats to our self-esteem, our pocketbooks, our ambitions, or our personal relationships.

We saw clearly, for the first time, how these resentments led only to unhappiness and shut us off from the very contact with a Higher Power that we desperately needed for our daily reprieve from suicide addiction. Therefore, putting aside what others might have done wrong, we looked at our own mistakes, asking ourselves where we had been selfish, dishonest, self-seeking and frightened. When we saw our faults, we listed them in black and white.

Next, we reviewed our fears. We put them on paper, asking ourselves honestly why we had them. Wasn't it because our own self-reliance had failed us so badly? We realized there is a better way: put our trust in God, not ourselves. We were in the world to play the role

---

[122] *Alcoholics Anonymous*, (New York: AA World Services, 1976), 64

God assigns. To the extent that we do this, God will match calamity with serenity. We asked God to remove our fears and direct our attention to what God would have us be or do.

Sex! We reviewed our conduct carefully. Where had we been selfish? Dishonest? Did we arouse jealousy, suspicion or anger? Who had we hurt? We put it all on paper and looked at it. We found the acid test for each relationship: was it selfish or not? We earnestly prayed for the right ideal and the strength to do the right thing. If sex was particularly troublesome, we threw ourselves into helping others, taking us out of ourselves.

If we had been thorough in our inventory, we began to learn tolerance and good-will toward all, even our enemies. We were ready for Step 5.

Step 5: Admitted to God, to ourselves, and to another human being the exact nature of our wrongs.

More than most people, suicide addicts lead a double life. To the world, we present a stage character. We take pride in our ability to keep a secret, to keep our stories straight, to keep our feelings hidden.

Such a strategy had a major payoff; we never had to deal with the consequences of our actions. We could even deny to ourselves that there *were* consequences. If ever anyone had a strong incentive to remain closed off from others, to hide the self from view, it was us.

Step 5 was our way to become open. If we didn't share with another person what we learned in Step 4, our sobriety was in danger. Our profound aloneness—both the root of our disease and its consequence—could be eased only by reaching out to another human being.

Many of us felt we needed to find just one person with whom to be totally honest. Most of us had tried being partially honest with different people. Total honesty with one human being was essential for humility. It was also necessary for breaking the isolation that had blocked us from the unconditional acceptance we so desperately needed.

So we pocketed our pride and went for it, illuminating every dark part of our past. Once done, we were relieved and excited. We could look people in the eye and begin to have a spiritual experience. Many of us actually felt the presence of God for the first time.

Step 6: Were entirely ready to have God remove all these defects of character.

In the first five steps we were moving away from the active disease. Now, at Step 6, we needed to make our first step toward re-building. To attribute all of our troubles to suicide addiction would have been a serious error, for our character defects affected our lives too. In becoming ready to give up our character defects, we were ready to give up that part of us capable of "the con".

Our old habits had subtle payoffs which were difficult to surrender. Often victims of emotional deprivation in childhood, we had learned to survive on anger and resentment. Because of our inner blocks, we had become incapable of intimacy with anyone.

Slowly our attitude toward our defects started to change. We began to move from surrender of our suicide addiction, toward surrender to a process which would prepare us for God's work. We understood that Step 6 only asked us to get out of God's way.

Step 7: Humbly asked Him to remove our shortcomings.

The whole emphasis of Step 7 is humility, and the basic ingredient of humility is a desire to seek and do God's will. But as long as we placed self-reliance first, reliance on a Higher Power was still impossible.

Although we had come a long way, we were still unable to shape our own lives in a consistently positive manner without a Power to continue to do for us what we could not do for ourselves.

So we called upon God to remove our shortcomings. When we were finally ready to do this, many of us chose the Step 7 prayer of the *Big Book*: "My Creator, I am now willing that you should have all of me, good and bad. I pray that you now remove from me every single defect of character which stands in the way of my usefulness to you and to my fellows. Grant me strength, as I go out from here, to do your bidding. Amen."[123]

---

[123] Ibid., 76.

Step 8: Made a list of all persons we had harmed and became willing to make amends to them all.

Learning to live in harmony with all men and women is a fascinating adventure. It is a task we may never finish. To accomplish it, we had to repair the damage done in the past to the best of our ability.

Using our Step 4 inventory, we made a list of all persons we had harmed, subjecting ourselves to drastic self-appraisal. Our list was often a long one, since we realized that our character defects—especially our selfishness and anger—had affected most of our relationships.

The problem now was to determine exactly what harm we had done others. A sort of generalized apologetic air was nowhere near enough: we had to see exactly how we had harmed others and how we could set that wrong to rights.

First, we stopped looking at the harm done to us. Regardless of what damage we'd suffered, we could not change another person. The only sins we could deal with were our own. So we closed the books on "wrongs done to us" and set out on our journey.

The prospect of amends could be terribly frightening. We could not imagine finding the courage to tackle some of the things we had done to others. So we simply asked God for the willingness to do so. We realized that if fear or pride kept us from making amends, we would go through life avoiding those we had harmed. We knew intuitively that there would be no real freedom in the future without taking full responsibility for our destructive behavior in the past.

Asking honestly what types of harm we had done, we considered the physical, mental, emotional or spiritual damage that we had done to ourselves or others. We had, for example, been abusive to our mates, blaming them for our own behavior, loading them with all the responsibility for our family life, and frequently taking out our anger on them. We had made their lives hell, and they had suffered real and lasting damage. We had neglected our children, depriving them of our love and care—and of course, they'd blamed themselves for our failure. And then there was the dreadful damage we'd done to ourselves, body and soul...Even if we could not imagine how we could possibly make amends for this sort of terrible injury, we wrote down what we had done, doing our best to be specific about the

393

injury. Without precise knowledge of what we had done to ourselves and others, we realized that we had no chance to stop harming ourselves and other people in the future.

In time we found that our commitment to recovery had moved us beyond simple survival to a higher plane, one born of a sincere desire to right the wrongs we had done during our active addiction.

Step 9: Made direct amends to such people whenever possible, except when to do so would injure them or others.

Step 8 would be meaningless unless we put it into action; it is the preparation for Step 9—a plan of action, but not the action itself. And the action had to be carried out, wherever possible.

In working Step 9 we cleaned up our past to the best of our ability. We did our honest best to make amends to people we had harmed. We prayed to be freed from the bondage of self, so we could free others in our lives from the pain our deception had caused.

The most important amends we made were those that were made face to face. As we looked at what we had done, it was clear that many on our list had gone on with their lives, burdened and twisted by the distortions of reality that we had inflicted on them. What we had to do for them, then, was to relieve them of the guilt that we had loaded on them and that they had accepted. We'd convinced ourselves and them that the problems had somehow been their fault—that they could have saved us from ourselves. We had to set the record straight, for their sakes, but also for ours.

It wasn't always simple. Some people had gone beyond our reach, either through death or disappearance. Others no longer wanted to hear from us under any circumstances. In some situations, full disclosure could only bring more harm, and we could make only partial restitution. In other cases, restitution had to be deferred till the time was right. And sometimes, we had to accept that we could never make direct amends.

While face-to-face was the best way, there were some people who we could not meet directly. In such cases, we wrote letters laying out the past frankly and fully and asking for forgiveness. If we had no way to make amends directly, all we could do was to say an honest prayer, admitting our wrongs and asking God to set the old wrongs to right on our behalf—and then we had to let the past go, trusting in the knowledge that we would be willing to make amends if we could.

In time we found that page 83 of AA's *Big Book* expresses a great truth:

If we are painstaking about this phase of our development, we will be amazed before we are half-way through. We are going to know a new freedom and a new happiness. We will not regret the past nor wish to shut the door on it. We will comprehend the word serenity and we will know peace. No matter how far down the scale we have gone, we will see how our experience will benefit others. That feeling of uselessness and self-pity will disappear. We will lose interest in selfish things and gain interest in our fellows. Self-seeking will slip away. Our whole attitude and outlook upon life will change. Fear of people and of economic insecurity will leave us. We will instinctively know how to handle situations which used to baffle us. We will suddenly realize that God is doing for us what we could not do for ourselves.

Step 10: Continued to take personal inventory and when we were wrong promptly admitted it.

Once we cleared away the old wreckage as best we could, we focused on clearing away the current mess, one day at a time. "It is a spiritual axiom that every time we are disturbed, no matter what the cause, there is something wrong with us."[124] During such a disturbance, a quick spot check proved to be very helpful. When we felt flooded by anger or fear, checking our own spiritual condition gave us much-needed perspective. We hung onto the knowledge that our daily reprieve from suicide addiction was contingent on maintaining our spiritual lives. We learned that our character defects, outrageous in the past, continued in milder form, and that we had to recognize them, realize that they were part of us, and keep them in check. This required our making frequent appraisals of our shortcomings during the day and then doing our best to set them right as they happened.

---

[124] *Twelve Steps and Twelve Traditions*, (New York: AA World Services, 1981), 90.

Kevin Taylor M.D.

Most of us found ourselves setting aside daily times for prayer and meditation to review the past 24 hours. Where had we been selfish and self-centered? Had we harmed others, and if so, who, how, and when? But self-examination aside, most of us learned to spend prayer time simply thanking our Higher Power for the day, its gifts, our accomplishments—even for our own failures.

In all of this we focused *only* on our own faults. We learned slowly that our own actions were the only ones that we could change—that we had always been, and forever would be powerless over the deeds of others.

Step 11: Sought through prayer and meditation to improve our conscious contact with God as we understood Him, praying only for knowledge of His will for us, and the power to carry that out.

By now we were convinced that spiritual reliance upon God was necessary for our relationships with others, at work and at home, and for all our daily endeavors. Therefore we found ourselves increasingly praying for God's guidance in all matters, big and little, spiritual and worldly.

We came to need prayer as much as we need food and water, for prayer sustained our very souls. Without it we suffered. The only requirements for our prayers were unselfishness and sincerity. We wanted to become channels of God's will, not our own will.

In order to become channels of God's will we had to keep our own wills out of the way. To this end we stopped praying for specific answers to specific problems. "Thy will, not mine, be done." became the basis for our prayers and conscious contact with God. Saying this prayer enabled us to clear a channel choked up with selfishness, self-centeredness, anger or simple misunderstanding. Using it more and more frequently during each day, we learned the power of prayer in all situations and in all circumstances.

After prayer comes meditation. Once we talk to God, we must listen carefully for answers. Setting aside time each morning, we reflect upon the upcoming day, we read favorite meditation passages, and we made ourselves be still in God's presence, listening for His word. We found, curiously, the more we sensed God's guidance, the less we seemed to need to make demands upon God. Asking (or secretly desiring) for thus-and-such to happen, we learned, only served to distort God's message. Prayer isn't a matter of making requests or bargaining for specific outcomes, and the more we learned to pray, the more we came to rely on God's will, not on what we wanted to see happen.

But when we were clear and open channels, focused solely on knowledge of God's will for us, intuitions came to us during these times of meditation and throughout each day. A word from another person, a thought popping into our minds, an idea for action emerging as we worked on our problems - all were likely to be knowledge of His will for us. The more open our channels, the more frequent the answers.

In time, we realized that "we intuitively knew how to handle situations that used to baffle us." [125]

Step 12: Having had a spiritual awakening as a result of these steps, we tried to carry this message to those who still suffer and to practice these principles in all our affairs.

---

[125] *Alcoholics Anonymous*, (New York: AA World Services, 1976), 84.

In Step 12 we reached out to fellow suicide addicts still in distress. In so doing we asked no reward for ourselves. Having worked all the steps, we found ourselves deeply involved in a new state of consciousness, an awareness that life is full of meaning after all, and that it is both a responsibility and a joy to spread that understanding to others.

We found ourselves fully, delightedly aware that we had been given a great gift: a second chance at life. Looking at newcomers who still doubted themselves, we could remember having been where they were now and really see the change in ourselves.

This brought us to the second part of Step 12: carrying the message. We learned that we had to give it away in order to keep it. And who better to give it away to than fellow suffering suicide addicts?

We attended Suicide Anonymous meetings and listened, providing support by our very presence. We talked when our turn came; we chaired meetings, organized eating meetings, and signed up for the phone list. When ready, we sponsored others in Suicide Anonymous. Here we experienced the kind of giving that asks no reward. Paradoxically, we found no greater satisfaction and no greater joy than that which we received in our selfless giving to others.

But could we actually carry the Suicide Anonymous spirit into our daily work? We discovered a wonderful feeling that we did not have to be seen as special or distinguished among our fellows in order to be useful and happy. We no longer needed to dominate those around us in order to bolster our sense of self-importance. Our goal was to live usefully and walk humbly with God. As long as we practiced the principles of these steps, we attained our goal—one day at a time.

Chapter 11

Does it Work?

"Keep coming back"
- Slogan of Alcoholics Anonymous

In the previous chapters we outlined the problem of suicide addiction and the solution that we found. Our stories told of the pain and agony of suicide addiction both for us and for those around us.

But does this solution really work? Can real people with real problems actually recover and get on with their lives? What about today? How are the people whose stories we read in this book doing today?

Raquel: *Today, after a difficult start, Raquel is alive and sober, active in Suicide Anonymous, Sex and Love Addicts Anonymous and Alcoholics Anonymous. Initially, Raquel continued to struggle with her sex addiction, relapsing several times, first in sex addiction,*

403

then in chemical dependence. She required several more hospitalizations. Finally surrendering her sex addiction, she established a strict aftercare plan and found a combination of medications which stabilized the cycles of her bipolar illness. Raquel credits Suicide Anonymous with saving her life and has been willing to share her story at suicide prevention conferences. She no longer practices nursing.

Remington: *Today Remington is alive and sober, active in Suicide Anonymous and Alcoholics Anonymous. He is happily married to Cindy (with no sexual acting out) and successfully practices medicine, with recent promotions. Remington has been free of suicidal thoughts and beliefs "one day at a time" since the beginning of Suicide Anonymous.*

Jacqueline: *Today Jacqueline is alive and sober, practicing medicine as a medical director in a small community.*

Thelma: *Today Thelma is alive and sober, active in Suicide Anonymous, Sex and Love Addicts Anonymous, and Alcoholics Anonymous. Despite her use of state-of-the-art medications, she still struggles with her bipolar illness, but she is free of suicidal behavior. As a result of her bipolar illness, she no longer practices nursing. Thelma too, credits Suicide Anonymous with saving her life and has shared her story at suicide prevention conferences. She sponsors other women in recovery.*

Mary: *Today Mary is alive and sober, active in Suicide Anonymous and Alcoholics Anonymous. Stable and on antidepressants, she has received promotions at work and is happily married to Stu. Mary started a Suicide Anonymous meeting and also does a great deal of rewarding Twelve Step work with other alcoholics and suicide addicts.*

Chastity: *Today Chastity is alive and sober, active in Suicide Anonymous and Alcoholics Anonymous. She is stable and on antidepressants, working full-time as a nurse and happily married. Chastity helped organize a major suicide prevention conference. She also served as an expert on a state panel which developed her state's suicide prevention strategy.*

Morgan: *Today Morgan is happily married to Kevin, both miraculously having survived the horrors of Kevin's suicide addiction. She has been active in the Suicide Prevention Advocacy Network (S.P.A.N.USA) and was instrumental in getting a suicide prevention resolution adopted by the Episcopal Church. Morgan co-chaired her state's first suicide prevention conference, an event which drew over 600 attendees. Since that first conference, Morgan has spoken at numerous suicide prevention conferences. She is Kevin's best friend and soul-mate.*

Epilogue

What about Kevin?

> "Life is difficult. This is a great truth,
> one of the greatest truths. It is a great
> truth because once we truly see this truth,
> we transcend it."
> Scott Peck, *The Road Less Traveled*[126]

For 15 years, I'd had no suicidal thoughts. But were they gone forever?

September 1982, 3 North, Monroe Mental Health Institute. Starting over in psychiatry was painful. My white coat, the keys to the unit, the beeper on my hip—they were all agony. Every single day, I wanted to run away. Without drugs, alcohol, sex, or suicide, how could I be a doctor? Whenever nurses or patients wanted to see "the doctor", so did I. *Where's Dr. Munford? Where's Bushy Brows? I want to go back to Woodlawn!* On night call for the first time, without a mood-altering woman with me in the call room to numb the fear and

---

[126] Scott Peck, *The Road Less Traveled* (New York: Simon and Schuster, 1978), 15.

pain, I fantasized that a 747 would crash into the hospital, leaving me to face thousands of dead or dying people. Mercifully, it was only a fantasy.

However much I wanted to run, my therapist Tom said, "Don't run away. Bloom where you're planted." I took it day by day, week by week. The months added up to years as I found my way back, slowly making peace with myself and my past. *Nothing about this is easy. Simple, maybe, but never easy.*

"Don't drink, don't drug, don't chase women, don't fantasize about suicide; take it one day at a time," Steve said at breakfast every week. "Then suit up, show up, and do your best." Morgan and my A.A. meetings were my lifeline.

June 1985. I'd been content with the prospect of working until I retired as Medical Director on 3 North, but God had other ideas. "Kevin, you'd be good in the addiction field," my friend Gene said one day. "Lakeview is looking for two doctors to run their program, and I'd like you to think about it." And so I did.

Associate Medical Director of the Addictive Disease Unit, Lakeview: a new career. I was scared but not terrified. Things clicked, and I began to thrive. When the doors of our Impaired Professionals Program opened in 1986, my eyes stung with tears of gratitude to God. Teaching doctors and nurses how to find the road back form hell was, for me, a natural. I knew where they'd been, after all.

April 1992, Medical Director, Dual Diagnosis Unit. The age of addiction treatment of the 1980s gave way to the "managed care" approach of the 1990s. Tougher times were starting.

And then 1997…in January, my good friend and sponsor of 10 years died. I was lost. Then I got hit with my first lawsuit. I was devastated. *All those years of craziness and no malpractice suits!* Suddenly my professional world felt unsafe. The answer to the managed care crunch seemed to be volume, and volume meant faster work. Faster work meant possible mistakes, and mistakes could turn into lawsuits. *This scares the shit out of me.* I couldn't see any way out. Managed care felt like a trap.

August 1997. My partner suddenly left. The physical and emotional load doubled. Grief and loss piled on grief and loss. I still stuck close to God, Morgan and my Alcoholics Anonymous, Sex and

Love Addicts Anonymous and Suicide Anonymous meetings. *I can get through this. I can.*

And then came September 4th. Going on call at 4 PM I found myself sickened by mold allergies from a water leak in my office. *Stupid, stinking allergies!* The beeper went off: an emergency. Fire 1! Then 2, 3, 4...It was one of those nights, with one crisis after another. I felt like a ship out in cold dark water, pounded by waves. And then I knew I was in trouble.

At exactly 10 PM, after 15 wonderful years sober, the thoughts hit, roaring through my mind like fire through dry grass. I found myself fantasizing about hanging myself in the attic, stabbing myself in the kitchen. *Oh, God, NO!* For almost two hours, the demons of death attacked me. I didn't want a drink or a drug or a mood-altering woman to numb the pain. I just wanted *out*.

In desperation I called on God in one long continuous prayer for help. With God's help, I refused to go back into that black hole that I'd spent 15 years climbing out of. Over and over, I said the Third Step prayer: "Thy will be done." I vowed fiercely not to run, not to act on my suicidal thoughts, and not to keep them to myself. After a couple of hours, the thoughts (blessedly) went away, as suddenly as they had come. My mind came into calm water and started to relax, but my body jerked and twitched until daylight. I felt like the survivor of a shipwreck, needing a warm blanket and medical attention, but still enormously grateful simply to be alive, and pulled from those cold dark waters.

"No job is worth my life," I told Morgan the next morning. At 8 AM that morning, I turned in my beeper, called Tom and went for a therapy session, and then made it to a Suicide Anonymous meeting. I was the impaired professional who got help that day!

I learned two important things that night. First, that the little flame of suicide at the back of my mind did *not* go out in 1982. It's still there, and will likely be there the rest of my life. At best, I can make peace with it one day at a time. Second, I learned that God had called me on the beeper that night, using one of my greatest fears to get my attention. He'd been saying in no uncertain terms: *I love you. Trust me. Get on with my work.*

Thanks be to God.

APPENDIX

THE TWELVE STEPS
AND
THE TWELVE TRADITIONS
OF
ALCOHOLICS ANONYMOUS

413

The Twelve Steps

1. We admitted that we were powerless over alcohol-that our lives had become unmanageable.

2. Came to believe that a Power greater than ourselves could restore us to sanity.

3. Made a decision to turn our will and our lives over to the care of God *as we understood Him.*

4. Made a searching and fearless moral inventory of ourselves.

5. Admitted to God, to ourselves, and to another human being the exact nature of our wrongs.

6. Were entirely ready to have God remove all these defects of character.

7. Humbly asked Him to remove our shortcomings.

8. Made a list of all persons we had harmed, and became willing to make amends to them all.

9. Made direct amends to such people wherever possible, except when to do so would injure them or others.

10. Continued to take personal inventory and when we were wrong promptly admitted it.

11. Sought through prayer and meditation to improve our conscious contact with God *as we understood Him*, praying only for knowledge of His will for us and the power to carry that out.

12. Having had a spiritual awakening as the result of these steps, we tried to carry this message to alcoholics, and to practice these principles in all our affairs.

The Twelve Traditions

1. Our common welfare should come first; personal recovery depends upon AA unity.

2. For our group purpose there is but one ultimate authority—a loving God as He may express Himself in our group conscience. Our leaders are but trusted servants; they do not govern.

3. The only requirement for AA membership is a desire to stop drinking.

4. Each group should be autonomous except in matters affecting other groups or AA as a whole.

5. Each group has but one primary purpose—to carry its message to the alcoholic who still suffers.

6. An AA group ought never endorse, finance or lend the AA name to any related facility or outside enterprise, lest problems of money, property and prestige divert us from our primary purpose.

7. Every AA group ought to be fully self-supporting, declining outside contributions.

8. Alcoholics Anonymous should remain forever nonprofessional, but our service centers may employ special workers.

9. AA, as such, ought never be organized; but we may create service boards or committees directly responsible to those they serve.

10. Alcoholics Anonymous has no opinion on outside issues; hence the AA name ought never be drawn into public controversy.

11. Our public relations policy is based on attraction rather than promotion; we need always maintain personal anonymity at the level of press, radio and films.

12. Anonymity is the spiritual foundation of all our traditions, ever reminding us to place principles before personalities.

Kevin Taylor M.D.

Index

About the Author

Kevin Taylor (pen name) is an award-winning psychiatrist specializing in addictions. He received the prestigious Diamond Award for lifetime contributions to the field of mental health, presented by the Mental Health Association of the Mid-South.

Dr. Taylor is a Fellow of the American Society of Addiction Medicine and a founding member of the American Academy of Psychiatrists in Alcoholism and Addictions. He has dedicated his life to helping impaired physicians and served on his state's Physicians Health Peer Review Committee.

With his wife, Morgan, Dr. Taylor appeared on the Oprah Winfrey Show, "Successful People Who Attempted Suicide." The Taylors organized and co-chaired their state's first-ever Suicide Prevention Conference in cooperation with Surgeon General David Satcher and their state's Department of Health.

Printed in the United States
977100003B